Newspaper Language

Titles in the series

Series editor: F. W. Hodgson

Newspaper Language

NICHOLAS BAGNALL

Focal Press
An imprint of Butterworth-Heinemann Ltd
Linacre House, Jordan Hill, Oxford OX2 8DP

℞ A member of the Reed Elsevier group

OXFORD LONDON BOSTON
MUNICH NEW DELHI SINGAPORE SYDNEY
TOKYO TORONTO WELLINGTON

First published 1993

British Library Cataloguing in Publication Data
Bagnall, Nicholas
    Newspaper Language
    I. Title
    808
ISBN 0 7506 0399 2

Printed and bound in Great Britain

CONTENTS

PREFACE

Many of the journalists whose words I quote in this book are colleagues or friends. They will I know forgive me if, to illustrate points of style, I have occasionally drawn attention to blemishes in their work which are not necessarily typical of them. Admittedly some journalists are consistently bad, but even the best of us make mistakes in haste or under stress.

I am grateful to my editor at Butterworth-Heinemann, Mr Freddie Hodgson; to Professor Stuart Sutherland of Sussex University for vetting my chapter on statistics (any remaining mistakes are mine) and for looking over some of my other chapters; to Mr Godfrey Bullard for reading the proofs; to Mr David Powell for inspiration and advice; to Mr Brian Davis for the surprising list of tautologies on page 93, and to Dr L. Horenstein for the interminable word on page 104.

My thanks are due, above all, to the many newspapers and journals from which I have quoted here.

Nicholas Bagnall

1 WHAT IS NEWSPAPER ENGLISH?

Clear your mind of cant. – Dr Johnson

The language of journalism is nearer the spoken word than business language is on the one hand, or academic language on the other. In fact it is closer to the spoken word than it ever was in the past.

Television and radio have made this happen. People are so used to getting their news from a live announcer, and their views from live interviewees, that they expect something like the same language from their newspapers and their periodicals.

But even before television and radio there was always a good reason why journalists should prefer what William Wordsworth called 'the common language of men' (and, he would have added if he had lived today, of women).

The common language

For example, you would have to be a very pompous journalist before you could write that someone was 'making every endeavour to locate a document'. You leave that kind of thing to your bank manager. You write, as you would say, 'He is doing his best to find it'.

Bank managers write in that way because they are unwilling to admit that they have lost something and they want to keep their dignity. But journalists who use such language are only putting themselves between the story and the readers.

The following advertisement is for a patent cure for leaky roofs:

Its special 35 mm foam application – combined if necessary with any external rectification work – solves all the problems of roof decay and helps prevent storm damage. It also prevents snow and rain ingress . . .

Why did the copywriter not put 'Stops the snow and rain coming in'? Because he needed to give the impression that his clients knew more about snow and rain than their customers did. Anyone can see how snow gets through a roof. But 'snow and rain ingress' is a different matter; you want a trained specialist for that.

The professional spokesperson, the white-collar worker with a stake in his firm, the landowner, the political careerist, the specialist jealous of her expertise, all use language as a shield to protect their particular interests.

> I like a style which is simple and natural, the same on paper as on the lip. – Montaigne

Politicians may use words which sound grand but have no actual meaning. Experts use obscure words and phrases to show that only they and their colleagues can understand the point at issue. (After all, their livelihoods depend on it.)

The journalist is the complete opposite. His or her task is to break down the shield and to disclose what others may be trying to conceal. A property developer who announces that he is 'sensitive to environmental considerations' may hope to disarm the green lobby. Good journalists are not fooled by such weasel talk. They discard the phrase, get at whatever truth may lurk behind it, and find the words which most accurately convey it.

Immediate clarity, then, is the aim. Clarity, and directness. The left-hand column below is a modest example of thesis-writer's language:

The present document has been divided into two sections. The second is derived partly from the work of Professor John Bloodnock and the author is grateful to him for his close scrutiny of the text.	I have divided this thesis into two sections. For the second section I relied partly on Professor John Bloodnock's work. He has gone carefully through my text and I am grateful to him.

There is nothing terribly wrong with the style of the left-hand version. But it is impersonal. Things and people have things done to them, but never do things themselves ('*has been* divided', '*is* derived').

The right-hand column says the same thing as a journalist might have written it. All three sentences have people *doing* something in them. Nouns give way to verbs. ('His close scrutiny of the text' becomes 'He has gone carefully through my text'). And the journalist feels no need to avoid using the first-person singular, 'I' or 'me', when necessary. He doesn't have to pretend he is someone else, with coy references to 'the present author'. There was a time, roughly up to the Second World War,

> For an explanation of grammatical terms, see the Glossary on page 209

when reports were usually unsigned and journalists referred to themselves as 'your correspondent' ('you' being the editor, of course). Those days are over. (More about the reasons for this in Chapter 8.)

Here is an example of too many nouns and not enough verbs, from a publisher's blurb for a book by the Archbishop of Canterbury:

> [George Carey] writes to redress two alarming trends: the low priority of the Cross in modern thinking and the multiplication of interpretations of the Cross in an ecumenical age.

How dead those long nouns sound! A journalist might have rephrased it:

> . . . writes to redress two alarming trends. Modern thinkers, he believes, pay too little attention to the Cross. And when they do write of it in this ecumenical age, they interpret it in too many ways.

Hazlitt's recipe

The best definition I know of the true language of journalism is by William Hazlitt. In his essay *On Familiar Style*, written in the early nineteenth century and still sound in this, he said:

> To write a genuine familiar or true English style is to write as anyone would speak in common conversation, who had a thorough command and choice of words, or who could discourse with ease, force and perspicuity, setting aside all pedantic and oratorical flourishes.

If we are to write in such a style, said Hazlitt, we must 'avail ourselves of the true idiom of the language'. It might sound easy, but it was not:

> On the contrary, there is nothing that requires more precision. . . . It is easy to affect a pompous style, to use a word twice as big as the thing you want to express; it is not easy to pitch upon the very word that exactly fits it.

Even journalists can fall into the same bad way of writing unless they are careful. There is so much of it about, and it may be catching. From the *Daily Telegraph*, reporting Kenneth Clarke, the then Education Secretary:

> Fears that popular classes such as aerobics or pottery would disappear or become prohibitively expensive were 'largely groundless', he said, stressing that ministers would maintain current levels of financial support for leisure and recreation in determining council funding.

This sounds like one of Mr Clarke's civil servants talking, rather than the man himself. But whoever inspired *ministers would maintain current levels of financial support* it wasn't natural, and since the reporter wasn't quoting anyone directly he could have translated it into something less offputting such as 'Leisure and recreation would be getting just as much support from central government as they were getting at present.' (I don't like *support*, but we have to have it because it means a percentage, depending on how much the councils put in – so we can't say money, otherwise we would have done.)

The first step towards writing naturally is to purge one's copy of words which sound 'pedantic and oratorical' when they have perfectly good equivalents in ordinary speech. Here is a list of some common words and (in brackets) a pedantic version of each:

answer	(respond)
ask	(request, inquire)
begin	(commence)
buy	(purchase)
choose	(opt, select)
die	(decease)
end	(conclude, terminate)
find	(locate)
find out	(ascertain)
get	(receive, obtain)
get worse	(deteriorate)
get home	(arrive at one's residence)
give	(donate)
go	(proceed)
go before	(precede)
have	(possess)
have	(contain)
help	(assist)
hurry	(expedite)
is in	(is located in, is situated in)
is	(represents)

is part	(forms part)
lead, take	(conduct)
learn	(apprehend)
lit	(illuminated)
live	(reside)
meet	(encounter)
need	(necessitate, require)
pay	(remunerate)
put	(place, deposit)
read	(peruse)
say	(state)
see	(discern, perceive)
send	(dispatch)
show	(demonstrate, exhibit, evince)
start	(initiate)
stay	(remain)
sweat	(perspire)
take part	(participate)
tell	(inform, apprise, acquaint, narrate)
try	(endeavour, attempt)
turn out	(eventuate)
use	(employ, utilize)
wait	(attend)
want	(desire)
was bruised	(suffered contusions)

All these words would have delighted Mr Borthrop Trumbull, the self-important small-town auctioneer in George Eliot's *Middlemarch*, who was

an amateur of superior phrases, and never used poor language without correcting himself . . .
'Oh yes, anybody may ask,' said Mr Trumbull, with loud and good-humoured though cutting sarcasm. 'Anybody may interrogate. Anybody may give their remarks an interrogative turn,' he continued, his sonorousness rising with his style. 'This is constantly done by good speakers, even when they anticipate no answer. It is what we call a figure of speech – speech at a high figure, as one might say . . .'

Seeing someone reading Walter Scott, he observes:

'I have bought one of his works myself – a very nice thing, a very superior publication, entitled Ivanhoe. You will not get any writer to beat him in a hurry, I think – he will not, in my opinion, be speedily surpassed. I have just been reading a portion at the commencement of Anne of Jeersteen [sic*]. It commences well.' Things never began with Mr Borthrop Trumbull: they always commenced, both in private life and in his handbills.

It is wrong to think (or as Mr Trumbull would put it, erroneous to suppose) that our ancestors made a point of using long words where we use short ones. Pomposity upset George Eliot just as it upsets us today. (*Middlemarch* was published in 1871.) Bad English was always bad English.

Mr Trumbull thought of an easy phrase then searched for a more dignified paraphrase of it, so that 'a very nice thing' becomes 'a very superior publication'. Good writers do the reverse of this: they go through their work and ask themselves whether they have written any-

> Bad writers are nearly always haunted by the notion that Latin and Greek words are grander than Saxon ones. – George Orwell

thing which can be put in a simpler, more direct and therefore more forceful way.

All the words in the above list, you may have noticed, are verbs. Here are some more common words and phrases, with their Trumbullisms in brackets:

house	(residence)	bowl	(utensil)
last	(final)	place	(location)
lucky	(fortunate)	way in	(ingress)
enough	(sufficient)	way out	(egress)
next	(adjacent)	pay	(emolument)
roughly, about	(approximately)	doubt	(dubiety)
wrong	(erroneous)	speech	(dissertation)
usual	(customary)	before	(prior to)
later	(subsequently)	steep	(precipitous)
limits	(parameters)	model	(paradigm)
time	(time factor)	weather	(weather conditions)
learning	(learning experience)	chalky	(of a calcareous nature)
part	portion	empty [house or flat]	
often	frequently		(vacant)

> Short words are best and the old ones when short are best of all.
> – Winston Churchill

* He was an ignorant fellow. He meant *Anne of Geierstein*.

People who are not used to writing begin by thinking what they want to say, then try to find important-sounding words for it, as Mr Trumbull did. So a parent whose child is ill writes to the school secretary:

I regret to inform you that due to an indisposition Jane is prevented from attending school today.

What she should have done, of course, was to forget the important words and use the ones which had come into her head in the first place:

I am afraid Jane is ill today and cannot come to school.

Pardon my Latin

My lists deliberately give the short, simple word first and the more elaborate one (derived in almost every case directly from Latin) in brackets after it. We shouldn't be thinking of the elaborate one first.

I am *not* saying that the right-hand column in those lists can be dispensed with entirely, as surplus to requirements. My point is that most of them have their own purposes and that to substitute one of them for the simpler word, when the simpler word is all that is meant, is a serious misuse of language and a mark of the amateur.

Some of the longer words, it is true, are mere luxuries. I can think of no occasion on which any journalist, or indeed any writer, even of po-faced legal documents, need use *subsequently* or *prior to*. Only comic butlers say 'I will endeavour to ascertain his Lordship's intentions' when they mean they will ask him what he wants.

Orwell's formula

But to suggest that we should *always* use the simple alternative is absurd. In his famous essay, *Politics and the English Language*, George Orwell says:

Never use a long word where a short one will do,

and his advice is often quoted by teachers of English. This has led to some misunderstanding in the past by the minimalist school of newspaper journalists (including some who have written books for young journalists) who have perversely taken him to mean that short words are bound to be better than long ones – whereas all he meant was that we shouldn't use long ones *unnecessarily*.

And sometimes the longer word is indeed necessary, or, if not necessary, at least more expressive. For example, it would be silly to prefer *see* to *perceive* every time: *perceive* has overtones which *see* lacks. It suggests a mental activity, not just a visual one. When Dr Johnson said to a friend: 'I perceive you are a vile Whig' he was implying that he had done a bit of thinking before coming to that conclusion. And, of course, his perception may have been wrong . . . None of this is implied by *see*.

Orwell's point was that it would be foolish – and not only foolish, but positively pretentious – to use *perceive* when *see* would do perfectly well.

To take another obvious example, there are certainly times when we need the word *deteriorate* (buildings deteriorate). But we apply the Orwell formula. We say: 'His condition got worse.'

My lists are not lists of synonyms, or exact meanings. Someone who always said *lead* instead of *conduct* would have no future as a music critic.

Let us now look more closely at some of the words in those lists:

- *Answer (respond)*: *Respond* suggests an emotional or physical reaction, not just an acknowledgement. It should be kept for this purpose. You *answer* a letter, *respond to* a stimulus.
- *Lit (illuminated)*: *Illuminated* is too good a word to waste on mere lighting systems. Useful, though, as a metaphor. (Metaphors: 'Words or expressions which describe one thing in terms of another.') 'I thank the Hon Member for his illuminating reply.'
- *Buy (purchase)*: *Purchase* should be never be used in news stories for *buy*. But we might need it occasionally as a noun. 'She left the shop festooned with her purchases.'
- *Say (state)*: Some people mistakenly think that *say* applies only to the spoken word and that *state* should always be used for the written word. So they write: 'He stated in his letter . . .' Don't fall for this. Write: 'He said in his letter' . . . 'The chairman's statement says . . .' etc. But: 'He asked her to state her terms.'
- *Find (locate)*: *Locate* is a technical term. It should be kept where it belongs, in engineering and real estate. You locate a sprocket on a shaft and a house is located in a district, though '*is* in' a district would probably do as well. A *location* is not just a place, but a place where a film is being made.
- *Start (initiate)*: People who write *initiate* when they mean *start* are just being sloppy. The person who initiates a project may not be the one who actually starts it.
- *Put (place)*: Sloppiness again. *Place* has its own meaning: 'Find a place for', implying deliberation on the part of the person doing the placing. So you do not *place* your foot in it, nor do you *place* the meat in the freezer. But you *place* a player in a team.

- *Try (attempt, endeavour)*: The two longer words are fine as nouns: 'The team is set to make the attempt; the public supports its endeavour.' I can think of no reason for using either of them in news stories instead of *try*.
- *Have (contain)*: Another bit of estate agent's jargon ('The house contains four bedrooms'). Terrible. Use *contain* where it has a point to make: 'The prison was too small to contain so many prisoners.'
- *Have (possess)*: *Possess* is hardly ever needed. But it is sometimes.

  It is a valuable work to possess. – Paul Johnson, book review in the *Sunday Telegraph*

  He means have on one's own shelves, not have in the sense of 'have available' or 'have been published'. *Possess* is right.
- *Show (demonstrate, exhibit)*: *Demonstrate* is useful in the laboratory. And an air hostess demonstrates the safety equipment, not shows it. Otherwise, *show* will nearly always do; but *demonstrate* is correct when used in the sense of *exemplify*:

  If by a 'classless society' Mr Major means, which I think he does, careers open to talent, then it arrived (as he himself demonstrates) some time ago. – Geoffrey Wheatcroft in the *Sunday Telegraph*

  Exhibit is for picture galleries and the like.

  The majority of police officers . . . exhibit a bravery of which we should be proud. – Leader in *Today*

  The rest of that leader was in good colloquial English. *Exhibit* was an odd man out here.
- *See (discern)*: It needs more effort to discern something than to see it. *See* would make sense in most instances, but *discern* has an extra edge to it – for use when, and only when, needed.
- *Meet (encounter)*: An encounter is more than just a meeting. It carries just an element of tension or surprise. Keep it for such occasions.
- *Wait (attend)*: Waiting on someone is a more menial activity than attending on them. *Attend* is what one does to weddings, funerals, etc., though it is better just to *go to* them.
- *Need (require)*: Hardly ever interchangeable. *Require* for *need* is butler's talk ('Do you require tea?'). I *need* a bath when I am dirty; I *require* a bath in the house I am buying.

  The launch of Britain's first Trident submarine yesterday marked the re-emergence of defence as an election issue, with the parties

split over whether three or four of the £600m vessels are required. –
Yorkshire Post

Why *required*? Isn't this just the sort of slightly pompous word Myles
na gCopaleen was laughing at in his *Catechism of Cliché*? (For more
about Myles see Chapter 2.)
- *Use (employ)*: Only employers employ.
- *Get (receive)*: Each of this pair has its own meaning and they should
not be confused. It should nearly always be clear which is needed.

> Getting and spending we lay waste our powers (Wordsworth)

becomes something altogether different if we change it to

> Receiving and spending we lay waste our powers.

One does not say 'I'm going to receive some sleep, then I'm going to
receive a meal'. On the other hand,

> It is more blessed to give than to receive (St Paul)

does not mean the same as

> It is more blessed to give than to get.

But personally I would rather use *get* even where *receive* would be
quite accurate. I would say 'Have you got my letter?' and 'I got a nice
surprise today'. And I would strongly advise you to do the same.
- *Go (proceed)*: Good writers never say *proceed* when all they mean is
go. Processions, or people in them, proceed; and perhaps, sometimes,
less formal groups of people. The rest of us just go, or walk, or drive,
or whatever. Policemen giving evidence like to say they were *proceed-
ing* to the scene of the crime because it gives a stately impression, and
pompous judges say to counsel 'Please proceed' because they are
pompous. Winston Churchill used to say 'pray proceed' to people he
was talking to, but he was born in 1874.
- *Die (decease)*: The two words are not synonymous. *Die* can be used
figuratively ('The thought died on my lips'). *Decease* cannot. It is a
euphemism among people who are frightened (as many of us are) of
death, and it should be allowed them. Apart from that, never say
decease.
- *Wrong (erroneous)*: These do mean different things, though their
meanings overlap. *Wrong* may carry a moral implication (it is wrong
to steal) but *erroneous* just means mistaken. People who admit that
their beliefs are erroneous are being mealy-mouthed.

- *End (terminate)*: Only trains and buses terminate. But *terminal* is a nice borrowing from the world of medicine, meaning final: a terminal disease is the one that's going to kill you. Avoid misuse, as here:

> He has never found a cure for his terminally short attention span and he probably never will. – Profile by Lesley White of retiring Tory MP Alan Clark, in the *Sunday Times*

Mr Clark's short attention span must have been deeply irritating to his friends, but it was not a fatal disease. The author meant *chronically*, another medical borrowing. If too many people said *terminally* when they meant *chronically* or *incurably*, the word would rapidly lose its flavour, which would be a pity. So do let's try to keep it alive.

These few examples should be enough to show that the longer, classically derived alternatives have their particular uses. When writers bring them on stage in roles to which they are unsuited, then we have every right

> Only a mechanical mind believes that the so-called Anglo-Saxon derivatives should always be preferred, and only the starched and stilted will persistently fall into the Latinate. – Jacques Barzun

to hiss them off. But to cut them out altogether would be to deprive ourselves of a vast range of ideas and our readers of a great deal of pleasure.

It might be worth seeing if there is a workable set of rules about when to use the Latinate words and when not. If the Latinate version never in any circumstances improves on the home-grown version, then there is no question about it. For example, there are many occasions when *give* does not mean *donate*, but none on which *donate* does not mean *give*. So by all means let us do without *donate*.

For the same reason, I, doubt if the English language would be seriously impoverished if it lost the following:

ascertain	eventuate	approximately
opt	necessitate	ingress
reside	utilize	egress
forms part	apprehend	emolument
participate	sufficient	concerning
remunerate	adjacent	prior to

Ordinary, everyday things are best given ordinary, everyday names. Call it a house not a residence, a meal not a repast, a place not a location, a letter not a communication or missive, a car or bus not a conveyance, a hand-out not a disbursement, salt and pepper not condiments, food not

> Don't accustom yourself to using big words for little matters. –
>
> Dr Johnson

comestibles, and so on. Grander things can support grander names, which are likely to be Latin-derived. The rich prince's house is entered by a portal, the poor worker's by a door. An inferno is hotter than a mere fire, or was before the hacks began overusing it.

And abstract ideas and emotions are often more emphatic when the words used for them are taken from Latin. *Terror* grips more fiercely than the Old English *fright* ('Were you frightened?' – 'I was terrified'), and there is no native English equivalent of the Latin *horror*.* Medieval English has *joyous*, but for something a bit headier Latin gives us *ecstatic,* which it took from ancient Greek. *Anxiety* gnaws more fiercely than *unease*. There seem to be more imported words for the emotions than there are native ones. There is no Anglo-Saxon word for *mollify* that I can think of. *Soothe* doesn't mean quite the same. *Pleasure* is a less evocative word than *gratification*, which is somehow much smugger.

I shall have more to say on journalists' use of Latinate words in Chapter 8, about style (see page 138).

Jargon

Dictionaries offer two main definitions of jargon: (1) specialized language (medical jargon, sports jargon) and (2) meaningless chatter, as of birds (the earlier definition).

The two definitions are not all that contradictory. What makes sense to the specialist may sound to the rest of us like mere barbarous noise. So it's pointless to advise: 'Avoid jargon.' Everything depends on who you are writing for.

Because all jargon is more or less exclusive – only certain people will be able to understand it – it is bound to annoy some and please others. The only worthwhile advice for those who write in non-specialist journals is: don't indulge in it just to show off. You are supposed to be telling

> The chief merit of language is clearness, and we know that nothing detracts so much from this as do unfamiliar terms.
>
> – Galen (second-century doctor and philosopher)

your readers something they didn't know before, not persuading them how clever you are. Of course, if you explain the jargon as you go along, that's a different matter: it can give authenticity to the piece.

* But see Chapter 3 for bad journalists' abuse of the words *horror* and *terror.*

Only slightly less tiresome than this sort of show-off jargon is *borrowed jargon* – terms which sound perfectly all right in their proper context but not in new ones, where they are probably inaccurate anyway.

What trick of car semiotics turned Hitler's cheap, no-frills gift to the master race into bags of fun? – *Guardian* article about the Volkswagen Beetle.

The introduction of a term from philology into a middlebrow piece about motor cars is just pretentious, and the use of the phrase *car semiotics* (what are they – a new scientific discipline?) is a clumsy way of doing it.

Dally is good, too, at pointing up the symbiosis between society and medicine. – Book review in the *Sunday Times*

Symbiosis is a biological term and it is silly to use it metaphorically in a piece about medicine; pompous too.

Before the Second World War the rage was for terms borrowed from medicine in general and psychiatry in particular: there was much talk of inferiority complexes and the like. *Syndrome*, a tired old word, is a hang-over from then, as is *the psychological moment*, misused so often that its meaning in psychology has been almost eclipsed and its lay meaning accepted by the dictionaries. Nowadays writers who want to be in the swim are more likely to take their language from that of commerce:

The 166 turbos were slightly more upmarket than the new 165 turbos on the Chiltern lines between Bicester North and Marylebone. – *Witney Gazette*, reporting the views of the chairman of a local railway pressure group.

Originally, of course, *to go upmarket* meant to offer a better or more exclusive class of goods which would appeal to richer customers. Then *upmarket* was for anything or anyone superior to other things or people. But we're not sure in what sense it is meant in the sentence above. Are the 166 turbos better – more powerful, say – or simply dearer, or both? Or is their engineering more advanced? (If they were better in this sense they could of course be cheaper.) The short answer is that *upmarket* is a vogue word. We must expect it to be heedlessly bandied about without reference to its meaning, if any.

The CAP reform is the bottom line so far as GATT is concerned. – Financial journalist, on BBC Radio 4

I wish I could be sure what this chap was talking about. Of course we know that the *bottom line* was the last figure on a balance sheet, so it came to mean the essential truth of a situation, showing what was really happening. But now it can also mean the *sticking point* or the *bargaining position* or the *crucial factor*, and I have a feeling that it was one or more of these things that our BBC man had in mind. It wasn't because he was being technical that I was confused – I knew what CAP and GATT were – but because he was *not* being technical. He was a financial journalist using a financial term in a non-financial sense. In short, another vogue word which conveys too many things and therefore ends up conveying not very much.

> The CAP reforms will have a negative effect on British farmers' incomes. – Another BBC man, on the same programme

This is not jargon, but it annoyed me so much that I couldn't help mentioning it. For mealy-mouthed, asinine pomposity it easily outclasses the trade-unionese 'We are hoping for a positive response from the membership' (he hopes they'll vote yes).

Here are some jargon words to be handled with care, if at all. On the right I offer alternatives; in effect, they are no different from what most people mean by the words on the left.

Axiomatic (from logic and maths)	Too obvious to mention, goes without saying
Charismatic (from religion)	Absolutely charming
Clinical (from medicine)	Cold fish
Concept (from philosophy)	Idea, thing
Image (from art)	Reputation
Interface (from physics and computing)	Relationship
Parameter (from maths and astronomy)	Limit
Scenario (from cinematography)	Situation, state of play
Spectrum (from physics)	Range
Traumatic (from medicine)	Upsetting

The first three, as it happens, are technically 'wrong' – the specialist meaning is not the same as the lay meaning. This hardly matters unless it's unclear which sense is meant. What does matter is that all these specialist words have become first modish then hackneyed. They are no longer the thing to wear.

Each 'group of interests has its own vocabulary. We have mentioned bank managers, estate agents, civil servants in Whitehall. By their words ye shall know them. If you read that someone 'rejects talking shops in favour of grassroots monitoring' you can guess without being told that they work in one of the caring professions and have an 'overall commitment to the community', where they will 'link and focus' a diversity of campaigning causes. 'The moral high ground', on the other hand, is politicians' talk. It is amusing to identify these argots, so long as we don't start unconsciously using them ourselves.

2 JOURNALISM AND JOURNALESE

It is as important, for the purpose of thought, to keep language efficient as it is in surgery to keep tetanus bacilli out of one's bandages. – Ezra Pound

Three important points arise out of Chapter 1:

1 Many people who put Latinisms into their copy don't really know what they mean. Yet the first skill an apprentice journalist aims for is factual accuracy; and this ought to include the accurate use of words. Everyone in the trade knows that 'getting the facts right' is harder than the readers think it is. But it can be just as hard to get the right words to convey them. Verbal and factual accuracy go together.
2 Every time someone uses a word in the wrong way, that word loses a little of its force, and will be less effective next time. Journalists who constantly bring on big powerful words to do the light work, which could easily be done by smaller words, are slowly bankrupting their vocabulary. (See Chapter 3 for more examples.)
3 There is only one way to acquire verbal accuracy, and that is by reading widely. A non-reading journalist is a lame runner.

I can think (for a start) of two authors in particular who are worth emulating, one from the eighteenth century, one from the twentieth. For simple, crystalline narrative, few can beat Oliver Goldsmith. No sentence of his *Vicar of Wakefield* ever needs to be read twice (except perhaps in the set-piece homilies, which, though amusing, are not strictly part of the story). Goldsmith doesn't try to avoid Latinisms, but each Latinism is there because it is the best word for the purpose. Here is a taste of Goldsmith: it comes from the first page of *The Vicar of Wakefield*:

We loved each other tenderly, and our fondness increased as we grew old. There was, in fact, nothing that could make us angry with ourselves or with each other. We had an elegant house, situated in a fine country, and a good neighbourhood. The year was spent in moral or rural amusement; in visiting our rich neighbours, and relieving such as were poor. We had no revolutions to fear, nor fatigues to undergo; all our adventures were by the fireside, and all our migrations from the blue bed to the brown.

Those who think of eighteenth-century prose in terms of Johnson or Gibbon should take a look at Goldsmith. Johnson was a marvellous stylist, but his style, with its almost cathedral-like splendour, is not a good model for journalists today. Goldsmith's is more like a small Georgian house, unpretentious and satisfyingly proportioned. Of course it has the rhetoric which everyone enjoyed in his day – note how his phrases mirror each other as he goes along – but note also how easy and simple it all is. The only word in the above passage which jars for us today is *situated*. We would have preferred *set*, or left out the verb altogether.

For a twentieth-century model I offer Ernest Hemingway. His tough-guy posture is slightly out of fashion at the time of my writing this, but not his prose style, whose purity is exceptional. Here is Hemingway on his life in Paris between the First and Second World Wars:

In the spring mornings I would work early while my wife still slept. The windows were open wide and the cobbles of the street were drying after the rain. The sun was drying the wet faces of the houses that faced the window. The shops were still shuttered. The goat-herd came up the street blowing his pipes and a woman who lived on the floor above us came out on to the sidewalk with a big pot. The goat-herd chose one of the heavy-bagged black milk-goats and milked her into the pot while his dog pushed the others on to the sidewalk.

It all looks so easy – yet Hemingway took years perfecting that style, cutting it back and back until it said for him just what he wanted it to, no more. There are no commas, nor any punctuation mark except the full stop. Most of us need commas, dashes and so forth to guide the reader around. Hemingway's syntax is so clear that he does without them.

Concrete and abstract

Obviously there is nothing to be said against abstract ideas. We could hardly think without them. But we should ask ourselves whether what we are writing or saying can just as well be put into more concrete form. If it can, it is likely to be more memorable and more compelling.

> There were many more accidents involving fatalities between the hours of 3 a.m. and 6 a.m.

I heard someone saying this on the radio. But he could have put the point more simply:

> Many more people died in accidents between 3 a.m. and 6 a.m.

However you look at it, that was what he meant. Never mind whether there were more or fewer accidents in the small hours than in broad daylight, the point was that during those hours more people got killed in them, or died later in hospital. So why didn't he say so? Partly it must have been a straight case of Trumbullitis: 'accidents involving fatalities' has a grander ring to it, though it lacks the directness of people getting killed on the road. It is remote from the carnage. And the speaker probably *was* remote. He had been analysing columns of accident statistics, perhaps with graphs attached, and had looked down the columns subheaded 'involving fatalities'.

It was also a case of too many nouns ('fatalities') and not enough verbs ('killed'). Compare that blurb for the Archbishop's book which I quoted from on page 3 – another instance of the same disease.

A good journalist doesn't write or talk like that. In the same programme someone else was mentioning 'low traffic densities', which was not a bad illustration of the point I was making just now about the accurate use of language. It is true that there is no ambiguity about low traffic densities: we know what they are. But it is not a proper use of words. Again the speaker had had his nose in the statistics. He had seen that the figures showing the number of vehicles per 1000 metres, or whatever, were *lower* at some times than at others. But density is neither high

---

To haggle over language *is* quibbling, of course. All precision is quibbling, whether about decimals in mathematics or grains of drugs in prescriptions. – Jacques Barzun

---

nor low. Density is thick or thin. The metaphorical content of that phrase was right off-course, which was why it sounded so dull. And isn't *traffic density*, after all, a pretty offputting expression? A journalist would surely have said that the traffic was light.

Two kinds of journalese

Editing a trade union magazine years ago, I used to be approached by the secretary of the sustentation fund, the organizer of the widows' and orphans' benevolent appeal and suchlike apparatchiks asking me to insert their copy in the next issue. It was always full of locutions like the ones above and I would politely suggest a rewrite, done preferably by someone on my staff rather than on theirs. 'Oh,' said one, 'I suppose you want to put it into *journalese*.'

I was too polite to answer: 'No, I only want to put it into English.' But he misunderstood what journalese is.

Journalese comes in two colours. One of them is a special language written only for the popular tabloids and imitated occasionally by some provincial papers. We shall be examining that in some detail in Chapter 3.

The other is, I'm afraid, sometimes found in Britain's quality and provincial press, and it is far closer to the sort of thing my union official was writing than anything I could have done with his copy.

For some journalists do seem to think that if they choose grand or pompous words instead of everyday ones their work will show a touch of class which it would otherwise have lacked, and that their stories will thereby become more authentic.

I have argued the case myself.* A man is knocked down by a hit-and-run motorist. 'They say he was badly hurt' says a bystander. The reporter writes: 'The victim is understood to have sustained serious injuries,' thus translating a bit of hearsay into something apparently more authoritative.

The best cure for this way of thinking is *The Myles na gCopaleen† Catechism of Cliché*, which na gCopaleen (also known as Flann O'Brien) wrote for the *Irish Times*. I strongly recommend this famous work, of which the first instalment appeared in 1939. It is described by its author as 'a unique compendium of all that is nauseating in contemporary writing . . . a harrowing survey of sub-literature and all that is pseudish, maldicted and calloused in the underworld of print', and it starts:

Is a man ever hurt in a motor smash? – No. he sustains an injury.
Does a man ever die from his injuries? – No. He succumbs to them.
Correct. But supposing an ambulance is sent for. He is put into the ambulance and *rushed* to hospital. Is he dead when he gets there, assuming that he is not alive? – No, he is not dead. Life is found to be extinct.

I am afraid this sort of thing is still being done today, though less often. Here is an example from a local paper:

Two Faversham firemen who gave their lives while attempting to extinguish a blazing aircraft at Luddenham are being honoured by Kent Fire Brigade – 51 years after the event . . .

* In *A Defence of Clichés*, Constable, 1985.
† Collected in *The Best of Myles*, MacGibbon & Kee, 1968.

The brigade is also anxious to trace Mr Beaumont's brothers, believed to be still resident in Kent.

Attempting to extinguish (for 'trying to put out') and *resident in Kent* (surely 'living in Kent'?) are pure na gCopaleen.

But why are they wrong? Isn't that how news stories should be written? No it is not. The trouble with putting newspaper reports into a journalese of their own is that it can make the events described seem *more* remote from reality, instead of closer.

Dictionaries sometimes define journalese as 'a hackneyed way of writing', and this may be true of tabloid journalese with its narrow range of clichés, but it is not quite the right definition for the journalese I am discussing here. For it's not the clichés that distinguish it: after all, clichés can be found all over the place, and are not confined to newspapers and periodicals. This journalese is a purposely special kind of writing which seems to say: 'Here is a news report. You can tell it's a report because of the way it's written.'

But why, I repeat, should such a report be believed because it is couched in that sort of journalese? Might not the reverse be the case? One Christmas Day the independent television company that puts on the soap opera *Coronation Street* decided that instead of interrupting the schedule with the Queen's traditional TV broadcast it would incorporate her speech into the soap and have the characters watch it. Later it was said by some that this was a mistake because it brought an unwelcome wind of reality into the escapist world of the Street. What it actually did, of course, was to take the Queen out of the real world and make her seem merely a character in a soap opera.

In the same way, journalists who prefer to tell their stories in a language of their own devising should not be surprised if their readers begin to think the stories are made up too.

Manly buzzwords

After the pomposities noted by Myles na gCopaleen comes news journalist's talk of another and almost opposite kind, with sharp little buzzwords like these:

ban	curb, slash
mercy dash	clash
(rates) freeze bid	drama
(police) probe	shock (adjective)
(minister) hits out	hell (adjective)
(councillor) slams critics	blast (explosion; to blast = to
crackdown feared	criticize)

which, as well as having a manly, no-nonsense immediacy about them, offer the advantage of brevity. They are very useful in large-type headlines, where they first became popular, only later invading the text itself. They certainly came in handy during the Second World War when the rationing of newsprint, not lifted till well into the 1950s, brought daily papers down to single-figure page numbers, and every line of print was thought valuable.

They are still with us today, though they are beginning to sound rather quaint. They remind me somehow of those cartoon hacks in belted raincoats with press tickets stuck in their hatbands, part of a legendary Fleet Street which may never have existed after all. However, they properly belong to the next chapter.

When journalese is needed

There are certain conventions in news writing which can be labelled 'journalese' but are necessary to the craft. We need them when our sources don't want to be identified, or when we want to help our readers distinguish between fact and rumour.

From a *Daily Telegraph* report on strikes by Liverpool council employees:

> There was growing concern in
> Whitehall last night that fur-
> ther strikes could push one of
> the country's biggest cities
> into total collapse.

And from *The Independent on Sunday* about the Charity Commission:

> There is growing concern among
> members of charities about the
> commission's willingness to
> exercise proper supervision.

From the same paper's business section:

> Speculation is growing that Olympia & York has substantial off-balance-sheet liabilities, which could mean that the ailing company's financial position is much weaker than previously believed. . . .
> Attention is focussing on Faisal Islamic Bank . . . which is believed to have made a transfer . . .

Concern was growing in the City last week that the company's financing may be much more complicated than has so far been revealed to the banks.

Growing concern is journalese. But civil servants hate being quoted. Even 'A Whitehall source said . . .' can give some of them the vapours. It is all part of the arcane system by which the British public is kept informed of government policies. It is quite unsatisfactory, but no one, as I write, has been able to do much about it.

In Chapter 1 we saw how the good journalist avoids abstract nouns and passive, impersonal forms – 'It is hoped that', 'The text has been subjected to close scrutiny' and so on – forms which leave things vague. But here the journalist *has* to be vague.

I don't know why the charities in that *Independent on Sunday's* report didn't want to be quoted. 'Growing concern among a number of charities' sounds like kite-flying to me. Even an unattributed quote would have strengthened the story; but no doubt there was a reason for their shyness. The Olympia & York story disguises, thinly, extreme caution among the paper's various sources, which in view of the stakes being played for is not surprising.

Anyway, there has to be a language to cover these situations. I translate:

Sources close to the Prime Minister (his press secretary)
It is believed (can't say who by, but probably true)
It is understood (firmer than the above)
I understand (exclusive story: can't reveal source, probably true)
I can disclose (exclusive story, certainly true)
I hear (a good gossip column version of 'I understand')
I learn (a good gossip column version of 'I can disclose')

The implications of *It is believed* and *I understand* are rather more subtle than the translation suggests. The journalist may know quite well that the story is true but may have been asked by his or her contact to make it sound like speculation. ('Mind, I never told you.')

Some quite respectable journalists resort to the formula 'There is growing concern among employers' (or trade unions, or whoever) to boost a speculative story. Others would call this an abuse of the conventions. We have only the writer's word for it. If used too often in this way, the device begins to backfire – readers stop believing in it.

3 WRITING FOR THE TABLOIDS

> Because the plain people are able to speak and understand, and even, in many cases, to read and write, it is assumed that they have ideas in their heads, and an appetite for more. This assumption is a folly. They dislike ideas, for ideas make them feel uncomfortable. – H. L. Mencken

Mencken, one of America's greatest journalists, wrote the above for the Chicago *Tribune* in 1926, when tabloid newspapers had only lately been invented. Mencken had never had a high opinion of the ordinary reader (then thought of as predominantly male) of mass-circulation newspapers. 'In all his miscellaneous reactions to ideas,' he wrote, 'he embraces invariably those that are the simplest, the least unfamiliar, the most comfortable – those that fit in most readily with his fundamental emotions.'

Pops and heavies

Mencken certainly underestimated the readers. But he was partly right. The aims of the popular press are quite different from those of the heavies. Of course, their functions overlap, but not much: so little, in fact, that good writing in the one might well be thought bad in the other, and vice versa.

And as the purpose is different, so is the language. I said in Chapter 1 that the language of journalism was nearer the spoken word than other kinds of language, and this is generally true. But it is much less true of the popular press.

Exclusive top-of-column news story in the *Daily Mirror*:

LABOUR WANT BRAVE JILL
TO STAND AS MP

Labour are to ask brave Jill
Morrell to stand for Parliament, the Mirror can reveal.
  They want the girl-
friend of freed hostage John
McCarthy to fight a crucial
by-election . . .

Here the functions of the pop and the heavy do overlap – such a story
would be of equal interest to either sort of paper. But the language the
Mirror used in the telling of it would obviously not do for a heavy. That
brave in the text, also picked out for the headline, would make any 'quality' sub-editor reach automatically for the Delete Word facility. But it is
part of the distinctive vocabulary of the British popular press

   Here is a formal and restricted language – as formal, almost, as that
of the old broadsheet ballads which were the forerunners of the mass-
circulation papers of today. (The word 'broadsheet' has changed since
that time, of course.)

   What we now call the broadsheets, or some call the 'serious' press, are
only too anxiously aware that their readers want something new every

---

The morning reading of the newspaper is a kind of realistic morning
prayer. It provides the same security as prayer, in that one knows
where one stands. – Friedrich Hegel

---

day: if not new facts (there may well be not enough of those to fill the
columns), then at least new ideas. Their aim is to make people sit up, to
stimulate and surprise them.

   The tabloids, on the other hand, are less in the business of new ideas.
Shock is a favourite tabloid word; but it is the shock of recognition that
the tabloids are offering. In this sense at any rate, Mencken did get it
right. A reporter for a popular paper, like his or her colleagues on the
qualities, is looking for a story. Unlike them, the popular paper reporter
wants a story that fits the readers' conception of the world, not one that
will disturb it – and uses language to match.

   The old ballads were the same.

The king sits in Dumfermline town
Drinking the blood-red wine.

The word *blood-red* was not put there just for information. The readers, or more likely listeners, knew very well what colour the wine would

have been, and in any case it was irrelevant to the story. But it was the word the balladmongers had always used when they sang of the wine drunk by kings and heroes; and when it was first heard it must have given a little frisson of pleasure, with its reminders of men's blood spilt, of blood ties, of strength and life. And perhaps even after meeting it a hundred times the listeners still heard its echoes. Anyway, such things stuck. They were part of the special way of telling a much-loved story.

The word *brave* in the *Mirror* story about Jill Morrell has exactly the same purpose. Everyone knew that Miss Morrell, who waited and campaigned for her friend during his long years in a Beirut jail, was brave. Her actions would have spoken for themselves even if she had not already been described as such in countless despatches. But, like the *blood-red* of the ballad, the word stuck, and was expected.

Popspeak, then, is another special language. It is quite different from ordinary speech, and is therefore an exception to the rule formulated in Chapter 1. The rule does hold good for the leaders in tabloids and for the more successful sort of regular signed column, whose authors do their best to make their language as much as possible like that of the man or woman in the street. A leader in the London *Daily Express* or *Sun* is nearly always a small masterpiece of simple and unaffected prose.

But news stories are another matter. They deal with a world in which blondes are *stunning* or, if at all attractive, *sizzling*, redheads *vivacious*

A simple test

If there is one single word by which you can distinguish a popular from a so-called quality paper it is *mum*, where a quality would have *mother* (DI'S MUM ILL). The test never fails. But see below for its application to the provincial press.

---

and dark girls *raven-haired*. Meanwhile, *sex romps* are also *sizzling*. Bereaved parents are *tragic*. Villages are *tiny communities*, but subject to *massive* upheavals when developers *send in the bulldozers*. And so on.

Writing in this way has a strong ritual flavour. As I say, it is highly formal. Since its stock of words is small, it is not hard to pick up. It is merely hard to do well.

For this is cliché-land. Clichés, much maligned as they are, have their place in popular news-writing. But they need to be handled with care if they are to have their intended effect. Too many dead clichés can turn good journalism into the tabloids' own unmistakable brand of journalese.

Provincials please don't copy

Because the vocabulary of Popspeak is so limited, one word may be called on to play many different parts. And because it seems so easy, the apprentice journalist is under a strong temptation to use it in newspapers where it is quite out of place – in provincial weeklies, for example, whose purpose is not the same as that of the tabloid dailies. An analysis of the news columns of the British popular press on any day of the week would probably show most column inches given to the world of entertainment, then to professional sport, then to crime, then to the doings of the very rich. Most readers of the local paper, I would guess, go to it for local news. So when we turn from one to the other we are turning from a world which is quite different from our own (for many people, almost a fantasy world) to one with which we are very familiar indeed. And we want to know what it's up to; it shouldn't need to be dressed up for us in the way we like stories in the pops to be.

Here, meanwhile, are some more examples of Popspeak gone wrong.

Words that are wearing out:

Bravery

We have agreed on the bravery of Miss Jill Morrell, who deserved her description. So, no doubt, did this policewoman:

GIRL PC IS KO'D BY LOUT
A brave policewoman was punched senseless after challenging a 6ft man in a multi-storey car park.

WPC Susan Snowdon lay unconscious for an hour before being found by colleagues worried that she had not responded to calls. – *The Sun*

And this celebrity·

BATTLING ANNE WINS COT DEATH VICTORY
Brave TV star Anne Diamond has won her crusade for a £2 million Government campaign to cut cot deaths.

And she will personally front an official television advert due to start screening in two weeks' time – five months after the cot death of her own baby. – *Daily Mirror*

But the bravery called for by the death of an infant, however heartbreaking, is not the same as that needed by the girlfriend of John McCarthy. In his *Dictionary of Clichés* Eric Partridge likens clichés to tired old workhorses which have become 'knock-kneed and spavined'. It is not a good dictionary – it is far too undiscriminating – but the phrase is apt. And when I saw this caption in the *Daily Mail* I really felt that *brave* was ready for the knacker's yard:

> Hollow triumph: brave Iain smiles through his fury at stumping up £37,000 for Bergerac's 'banger'. [Picture of man at wheel of old car.]

The story was about someone who had bought a Triumph roadster, used in a TV serial, for more than its real value.

Writers who shove *brave* in front of the name of anyone who happens to have suffered a minor misfortune have abandoned journalism for journalese. They are flying on autopilot.

Tiny

The cot deaths story quoted above continues:

> Britain has 1,400 tiny victims from the
> mystery killer every year.

Well, people who sleep in cots generally *are* tiny, aren't they? So the words tell us nothing, but at least it's accurate. It's just another ritual word like the *blood-red* of the ballad, and as such is harmless. What about this, though?

> ### GROTTO GRAB BY BOY, 12
> A tiny tearaway who couldn't wait for Christmas staged his own prezzie raid on Santa's grotto.
>   The 12-year-old hung around till Santa turned his back . . . –
> *News of the World*

How tiny is tiny? Perhaps it was the alliteration of 'tiny tearaway' that beguiled the reporter into using the adjective to describe a 12-year-old. But if we must use this overworked word, let's keep it for when it really makes sense.

Or find another term. A *Daily Express* story about a three-year-old girl savaged by dogs called her 'the tiny blonde child' (was she small for her age or what?) with another story under it about a six-year-old also savaged by dogs. But *he* was called 'a little boy', and it was probably for this reason that I found his story more affecting.

Stunning

This word used to be quite a knockout, but it has been so grossly over-worked by the pops that it hardly longer carries any punch at all.

> *Today's* Mike Moore has been named photographer of the year for this stunning picture of British troops capturing Iraqis.
> Mike was on the front line at the height of the Gulf War when he photographed Sergeant Tom Gorrion of the 1st Royal Scots during an assault on Iraqi armoured personnel carriers.

At one time *stunning* carried a strong connotation with pleasure, as in a pretty face or a landscape, but now it describes anything that is visually striking. A word which can be used as easily of unpleasant war pictures as it can of come-hither blondes is well down the scale. No word whose application is so general is likely to overexcite the readers.

> Her stunning Mayfair home in Hays Mews, behind Claridges, is soon to be the centre of Labour Party gatherings. – Article in the *Daily Mail* about Doris Saatchi

Wake me up when it's over.

Horrors

A newspaper cliché can be declared dead when it no longer has an effect on the emotion of the reader. This splash story from the *Sussex Express* will show what I mean:

POSTMAN KILLED IN HORROR CRASH
Car catches fire after collision with lorry
A Lewes postman died in a horror crash at Beddingham on the A26 on Saturday morning . . .

Here the word *horror* has become quite perfunctory. ('What sort of crash did they say it was?' – 'A horror crash, I believe.') It carries no more drama than the world *milk* in 'milk float'. Certainly it no longer causes the hair to stand on end, as it did when the English first took the word from the original Latin (where it meant the act of *quaking* from fear).

DOG RIPS NEWBORN BABY'S EAR OFF

A week-old baby boy had his right ear torn off in a horror attack by the family Jack Russell terrier.

His mother had just left the room when the blind dog savaged the child as he lay on a settee . . . – *Daily Mirror*

The words *in a horror attack* add nothing to the story. If anything, they diminish its impact. It could have started:

A week-old baby boy had his right ear torn off by the family dog, a blind Jack Russell terrier

which would also have brought out the interesting fact of the dog's blindness, instead of noting it *en passant* in the second paragraph. I have even seen *Horror* as a single-word crosshead in a *Daily Mirror* story. It was round the time of the Gulf War, but it was not about that. It was about a 'lucky toddler' who had survived a road crash with a minor bruise on the head ('Amazing escape of boy, 3').

Terror

Horror's twin sister. Used, of course – and very properly – of the *deadly missions* of IRA bombers and their like:

TERROR AT QUEEN'S CAVALRY CONCERT

A man was killed last night when an IRA car bomb exploded as a top Army band performed at a concert . . . – *The Sun*

but also for small domestic mishaps, as here:

WHIRLPOOL TERROR OF LONG-HAIRED SWIM GIRL

A schoolgirl almost drowned after her waist-length hair was sucked into a pipe in a leisure centre's whirlpool bath.

Carolyn Davidson, 12, struggled frantically to keep her head above the bubbling surface for ten minutes while her sister Louise tried to free her pony tail . . . – *Daily Mirror* [Caption: Horror ordeal . . .]

Why should Popspeak so restrict the number of words it uses that it has to recruit *terror* for both these very different occasions?

Massive

Badly overworked, and not only in the popular papers.

> Massive provisions against possible losses on the Channel Tunnel project. – *Independent on Sunday*
> Philips . . . is undergoing a massive restructuring. – The same, City pages
> A massive barrage of Allied bombing. – *Daily Star*
> A massive clean-up operation. – *Today*
> A massive irony. – Jonathon Green on Radio 4
> These figures [for rapes] are just the tip of a massive iceberg. – *Today*

Originally, *massive* was a word for anything solid and heavy (like the iceberg in the last example). Overuse has now diminished it so that it is hardly more than a shadow of itself, and just means *considerable*, with no notion of weight or volume. It is probably beyond rescue at this stage, but it certainly needs a rest.

The stronger the word, the more quickly it loses its strength.

Mysteries

Mystery is a favourite Popspeak word for use when reporters haven't been able to find out as much as they had hoped. Here is an extended caption in the *Daily Mirror*:

> Whacky Naomi Campbell has met her match – a date whose outfit is as weird as hers.
> The mystery pal, seen leaving a New York art gallery with the London-born model, is a vision in crushed velvet, boots and goggles.
> But Naomi shows her mettle in a chainmail mini skirt and Madonna-style boob protectors over a figure-hugging body suit.

It's certainly a stylish caption. But the only mysterious thing about Naomi's fella was that the journos didn't get his name. Another *Mirror* caption, under what that paper called a Pap Snap:

> Prince the singer may have a new girl in his life, but what about Prince Edward? The Queen's youngest son was with a mystery escort at a National Youth Theatre ball. The beautiful blonde looks as if she can shoulder the responsibility of mixing in royal circles. [The girl has an off-the-shoulder dress. See note on puns, below.]

They didn't get *her* name either. Now for two stories from the *Sunday Mirror*:

PILOT'S LAST FLIGHT RIDDLE

Mystery surrounds the death of a British stunt pilot found yesterday in a plane dragged from the sea.

It was believed to be ex-RAF officer John Hawke, once at the centre of a US political scandal when he was accused of smuggling bombers.

His six-seat private aircraft was recovered . . .

MYSTERY BODY FOUND AT SHOP

Mystery surrounds the discovery of a man's body after a break-in at a city bookstore yesterday.

Police are trying to identify the dead man, aged 25 to 35 – and to find out how he died.

The body was found in a yard at the back of Dillon's bookshop in Leeds.

Either of these intros might have been acceptable if they hadn't unfortunately appeared on facing pages of the same issue. Too many mysteries surrounding things and the readers might think there was something fishy going on. Perhaps reporters weren't staying with their stories long enough?

Perish the thought. To avoid such vile suspicions, we should think of fresher intros. Actually, the right-hand one above would have caught the eye just as well if the first sentence had been left out altogether:

Police are trying to identify the body of a man aged 25 to 35 found yesterday in a yard behind Dillon's bookstore in Leeds – and to find out how he died. . . .

The trouble with these minor mysteries is that they spoil the market for the bigger ones, like this story in the London *Evening Standard* written from Tenerife:

MAXWELL: NEW YACHT MYSTERY

A mystery yacht shadowed Robert Maxwell's *Lady Ghislaine* the day before he disappeared overboard, it has emerged here.

The vessel was seen in company with the dead publisher's yacht at Bunta de Abona, a picturesque bay in southern Tenerife where Maxwell spent several hours last Monday . . .

That looked like a proper mystery all right, with some of the ingredients of a good paperback from the Mystery and Suspense section of the lending library. But the poor old word has been so overworked that, in newspapers at any rate, it no longer casts much of a spell. Let's give it a break.

Bitterness

There is life in the old word yet, but I guess it is terribly tired and wants to lie down. From the *Daily Star*:

SECRET AGONY OF BOY SOLDIER
Boy soldier Vincent Stott went to war in the Gulf nursing a secret heartache.
His mum and dad are in the middle of a bitter divorce.

This sounds like what we call 'a human story' until we learn lower down the column that the divorce was, if anything, reasonably amicable, that the parents stayed together for as long as possible for the sake of the children, that the split took place a year earlier and that, according to the lad's father, 'Vincent hasn't allowed the situation to affect his Army life'.

In other words, 'bitter' is just a come-on. Or rather a mere reflex on the part of the reporter. Also from the *Daily Star*:

NO ELTON AT DAD'S FUNERAL
Megastar Elton John shunned his father Stanley Dwight's funeral yesterday – the final snub in a bitter 18-year rift . . .
Elton, 44, has said that as a child he was afraid of his father, 66.

And from the pro-European *Daily Mirror*:

(From Alastair Campbell in Maastricht) Britain was left completely isolated in Europe yesterday as Premier John Major almost wrecked the EC summit.
He stubbornly refused to sign the historic treaty of Maastricht unless a whole chapter on social policies was dropped . . .
The dropping of the social chapter, which includes a charter on pensioners' rights, was a sensational ending to two days of bitter argument.

Those who may have read of the far from bitter divorce are the less likely to believe in the bitterness of the pop star's rift with his father; and if they decide to graduate to the *Daily Mirror* they will also wonder whether the Maastricht talks were as bitter as the reporter assures them they were.

Bad currency drives out good. If we have doubts about the bitterness of the talks, we may also begin to take an equally cynical view of that 'stubbornly' in Alastair Campbell's second par – which would be a pity, since it is an important word in his deftly angled report.

Here we go again:

> Prince Charles was at the centre of a bitter row yesterday after taking his seven-year-old son Harry on a hunt in which two hares were killed.
>
> Princess Anne's daughter Zara, ten, was also among the 20 children in the party of 50 riders.
>
> Angry anti-blood sports campaigners attacked Charles for encouraging the youngster to kill animals . . .
>
> But joint hunt master Roger Bradbury did not think the royals saw animals killed . . .
>
> Another member said: 'The royal visitors joined the chase. Whether they saw any hares, I don't know.
>
> 'None of us is bloodthirsty and the killing is minimal' . . . – *Daily Mirror*

An interesting story. But couldn't the reporter have come up with something more exciting than 'a bitter row'? You will notice that in this case there was not, in fact, a 'row' at all. The hunt saboteurs and the League against Cruel Sports were certainly outraged, but the hunt people were keeping a very low profile.

Ironically, if there *had* been such a row I am pretty sure the reporter would have used another form of words. For 'bitter row' is feeble stuff. Seeing the phrase, readers might think the story was not up to much.

There was an add to that story, starting 'The hunt storm was the latest in a series to hit the Royal Family'. So if the reporter had wanted to keep his intro, but avoid the 'bitter row' turn-off, he would have been justified in starting:

> Prince Charles was at the centre of another scandal yesterday after he took his seven-year-old son Harry on a hunt in which two hares were killed.

But to make them really sit up, couldn't he have cut the cackle and gone to the stark point?

> Prince Charles was accused yesterday of encouraging his young son and niece to kill animals.
>
> Anti-blood-sports campaigners were outraged when he took his seven-year-old son Harry on a hunt in which two hares were killed. Princess Anne's daughter Zara, ten, was also among the 20 children at the hunt. . . .

Meanwhile I learned from my *Daily Express* that Sinn Fein candidate Gerry Adams was beaten at the 1992 General Election because of the tactics of his 'bitter enemies'. How did he feel about that? You guessed it. 'Bitterly.' But by then the readers were so used to all this bitterness that they probably didn't notice.

Dreams and nightmares

Nightmares are suffered by political hostages ('His sunken eyes and thin face reveal his nightmare' – *Daily Mirror* caption under picture of Terry Waite). They are also what dreams turn into.

WEDDING OFF AT HEARTBREAK HOTEL
A dream wedding in paradise turned into a holiday nightmare for a young Oxfordshire couple.

They returned home unmarried midway through the trip after finding the hotel ceiling leaked, rooms were dirty, the restaurant floor was being dug up with power drills and the food was often cold

– *Oxford Mail* [Caption: Nightmare . . .]

Then there was the reported collapse of Olivia Newton-John's leisurewear company, which left 'the trail of trusting fans . . . claiming its slipshod business practices shattered their dreams', according to *Today*. It went on to tell us that Miss Newton-John was advertised as 'a strong glamorous lady who has many dreams and the ability to make those dreams come true' but that 'the dream quickly turned into nightmare'.

This is tedious stuff – not because of the subject matter, which no doubt also made the City pages, but because of those clichés. It should not be imitated, unless you wanted to write for *Today* (which may have improved since that piece was written).

Exaggeration

A tendency to exaggerate is natural to my profession: we want to make *our* version of the story more interesting than our rivals'. Popspeak is particularly vulnerable to this temptation; and it succumbs to it, as we have seen, by cramming in a limited range of emotive words. The *Daily Star* shows the method in full flower in this court report (my italics):

LOCK ME AWAY FOR EVER BEGS SEX BEAST
Young sisters stabbed by rape-bid monster

A *psycho sex monster* begged to be *caged* forever after *viciously* attacking two young sisters.

And yesterday a judge obliged – by handing *lust-crazed* James Hattel FOUR life sentences.

Just a month before *pouncing* on the girls, aged 13 and eight, *madman* Hattel had been released from jail three years early, the court heard.

The 24-year-old bachelor *terrified* the elder girl so much that she *leapt* from a 23ft-high window and suffered serious back injuries.

After *bursting* into their house he had threatened her with a screwdriver and was *tearing* off her clothes to rape her when her sister entered the room . . .

Seconds later the *frenzied sex fiend* stabbed the girls with the screwdriver.

This might seem fairly harmless, if language did not devalue so easily. Unfortunately, the resulting inflationary spiral means that popular journalists have to make more and more journeys to the treasury in search of

> The story is told of a couple outside a cinema looking at a garish sign which says: 'COLOSSAL! STUPENDOUS! The Greatest Cinematic Attraction of All Time!' And the woman turns to her husband and says: 'I wonder if it's any good, dear.' – Randolph Quirk.*

stronger and stronger words. You may have noticed, for example, that hardly anyone is angry these days, if we are to judge by reports in the tabloid press. They are always *furious*. (No doubt *furious* will eventually lose its power of attracting attention, and we shall be reading: APOPLECTIC RATEPAYERS DEMAND REBATES.)

Exaggeration becomes a serious matter when it leads to factual distortion, as it may have done in the *Daily Mirror* report of Terry Waite's release already quoted from.

Joyful Terry Waite [it says] flashes a smile of freedom . . . yet it cannot hide the terrible toll exacted by the man of God's 1,763 days in hell.

The 52-year-old church envoy looked sunken-eyed and desperately tired last night as he faced the world he left behind nearly five years ago.

*Originally, I think, a *Punch* cartoon.

But down-column the *Mirror* quotes Waite's cousin John as saying that Terry didn't look too bad. The reporter's problem was: which way should he treat it? Which of the two possible angles should he choose? How well Terry looked – or how ill? Once he had plumped for the latter, he had to go for it with all he'd got.

Bad habits are hard to break. Take these two reports:

1   MASSACRE: B52 BLITZ WIPES OUT IRAQI HORDES
Thousands of Iraqi troops were dead or wounded last night as the might of the Allies' bomber force relentlessly blasted their columns.
Five or six brigades – up to 60,000 men – were trapped in a 15-mile convoy of carnage.
More than 1,000 tanks and armoured vehicles had been ordered by Saddam Hussein to thrust out of Kuwait to invade Saudi Arabia. They faced a massacre in the desert.

Blasted
America's huge B52 bombers dropped awesome 'sticks' of 2,000lb bombs, which leave 40-ft craters stretching for a mile . . .
Harriers also blasted the Iraqi armour with bombs and missiles . . .
Apache tank-killing helicopters blitzed the Iraqis' Soviet-built tanks with hellfire missiles, incinerating the crews on impact.
American A-10 Thunderbolt jets are also believed to have scored massive successes.
Their fearsome Gatling guns spewed out a deadly hail of armour-piercing bullets. – *The Sun*

2   STORE WARS: XMAS SHOPPERS CASH IN AS PRICE WAR RAGES
A Christmas price war erupted between Britain's big supermarket chains yesterday.
Asda fired the first salvo by freezing the price of more than 30,000 items until the New Year.
The sudden attack left rivals Sainsbury's, Tesco and Gateway reeling. But by last night they were set to blast back with volleys of discounts and reductions. – *Daily Mirror*

Both appeared in the same year, 1991. I needn't say much about *The Sun's* war report, with its great clumps of cliché hardly worthy of a boys' second-rate comic. The *Mirror* report could just about be accepted as a take-off – but how sad that its reporter could only think of those tired old images!

Real reporting: a comparison

Clichés are substitutes for experience. Two further reports from the Gulf War, both from the same issue of *Today*, make an instructive contrast:

1 A desperate attempt by Saddam Hussein to invade Saudi Arabia has been stopped in its tracks by a massive Allied air strike.

   Wave after wave of American B52 bombers queued up to wreak havoc on a 10-mile Iraqi tank convoy heading across the desert.

   Dozens of enemy tanks were ripped apart as thousands of tons of armour-piercing bombs rained down.

   Many of the crews were killed by the shockwave as the powerful missiles ripped apart the metal casings . . .

   US Marines battered the target with heavy artillery fire, while B52s, Harrier jump-jets and Cobra anti-tank helicopters roared in overhead . . .

   The sinister-looking AH-64 Apache attack helicopters swooped down, then hung menacingly in the air as their Hellfire laser-guided missiles streaked across the sky . . .

2 They were pinned down by shellfire, explosions pounding around their bodies.

   Someone was watching the Allied soldiers, guiding the enemy bombs into their path – kicking up 6ft craters in the Saudi desert.

   They looked anxiously towards their signalman who was desperately trying to alert his recce unit in Khafji town centre.

   The American Army captain became frustrated by the Iraqi 'sniper spy'. As a shell hit the sand just 20 yards from a petrol station where his wagons were circled, he ordered 'Find him'.

   Seconds later, the radio man spun round. 'We've got him. Jeezus, he's in the water tower.'

   As air support was called up, the captain trained his eyes on the smoke-palled face of Khafji just one hazy kilometre away and picked out the soaring, sand-coloured rectangular tower. It was the obvious position for the Iraqi forward artillery controller.

The first is like a child's drawing of war ('Kerpow!!'). It is datelined

> Epithets are used for their likely effect on the reader, not to catch the nature of what is being described.
> – Richard Hoggart, on bad autobiographies

Riyadh, the Saudi Arabian capital. The second is datelined Khafji, the desert township the Allies are supposed to have taken, and it has no need of war-clichés – all the reporter has to do is tell us what he saw. It is therefore more compelling and more credible than the first, which reads rather like the imaginative interpretation of a press briefing, presumably the same briefing given to the *Sun* reporter quoted earlier. It may be that the *Sun* man was congratulated by his foreign editor for having made more out of that briefing than did his colleague from *Today*. In a sense he did do better: he got more figures in. In another sense he did worse, because his cliché-count was that much higher.

Bias

One of the most notable differences between Popspeak and other kinds of journalism is to be found in its treatment of news. A news item in a good broadsheet may well be biased, intentionally or otherwise, but the bias is likely to consist in selected quotes or the omission of certain facts. Bias in tabloids, on the other hand, is blatant and unashamed. It is simply a question of bombarding the reader with emotive words and phrases. A *Daily Mirror* splash:

> The two bungling American pilots who slaughtered nine British soldiers were branded as reckless killers last night.
>
> Relatives of the Desert Rats who died clapped and cheered as the 'friendly fire' inquest ended in sensational verdicts of unlawful killing. The unnamed Top Gun pilots had already been condemned as cowards without honour for refusing to give evidence at the Oxford inquest (etc.).

Bungling, slaughtered, reckless killers – such words are pure opinion-form-ers. (The headline is DISHONOUR AND DISGRACE.) Many other journalists pointed out that mistakes of the kind made by the admittedly

> Newspapers . . . should distinguish clearly between comment, conjec-ture and fact. – Newspaper editors' agreed Code of Conduct

incompetent Americans in this Gulf War incident are common in all wars. The *Daily Mirror* chose to exploit the relatives' grief and the chau-vinistic feelings which naturally went with it.

The *Mirror* was entitled to its opinion. The important difference, though, is that the broadsheets put their views on the affair in leaders or features, not in their news columns.*

* But see page 122 for a blatant example of biased 'reporting' in *The Observer*.

Such biased news reporting is not difficult to write, and I have known many colleagues who have been very good at it, though some have been distressed when their editors' prejudices happened to conflict with their own.

A new catechism

MYLES na gCopaleen, as mentioned in the previous chapter, devised a Catechism of Cliché to shame the hacks. His Catechism being now more than a quarter of a century old, I offer a short update.

How did the kidnapped man look when he got back? – He was tired.
Of course, but how tired? – I would say desperately tired.
What sort of prison was he held in? – It was a hell prison.
And what is his next move now? – To recover from his nightmare.
Very good. And what did his wife do when she saw him? – She wept.
How did she weep? – Openly.
And what? – Tears of joy.
Was that all she did? – No. She fell into his arms.
What does she look like? – She is beautiful.
Bubbly blonde, or curvy brunette? – Do you mind? This is a serious horror story, not a showbiz story.
I beg your pardon. Would you call his captors violent? – They were brutal killers.
Is that all? – No.
What else then? – They were callous.
Quite so. And how long was he held for? – They were his 80 days of terror.
I suppose his relatives were uneasy? – Their prayers were anguished.
And how often did they pray? – Night and day.
I understand his prison caught fire. – It did not. It became a blazing inferno.
How long did it burn for? – It raged for three hours.
Wasn't he hurt? – No.
How not? – It was his miraculous escape.
But his colleague died in the fire? – No.
What then? – He perished in the blaze.
What does a nation do on such occasions? – It mourns.
And how is his *tragic* widow looking? – She is beautiful, etc.

Pop glossary

Now, as a further service to any of my readers who may find themselves working for a Fleet Street tabloid, I append a short glossary.

Brave   of anyone who has been inconvenienced.

Terror   an unhappy experience.

Ordeal   ditto, but lasting longer.

Horror   ditto, usually involving physical hurt.

Horror (adj.)   hurtful or alarming (a horror crash).

Hell (adj.)   uncomfortable (homeless in hell hostels).

Stunning   better than average.

Curvy   female; replaced *curvaceous*, now obsolete.

Chilling   of anonymous messages (the chilling tape).

Callous   of any criminal or wrongdoer. 'A callous motorist mowed down a schoolgirl on a pelican crossing and left her screaming in agony.' – *Today*. 'A boy aged eight was callously shot in the head while screaming for mercy during a terrorist attack on a bar yesterday.' – *Daily Mirror*.

Tiny   of any village or child.

Giant   big (mostly concrete: a giant steelworks).

Massive   ditto (more abstract: a massive increase, a massive police operation).

Accident-prone   of a politician.

Probe   any investigation.

Bitter   of a difference of opinion, or any divorce.

Star-studded   including some showbiz people.

Mystery   wouldn't give his name.

Fury   a feeling of regret.

Furious   displeased.

A note on puns

Puns are a speciality of the tabloid press, and anyone with ambitions to write for it must learn how to perpetrate them. They are mainly of two sorts.

The first is a mere play on the sound of names, and need not be particularly witty. A favourable review of a play starring Joely Richardson is headed 'Joely Good Show'. A par in Anna Raeburn's *People* column is headed 'Re-Joyce with a Wise Old Lady' for no better reason than that someone whose views Miss Raeburn agrees with is called Joyce Skinner. And dishy Diane Harman, *The Sun's* Essex Girl of the Year, is described in that paper as having 'Essex appeal', a pun which so pleased the subs that they headed the story 'Di's real Essex-y'. (Only the weakest puns need hyphens.)

An even feebler sub-category of the above is the pun which plays on mere word sounds, like this:

FIN-TASTIC
Nigel's a reel star

Racing driver Nigel Mansell had a reel battle on his hands when he went sea fishing . . . – *Daily Mirror*

A single further example will, I hope, be enough. It is the caption to one of the topless girls from *The Sun*, and I have italicized the puns in it:

Ward a bit of luck! Lovely Amanda Jayne Forbes got *sick* of her job as a nurse – and vowed to *inject* some glamour into her career.

Fellas *feel better* since the 22-year-old Leicestershire beauty decided to *op* off and become a model. Well, it's *patient-ly* obvious – she looks such an *angel* on page 3.

Ward, op and *patient-ly* (a poor pun on *patently*) are in this category.

The other puns in *The Sun's* caption are of the second sort. They deal not in double sounds but in double meanings; and though those above are clumsily contrived (any pun will do for a Page Three caption) they give more room for wit. I quite liked this effort in *The People*:

LOVE FOR £2M WIFE A WASHOUT

Plumber Derek Tull was driven round the bend by the cruel insults of his nagging millionaire wife . . .

The henpecked husband's 23-year marriage finally went down the drain after a sympathetic judge granted him a divorce.

And this London *Evening Standard* headline had some style:

GOLFERS TAKE A SWING AT CRIME

(It was about a golf club which started a Neighbourhood Watch scheme.) So had this brief item from the *Daily Mirror*:

A firm that struck gold making Maggie Thatcher garden gnomes has closed at Gateshead, Tyne and Wear, for lack of orders.

The heading? Mrs T ON SHELF.

The tabloids are by no means the only ones to go for puns, though in other papers they are not compulsory. I must admit I admired a 1992 election sketch by Mark Lawson of *The Independent* which managed to keep punning for five long paragraphs without sending me, groaning, to sleep. It reported Tory MP Kenneth Clarke's visits to some butchers' shops, and I give a taste of it here:

> IN A last attempt to save the bacon of a Tory campaign widely thought to lack beef, Kenneth Clarke went to the butchers on Saturday afternoon. In one street in the Wolverhampton North-East constituency, held in 1987 by Maureen Hicks by an extra-lean cut of 204 votes, the Secretary of State for Education visited three rival meat-and-pie kings . . .
>
> More worrying for Mr Clarke was the number of grouses hanging around the butcher's shops. . . . Less chicken than most modern politicians when hooked, Mr Clarke grilled him on the Uniform Business Rate and suggested that the last few months had been economically less bloody. The butcher felt that this is what Chris Patten calls a 'porkie'. Momentarily stuffed, the politician left the shop.
>
> Back on the streets, a large number of shoppers took one butcher's (Patten rhyming slang for 'look') at Clarke and flew past or cooked him with a look. 'Not today thank you, Mr Clarke, I don't agree with you one bit!' shouted one shopper, his Midlands whine rising like a cleaver.
>
> Such a choppy reception would dismay some politicians . . .

Mr Lawson ended:

> If the Conservative gravy train is halted on Thursday, he will still emerge from the abattoir of Tory hopes with a juicy stake, perhaps even that of leader. For his colleagues in the marginals, though, it looks like slaughter.

Only in the last par did the piece falter, with its pop-style sound-pun *juicy stake*.

Good puns like these need to be *apposite*. Otherwise they are like meaningless jingles. A punning headline should be reflected in the copy, like this one from *The Independent on Sunday*, over a story about a merry party for former subjects of the radio programme *Desert Island Discs*:

DESERT ISLANDERS GO FOR THE JOCULAR

This one, put up by a *Sunday Telegraph* colleague (now retired) over the Music Critic's piece, sounded promising:

HAYDN SEEK

and the piece was certainly about Haydn, but one looked in vain for its justification. An attempt at punning by the *Sunday Times* over a story of supposed cruelty to horses –

ANIMAL LOBBY BRIDLES AT SIENA RACES

– was, I fear, not much better than Page Three standard. But puns *are* difficult, partly because any fool can make them. The only sound advice is: don't force them.

4 WAYS TO START A STORY

'Begin at the beginning, and go on until you come to the end. Then stop.' –
King to White Rabbit, *Alice in Wonderland*

Everyone knows the old saying: if you can't get their attention in the first
sentence (or the first eight seconds) they won't bother with the rest. And
news editors want to know 'what's the point of the story?'

First things first: A Sussex tale

In the following elementary example, from a local weekly, the point of
the story appears only in the third paragraph. It is a boxed column-lead
in a full-page news feature, and the subject is an £80 million road
improvement scheme in the valley of the Sussex Ouse:

A LIVELY DISCUSSION

Members of Glynde and Beddingham parish council staged a public
meeting to discuss the road proposals.

There was a very lively discussion and parish council members
went into detail about the plans, especially about the proposed
works below Mount Caburn and the route of the A27 past
Beddingham.

At a vote of the councillors, they opted to recommend rejection of
the DoT red and green routes for the A27 and press for the dual car-
riagewaying of the present road with roundabouts rather than
flyovers or bridges.

For the A26 they did not like any of the DoT proposals and preferred a single carriageway west of Beddingham along the line of the
suggested pink route.

Andrew Lusted, *Sussex Express* correspondent for Glynde,
Beddingham and Firle, who was at the meeting, said: 'It seems to me
that the recommendations for the A27 have several problems . . .'

This story starts at the third paragraph. The first two merely tell us that there was a public meeting and what it was about. Not very exciting. (In fact, since those contentious routes apparently went slap through their parish, there would have been a good news story if the councillors had decided *not* to hold a meeting.) But in what way was it lively? We long for details which we don't get.

Obviously the third paragraph (adjusted a little) should have come first – something like this:

> Glynde and Berwick parish councillors have rejected both the DoT's proposed routes – the red and the green – for the A27. Instead they want the present road made into a dual carriageway, with no flyovers or bridges – only roundabouts.
>
> Nor do they like any of the DoT's proposals for the A26 . . . (etc.)
>
> The councillors' vote came at the end of a lively public meeting which discussed the plans in detail, particularly the proposed works below Mount Caburn and the route of the A27 past Beddingham. . . .
>
> Our local correspondent Andrew Lusted writes: . . .

There are, of course, further difficulties about this story (one of them being that the person who wrote the first four paragraphs apparently wasn't there). The sentence starting

> At a vote of the councillors, they opted to recommend rejection

is a puzzle. We know what 'opted to recommend' means ('recommended' would have been good enough) but why did only the councillors vote at this public meeting, and to whom did they recommend their proposals? (It is not good enough to say that wise local citizens knew the answers at the time; the story will have gone on file, to puzzle those coming across it later.)

But these are minor matters, and are aside from my immediate concern, which is: *Start at the beginning.*

The story below this one on the same page does better:

Hughes adds his objections

LibDem MP Simon Hughes, the party's environmental spokesman, has added his voice to local objections to the Department of Transport's options for the A26/A27 improvements.

After studying the proposals, meeting local councillors and touring the area, including Mount Caburn, on Monday he said the Department's schemes were 'exaggerated'.

'Improvements are needed but there is no justification for flyovers in an Area of Outstanding Natural Beauty,' said Mr Hughes. . . .

The first sentence does tell us something – that the locals have the support of Mr Hughes – but not his reasons, which emerge only in the second and third pars. Another way of doing it might have been to kick off with that rather good quote in the third:

Hughes adds his objections

'There is no justification for flyovers in an Area of Outstanding Natural Beauty,' said Mr Simon Hughes, LibDem environment spokesman, on Monday.

Mr Hughes had been making a tour of the area covered by the DoT's plans for the A26/27, including Mount Caburn, and had studied the DoT's proposals and discussed them with local councillors.

He agreed that improvements were needed, but the Government's schemes were 'exaggerated', he said.

The main story on the page gets to the point straight away:

'GO BACK TO THE DRAWING BOARD'

More than 300 people packed into Lewes Town Hall last Thursday to oppose the new £80 million A27 road scheme.

Department of Transport men were told in no uncertain terms to go back to the drawing board.

At one point, when someone showed a preference for trains, a clearly irritated DoT man Colin Wood told the audience: 'We have come all the way here to discuss a road, not your idealism.'

County engineer Brian Kermode told the meeting – organised by the district council – that the A27 east of Lewes carried about 22,000 vehicles a day . . . (etc.).

Here the reporter has put the best bits first; he doesn't have to tell us that it was 'a lively meeting'. We know it was from the text. The less interesting (but essential) details, such as who organized the meeting, are tucked away between dashes.

Beneath his report is another story which starts:

IMPROVEMENT LONG OVERDUE

Improvement of the A27 is long overdue and the Friends of Lewes warmly support the dualling of the route between Lewes and Polegate.

However the society cannot support any of the options proposed between Lewes and Beddingham . . . (etc.)

This looks rather odd, until you realize that it is simply the unsubbed transcription of a statement put out by the local amenity society. If the edition loomed and there was no time to write up the story, it could have started:

> The Friends of Lewes have also come out against all the DoT's plans. Their statement declares: . . .

and then carried the statement. It would have been the work of a moment, and would have at least told readers in the first sentence what it was really about. The headline, which has nothing to do with the main thrust of the statement, could have been altered at the same time. Here endeth the lesson from Sussex.

One thing at a time

Often a story is complicated and it is hard to explain what is going on in the space of a moderately sized introductory paragraph. At this point the temptation to cram as much as possible into the first sentence is very strong.

But it should, if possible, be resisted. Otherwise we can too easily get something like this:

> John Major and his closest ministers decided yesterday to meet head-on the expected onslaughts by Mrs Thatcher over the betrayal of her legacy rather than repeat recent attempts to persuade the deposed prime minister to tone down her speeches or even to gag her completely.
>
>   Mrs Thatcher . . . has already vowed to end her self-imposed domestic silence . . . – Political Correspondent, *The Guardian*, 20 July 1991

Even readers of *The Guardian*, who are rightly or wrongly supposed to have more leisure for reading than most people, might have found the first sentence too crowded for their liking.

A more downmarket paper, if it had had the story, would have made it much easier for their customers:

> Premier John Major has at last decided how to cope with an embarrassing problem – the wrath of Maggie.
>
>   The deposed Iron Lady believes that her successor is betraying her ideals. And from now on she is not going to be afraid to say so.
>
>   Yesterday the prime minister and his closest colleagues plucked up their courage and agreed: there is only one solution.

To answer back.

Up to now they have tried to persuade Mrs Thatcher to tone down her promised attacks. They even thought they might be able to shut her up altogether. Perhaps they should have guessed that it wouldn't work . . .

– and so on. But *The Guardian's* news columns are not quite the place for this mildly jocular talk, though there is plenty of it in other parts of the paper.

The real problem, perhaps, with that *Guardian* intro is the long clause 'to meet head-on the expected onslaughts by Mrs Thatcher over the betrayal of her legacy'. Apart from its length, it has the disadvantage of being in a passive form. And it seems to need more verbs, fewer abstract nouns. A more direct version would read:

John Major and his colleagues decided yesterday to meet Mrs Thatcher head-on when, as expected, she begins to belabour them for having betrayed her legacy.

There would be no harm, I should have thought, in breaking off there and starting a fresh sentence. Perhaps we should also do something with 'repeat recent attempts to persuade', because as it stands it is too impersonal: it doesn't make clear who has been making the attempts. So we could restart it (assuming that this is what the writer meant):

All their recent efforts to persuade her to stay silent, or at least to tone down her speeches, have clearly failed.

Let us now put the two versions side by side (new version on the right):

John Major and his closest ministers decided yesterday to meet head-on the expected onslaughts by Mrs Thatcher over the betrayal of her legacy rather than repeat recent attempts to persuade the deposed prime minister to tone down her speeches or even to gag her completely.	John Major and his closest ministers decided yesterday to meet Mrs Thatcher head-on when, as expected, she begins to belabour them for having betrayed her legacy. All their recent efforts to persuade her to stay silent, or at least to tone down her speeches, have clearly failed.

This keeps the shape of the paragraph but gives the reader a breathing-space in the middle of it. Some people, however, might think the second sentence – about John Major's failure to gag Mrs Thatcher – was the more compelling, likelier to engage readers' attention than the news about what he was going to do about it. Admittedly it makes a negative start, but it does put things in the order in which they happened. Let's try it (new version on the left):

John Major has had to give up his attempts to muzzle Mrs Thatcher when, as promised, she ends her self-imposed domestic silence. He had hoped at least to persuade her to tone down her speeches. But yesterday he and his closest ministers decided to meet head-on her charge that they have betrayed the legacy she left them.

John Major and his closest ministers decided yesterday to meet Mrs Thatcher head-on when, as expected, she begins to belabour them for having betrayed her legacy. All their recent efforts to persuade her to stay silent, or least to tone down her speeches, have clearly failed.

Mrs Thatcher . . . has already vowed . . . etc.

The left-hand version is certainly a bit smoother. The rest is a matter of taste, or news judgement.

Running stories

The hardest intros to write are those which take up a running story. This item in *The Times* gets itself into complications by trying to keep too many balls in the air at the same time. It begins:

> John Major yesterday invited the administrators who moved in to take control of the Canary Wharf project to put forward their plans for the troubled development in London's Docklands.
>
> The move came after 11 banks refused to put up more money for Olympia & York, the Canadian developer behind the biggest property scheme in Europe.
>
> The prime minister appeared to rule out any government rescue package or a change in its insistence that it would help to pay for the Jubilee Line Underground extension, which is seen as vital to the success of Canary Wharf, only if the private sector makes a substantial contribution.

The first paragraph wants to explain that Canary Wharf has gone bust *and* how the prime minister reacted to the news. To do so it has to have an unwieldy noun-clause in it ('the administrators who moved in to take control of the Canary Wharf project') which holds things up and makes one reluctant to read further. But it is the third par that is the real trouble.

The structure of this 50-word sentence suggests that it was run up in a bit of a hurry and is in danger of imminent collapse. It is certainly far too complex for a news update. Its weakest point, of course, is the sub-sub-clause 'which is seen as vital to the success of Canary Wharf': the necessary comma after 'extension' momentarily misleads the reader into thinking that the prime minister was still insisting on subsidizing the Jubilee Line extension. Only after we have got through the sub-sub-clause and reached the qualifying clause beyond it do we realize what the sentence is really about.

It was a tricky story to handle. But the *Daily Telegraph* showed how it could be done. Its splash that day started:

> Mr Major ruled out last night any immediate Government rescue package for the debt-ridden Canary Wharf development in London Docklands which the High Court placed in administration earlier in the day.

This is actually five or six words longer than *The Times's* first paragraph but feels shorter because its structure is simpler. More important, it tells us immediately what the point of the update is – the prime minister's apparent refusal to bail out the developers – which *The Times* left to its third par.* (His invitation to the administrators would have been of less general interest, one would have thought.) Most important, though, it doesn't try to tell us everything at once. The fate of the Jubilee Line comes later, after a fairly leisurely explanation (which I have not quoted) of what it means to be 'placed in administration'. And because the Jubilee Line is dealt with on its own, rather than mixed up with the future of Canary Wharf, the situation can be put far more lucidly:

> The Prime Minister stressed that the Government was sticking to its policy that the Jubilee Line Underground extension to Docklands, seen as vital to saving the project, would not go ahead unless the developers came up with a substantial contribution towards the cost.

This is quite a lot neater than the quasi-negative *appeared to rule out . . . a change in its insistence* of the *Times* version.

* Strangely enough, the *Times* subs picked out the subject of the *Telegraph's* nose for their headline (RESCUE DOUBTS GROW AT CANARY WHARF) while the *Telegraph* subs – or someone in the office – did the reverse, heading the story MAJOR READY FOR TALKS ON CANARY WHARF. No doubt there were reasons for this interesting paradox.

I contrast these two treatments of the same story not to rubbish *The Times* but to show how hard it can be to squeeze an involved situation into a few words which explain accurately and unambiguously what's been going on. It needs practice.

Some journalists can practise on the news editor, the trick being to finish telling him or her the nub of your story before his eyes have strayed back to his screen, or to the papers on his desk. If that busy person stops listening before you've got there, you've failed: you should have managed it in fewer words still. Others, away from the news room, perhaps have to do the same thing from a callbox, which can also concentrate the mind. One former editor of mine used to advise us to try what he called the Soup Test. You had to imagine that your neighbour at a dinner party had turned to you during the soup course and said 'Just what *is* that story you're on about?' and you had to finish your answer before they took the next mouthful. (If you stop the spoon midway between plate and mouth, you've probably got a good one.)

One can practise mental self-subbing at any time. Imagine you have to go back to hospital for a check-up after an operation and are anxious to know whether your recovery is on-course. The surgeon is in a terrible rush. Breathlessly you ask:

'I seem to be progressing rather slowly, do you think the recovery rate is likely to speed up later?'

By the time you'd finished saying this the surgeon would have been half-way out of the room. So you sub it down:

'Does recovery usually start slow and end fast, or the other way round, would you say?'

Still too wordy. Try again:

'Will I be getting better any quicker from now on?'

That, with any luck, will stop him in his tracks.

Such mental exercises can be applied to all sorts of imaginary situations and can help stave off boredom.

5 SEQUENCE AND STRUCTURE

The classic rule says that no newspaper story should need to be read twice, even by a jaded commuter squashed into a bumpy train. The rule is harder to observe than it sounds, as these further examples show.

Storytelling props: 'As'

Another good example of the running story was the stolen papers scandal in the run-up to the general election of 1992. A document taken from the offices of Paddy Ashdown's solicitor seemed to suggest that he had had an affair with his secretary some years earlier, and the first question (soon answered) was whether this would affect his career as Liberal Democrat leader. But then came evidence of other recent break-ins. The newspapers had to keep their readers abreast of the latest *revelations*, which were not, however, the latest *events*. It was all very complicated. *The Independent* solved the problem by using the 'as' construction – linking two different statements with an 'as' and leaving the reader to sort out the relationship between them. Its front page started like this:

> Fresh evidence of break-ins at Opposition MPs' offices emerged yesterday as some Labour MPs demanded an inquiry into possible intelligence service or Conservative Party involvement in a series of thefts of computer disks and equipment.
>
> The Liberal Democrats revealed that, away from Westminster, they had suffered apparently similar thefts of computer records as reported by five Labour MPs in the Commons.
>
> Peter Hain, Labour MP for Neath, called for inquiries into 'possible intelligence services' involvement and that of Conservative Party supporters' . . .
>
> The fresh row came as senior figures in all parties called for an end to political smears and personality attacks . . .

There are a number of things happening on top of each other here, and it is not clear in what order. What is the story? Is it the news of the LibDems' revelations about their break-ins, or Labour members' demand for an inquiry into *their* break-ins? Or should it have been the ugly' suspicions of Mr Hain and his colleagues?

That is the trouble with the 'as' construction. There are two examples of it above – 'emerged yesterday as' and 'the fresh row came as'. It hardly ever works. Here the reporter should have decided firmly what the most important part of the story was and taken it from there. He should have tried the Soup Test.

The Sun's man in New York apparently couldn't make up his mind about the following story, so he used an 'as':

Rap stars battled to save fans as eight youngsters were crushed to death after a mob of teenagers burst into a charity basketball game.

For readers who weren't rap fans the story was obviously the unpleasant deaths of eight young people, then the guilt of the promoters who oversold. But the reporter (or a rewrite man in London?) decided that the fans were more important, so he stressed the rappers' heroism. If he really thought that, shouldn't he have done it properly and given the rappers his undivided attention in the first sentence, instead of trying to cram three different points into it? Some would argue that this was a neat way of encapsulating the scene. I am not so sure.

'After'

One way of coping with the running story is the 'after' technique. *The Times* used it in its story about Canary Wharf quoted above; so did *The Sun* in the example I have just cited. Here is how one quality daily told of the BCCI crash of 1991 (my italics):

The Bank of Credit and Commerce International, which has assets of £13 billion, was closed down yesterday *after* the discovery of suspected fraud which Mr Robin Leigh-Pemberton, Governor of the Bank of England, described as 'large, extensive and going on for a long time'. Assets in this country, which have been frozen, include £250 million held in about 120,000 accounts belonging to individuals.

The closure came *after* unprecedented international action led by the Bank of England. . . .

The bank of England moved quickly *after* a report from Price Waterhouse, the auditors . . .

The sequence of events was

1　Price Waterhouse's report
2　Bank of England learns of fraud
3　BCCI shut down

and what the writer has done is to tell the whole thing backwards. The most interesting part of this story is its climax – the closure of the bank – so (3) changes place with (1). Hence the repeated use of 'after'.

This report from the *Cambridge Evening News* uses the same reverse-order technique:

> Police arrested a man at gunpoint after he armed himself with an air-gun and a knife when his girlfriend ended their relationship, a court was told.
> Jason Clark, 20, had several drinks then went to the hotel where the girl worked . . .

But it is not too well managed, with its awkward clause-within-a-clause (*after . . . when*). The reporter evidently thought that the gunpoint arrest was the most important thing about the story so he turned it round, but this time it would probably have been better to put things in their original sequence, bringing in a good quote from down-column:

> Jason Clark was so upset when his girlfriend broke off their relationship that he armed himself with an air-gun and a knife, went to the hotel where she worked and told her: 'You are dead meat', a court heard.
> Clark, 20, was arrested at gunpoint by armed police . . .

Another 'after' story, this time from a national paper's legal correspondent:

MACKAY THINKS AGAIN ON 'NO FAULT' DIVORCE
The Government is backtracking on plans to abolish fault in divorce, after objections that the move would weaken the institution of marriage.
Lord MacKay, the Lord Chancellor, who supported the recommendations in a Law Commission report a year ago, is considering inserting a provision allowing the court to refuse a divorce where the spouse resisting it is held to be blameless . . .

The reporter has certainly encapsulated the story in a single first sentence. But it is not natural English. This time it doesn't pass the Hazlitt Test. No one, asked to tell the story to a perhaps not very attentive neighbour at the dinner table, would say 'after objections that'. They would say 'because some people have objected that'. In short, they would avoid being impersonal about it, as this newspaper's storyteller was. The not very attentive neighbour might then prick up his or her ears and ask 'What people?' (It turns out that the writer didn't know, the names having been suppressed.)

'Plans to abolish fault in divorce' is also a bit impersonal. The situation is lucidly explained lower down the column, but the first sentence is not much of a come-on. A more human, and rather clearer, intro might be:

> The Government is having second thoughts on proposals to make divorce easier. The proposals, recommended by the Law Commission a year ago, would remove the concepts of guilt and innocence in divorce cases, and the Lord Chancellor, Lord Mackay, originally backed them.
>
> But some people have objected because they say this would weaken the institution of marriage. The Lord Chancellor's Department has declined to name the objectors, arguing that such information is 'confidential'.
>
> The Chancellor is now considering . . . etc.

The weakness of impersonal-sounding nouns ('after objections that' and so forth) is not just that they are boring, but that they are uninformative, which, when you think about it, comes to the same thing. They don't tell readers what they want to know.

If the journalist writing the piece doesn't know either, they may be unavoidable, but they should surely never be used unless they are absolutely necessary – indeed, they weren't really necessary here.

The advantage of the 'after' device is that it doesn't commit the writer to saying outright that the first event actually *caused* the second. It leaves the readers to draw their own conclusions. But if you really do know that the first caused the second, a 'because' is much stronger – as in this example (my italics):

A reproduction of Goya's painting, Naked Maja, has been removed from the walls of an American university *after* a woman professor complained that its display amounted to 'sexual harassment.'	A reproduction of Goya's painting Naked Maja has been removed from the walls of an American university *because* a woman professor complained that its display amounted to 'sexual harassment.'

The left-hand version is how the story appeared. The right-hand one makes a pleasingly absurd story sound that much absurder.

Too many 'afters' can be irritating. London *Evening Standard* caption:

> Ending a year in captivity, a pilot whale is returned to the ocean by a US Air Force Blackhawk helicopter after the animal beached itself in Key West, Florida. It was one of 15 whales rehabilitated by Miami after the stranding in March last year.

Here we have two consecutive sentences with the same pattern. (Good storytellers vary their sentence construction.) Such repetition can, of course, be done on purpose, for effect – in oratory,* for example. But in a caption like this it only grates.

'Following'

This is another device for altering the sequence of a story so as to put the important fact first. It is hardly used anywhere except in newspapers, so I suppose some would class it as journalese. It is certainly never found in a 'genuine familiar and true English style'. But sometimes it is hard to avoid, as here:

'CUSHIEST JAIL' BOSS NICKED IN CASH QUIZ
A prison boss has been arrested following an investigation into finances at his jail, it was revealed yesterday.

Assistant governor Trevor Phipps was questioned by detectives for several hours.

His arrest followed a police probe into the running of Leyhill open prison near Bristol – dubbed Britain's cushiest nick.

A police spokesman said: 'A member of staff was arrested in connection with offences allegedly committed during the course of his duties. He has been given bail.'

Again the order of events – police probe, investigation into finances, arrest – has been reversed, and to do it the reporter has had to use a *following* followed quickly by a *followed*. Since the police spokesman declined to say what the man was arrested for, there wasn't much option here (*followed*, like *after*, doesn't necessarily imply a cause and an effect). But to bring on this device twice in the space of three sentences is not a good idea.

*The most notable example I can think of being Christ's Sermon on the Mount, with its reiterated 'Blessed are . . . Blessed are . . .'

The writer could at least have got rid of one of them, perhaps by starting the third paragraph

Police had been looking into the running of the open prison at Leyhill, near Bristol (etc.).

Again it is wise to avoid tedious repetition:

Swale Council is offering a £250 reward following a vandal attack on the toilets in Faversham Central Car Park.

More than £500 damage was caused after thieves forced the door to the women's toilets after breaking the metal grill.

A Swale Council spokesman said: 'We are offering £250 for any information leading to the prosecution of the thieves. This is a standard reward and we would be delighted to be able to pay it out in this case.'

With this reporter *after* seems to have become a habit. The point of the story is obviously the offer of a reward – smashed-up lavatories are not news – and this was the last item in the sequence of events. But the reporter didn't actually need any *afters* or *followings* to get the reward into the first line. They could have put:

Swale Council is offering £250 for information about the thieves who vandalised the women's toilets in Faversham Central Car Park on [date].

The thieves caused more than £500 damage. They broke the metal grill, forced the door, ripped dispensers from the walls and stole about £150.

A Swale Council spokesman said: 'This is a standard reward for information leading to prosecution . . .'

'Before'

Some reporters rely on a *before* to hurry their narrative along, as in this example from the *Oxford Mail*:

A manic depressive tried to burn down his landlord's Witney home before travelling towards Beachy Head to attempt suicide again.

After causing £10,000 of damage to the house, Russell O'Gallagher turned himself in to police with the words 'I think I need help', Oxford Crown Court heard.

But this is most confusing. Immediately after the 'before' we get an unexpected 'after' – and it takes us not to Beachy Head but to an unnamed police station. Only a careful reading of the rest of the text makes it clear that the man never *got* to Beachy Head. Rather than jerking the reader back and forth in time with *befores* and *afters* it's best to tell the story straight:

> A manic depressive tried to burn down his landlord's Witney home, causing £10,000 of damage, then made for Beachy Head for another attempt at suicide.
> But Russell O'Gallacher never got to the clifftop, Oxford Crown Court heard. On the way he turned himself in to police with the words 'I think I need help.'

Before can conceal a dangerous boobytrap. The *Daily Telegraph* fell into it with this intro on another running story:

> Prison authorities were told how two IRA suspects planned to escape five months before they broke out of Brixton jail, but the warning was not passed on to key staff, it was disclosed yesterday.

This doesn't mean that the escape was planned five months before, as the order of words might suggest: it means that the authorities were told about it five months before. The meaning is clear by the time we get to the end of the sentence, but there is an awkward little doubt at first. The only way to dispel it would have been to turn the sentence round:

> The plan by two IRA suspects to escape from Brixton jail was known to prison authorities five months before the break-out, it was disclosed yesterday. But the warning was not passed on to key staff.

Ways of avoiding clutter

Now for an intro of the 'man narrowly fails to bite dog' sort. It comes from the front page of *The Independent*:

> The space shuttle Atlantis was forced to swerve to avoid the remains of a Soviet rocket on Thursday in a dramatic illustration of the dangers of 'space junk'. The near-catastrophe happened within weeks of a Nasa project to investigate such litter problems finding itself beset by severe financial problems.
> The shuttle, which put a military spy satellite into orbit five days ago, was travelling at about 18,000 mph . . . [The story then goes on to give details of the incident.]

This is another example of a reporter taking hold of the reader by the lapels and shaking him hard to make sure that he is listening. It says: 'Now then, mind you get the point of this story!' The result is that these first two paragraphs are crowded with unnecessary matter.

> The space shuttle Atlantis was forced to swerve to avoid the remains of a Soviet rocket on Thursday

is a startling enough statement by itself, but the reporter felt she had to batter the point home by adding

> in a dramatic illustration of the dangers of 'space junk'

and calling it 'a near-catastrophe'. Incidentally, the important difference between a catastrophe and a near-catastrophe is that a catastrophe happens but a near-catastrophe doesn't, so the choice of 'happen' was a bit unlucky here, but this is a quibble; it is not what is really worrying about that second sentence. The trouble, as so often with openings, is that it tries to tell us too much at once, so that we have dependent clauses tripping over each other to get on to the bus. It would have been better to marshal the facts in an orderly queue:

> The space shuttle Atlantis was forced to swerve to avoid the remains of a Soviet rocket on Thursday, it was revealed yesterday. Though Nasa has been investigating the dangers posed by tons of space junk, it announced only a few weeks ago that the investigation was running out of cash.
> The shuttle had put a military spy satellite into orbit five days ago and was travelling at about 18,000 mph . . .

One can see why the reporter didn't do this. The 'severe financial problems' announced by Nasa had already been reported, and she didn't want to write the story as though she thought this was new, so she had to put it into a dependent clause, as an aside, to show that she knew all about it already and was only reminding us about it. But journalists are not writing for fellow-journalists. The reader doesn't mind being told something again, as long as it is relevant.

Clauses within clauses

Here is Nigel Dempster of the *Daily Mail*. He, too, is bringing us up to date on a running story:

There is good news for Ethiopian beauty Meriam Bailey who has been attempting to trace her husband, the grandson of London landowner Earl Cadogan, and prove he is the father of her twins, as I revealed three weeks ago.

Meriam, 34, has learned through solicitors that Alexander, believed to be working in South Africa and whose mother Lady Daphne Bailey is Cadogan's daughter, has agreed to return to this country for blood tests to establish paternity.

This is rather like one of those nightmares where you are lost in the corridors of a strange hotel and can't find the lift that will take you back to the reception area – and when you do get to the lift it is crammed with people. There are at least five of them in that short first paragraph: the Ethiopian beauty, her husband, his grandfather and the disputed twins. In the next par someone called Alexander joins the party. Perhaps he is a new character? No, he must be the husband, and he has brought his mother with him. Let me out of here!

In his effort to introduce all these characters at once Mr Dempster has had to construct two highly complicated sentences infested with asides and digressions of one sort or another. No sooner has be brought us the point where he is going to tell us Meriam's good news than he has to interrupt himself to tell us who her mother-in-law is. ('And whose mother' is particularly awkward, because we haven't had a 'who' or a 'whose' before we get to this one.)

It would not be difficult to unpick these two sentences, but it would need a little more space than Mr Dempster allowed himself. It would also need a more relaxed approach – something like this:

You may remember my telling you about the trials of Meriam Bailey, the Ethiopian beauty. She is anxious for a word with her husband Alexander, grandson of London landowner Lord Cadogan, so that he can prove that he really is the father or her twins. But where is he?

Now comes some good news for 34-year-old Meriam. She has learned through solicitors that he has agreed to come home and have a blood test.

Alexander is believed to have been working in South Africa. Wherever it was, his prodigal-son act will certainly please his mother Lady Daphne Bailey, Cadogan's daughter.

The objection to this rewrite is that the news – discovery and impending return of absent father – does not come in the first paragraph, which is merely a recap of the original story. That, however, is just what the readers want. How can we be sure that they have remembered, or even read, the earlier item? And it is they, not the columnist's self-regard, who matter. The opening makes it obvious in any case that they are going to be given a fresh titbit.

My own effort fails because it has a slight air of cynicism, conspicuously absent in Dempster. That is not his style. But perhaps there is little point in trying to tidy up a column whose main aim is to show how many well-connected people the diarist knows, and to give us a glimpse, as from the servants' hall, into that splendid world. It hardly matters if we don't quite grasp the ins and outs of the story, because the column is not meant to be looked at in that way. (Never mind the notes, just listen to the music.)

It is worth comparing Dempster's way of writing with that of a much sharper column under John Junor's name in the *Mail's* sister paper the *Mail on Sunday*. Here is a taste of the Junor style:

> The Prime Minister is said to be quite relaxed about the timing of the General Election.
>
> He takes the view that the worst of the recession is over, things are getting better and will continue to get better and therefore there is no urgent need to go to the country . . .
>
> I agree with his thinking. Save for one vital thing. Has he considered the possibility that if he delays until May he may lose his greatest asset, the one thing which now makes a Tory victory inevitable? Has he considered the horrifying possibility that if he waits until next year the Socialists may find a way between now and then of dumping Mr Kinnock?

Junor is only making a small political point which he could easily have done in a couple of short sentences, but that doesn't bother us. We are carried effortlessly along from one idea to the next so that we hardly notice how long the journey takes. There are no hairpin bends, no turning back to pick up an incidental fact, no darting down sidestreets. It was all the more odd, therefore, that lower down the same page and under the same byline I found the following. It could almost have been written by Nigel Dempster:

> . . . According to the *Daily Mail*, which broke the story in quite brilliant fashion and which throughout has been so well-informed and so far ahead of Fleet Street as to make one almost suspect that the intelligence was coming from a family source, Princess Diana and her two sisters, Jane and Sarah, are considerably upset by their stepmother's conduct and their brother Charles, Viscount Althorp, heir to the Earldom, is spitting mad.

More than half of this 73-word sentence has been broken into by a long interruption in the form of two *which* clauses, the second of them having a further dependent clause attached to it, so that a deep breath is needed just over half-way (after 'family source'). Even the main part of the sentence is encumbered with explanations of who the characters are, making the whole machinery uncomfortably jerky. What a contrast between this sentence and my earlier quotation from the same page! Can this second one really have been from the hand of John Junor, that elegant craftsman? It looks very much as though it was written by an inexperienced aide, with perhaps a third person, under instruction from above, inserting the plug for the *Daily Mail*. However it came about, such a sentence had no business there.

But it is easy going compared with the opening sentence from a column by Anne Robinson in the *Daily Mirror*:

> It is difficult to find a concise example of the hopelessness and power-fulness of obsessive love but a quote I spotted this week in an absorbing new biography of author Elizabeth Smart who had four children by the notorious womaniser and poet George Baker and received from him not one iota of financial or emotional support, sums it up.
>
> 'Even if he had quintuplets in every village in England,' she wrote, 'and sleeps with his mother and the whole US airforce I can't help it. I love him.'

I have set this monster out in the same number of lines it took in the 9½-em column of the original. Such a sentence, which, as Alexander Pope said of a long line in poetry,

like a wounded snake drags its slow length along,

is quite unsuitable for such a narrow measure. But even if it were given a more generous column width it would still leave us dazed and winded. (For an alternative version see page 69.)

Chinese puzzles

The temptation to complicate sentences cluttered with relative clauses ('which . . .', 'who . . .', 'whose . . .') is understandable. Try rewriting this fragment from one of the quality Sundays (it comes from a piece about a notorious case of ritual child abuse, in which the defendants were cleared):

> Mrs Ridewood, 57, and Gibbard, 58, are united by fervent Christian commitment which involves them in prayer meetings and charitable work, in particular with New Bridge, whose founder members include Lord Longford, which helps offenders in prison and when they return to the community.

The amount of information crammed into those 44 words is quite remarkable. It is also admirably clear, except for the phrase *which involves them*, which is rather vague. Perhaps the writer used it on purpose, not knowing quite what the connection with prayer meetings was: did they just go to them, or did they organize them themselves? *Involves* is a fudger. But the *which . . . whose . . . which . . .* construction is uncomfortable. Obviously the idea was to give as many facts as possible without holding up the story. I am not sure that *which* clauses are the best solution to this problem.

Too often (like the bit about Lord Longford) they *look* like afterthoughts, put on to the screen at the last minute. And I wonder whether long, highly complicated single-sentence pars really do carry the reader along any quicker than a series of shorter sentences. Supposing we broke this one up:

> Mrs Ridewood, 57, and Gibbard, 58, are united by fervent Christian commitment, involving them in prayer meetings and charitable work. They do much for a charity called New Bridge, which helps offenders in prison and when they come out; Lord Longford is among its founders.

We have got rid of one *which* and have avoided the rather awkward clause-within-a-clause construction of the original. Some old hands would object that we have cheated by using a semi-colon, a punctuation-mark they despise as being fit only for the arts and review pages.* This is a foolish prejudice.

A semi-colon would have come in useful in this sentence from the *UK Press Gazette*, about a libel writ brought by Robert Maxwell against the BBC and one of its football commentators, Graham Richards:

---

* For more on punctuation see Chapter 9.

The writ relates to remarks made in Richards's 'Sportscene Talk-in' about Derby County, which is chaired by Maxwell, whose family bought the club.

The ugly clause-within-a-clause could have been avoided:

The writ relates to remarks made in Richards's 'Sportscene Talk-in' about Derby County, which is chaired by Maxwell; his family owns the club.

Or if the nitty-gritty old *UK Press Gazette* thought a semi-colon was too affected or precious, it could avoid that too:

The writ relates to remarks made in Richards's 'Sportscene Talk-in' about Derby County. Maxwell chairs the club, which was bought by his family.

or, if we want to avoid a 'which':

Maxwell's family bought the club and he is its chairman.

The fact that even good writers are found guilty of this lapse of style – the double *which* – should be no mitigation. Here is Anita Brookner in *The Spectator* struggling to explain a plot by fellow-novelist Nina Bawden:

Fanny is a cheerful woman, though subject to flashes of irrational dislike; she agrees with her son to sell, and plans to give a large part of the money thus realised to her dear friend and daily help, Ivy Trench, a plan which horrifies her children who, not unnaturally, see their patrimony dwindling to nothing.

There is nothing *grammatically* wrong with this. Plots of novels are famously hard to epitomize in a few words, and it might well be thought that readers of *Spectator* review columns could easily cope with sentences which wander from clause to clause as this one does. But there is no doubt that a *who* clause inside a *which* clause is an inelegant device. It jars.

It is a particularly easy habit to fall into among observers of the social scene, as in the following item from the *Evening Standard*. Lady Helen Windsor, it tells us, went to dinner at the Tate for the annual Turner Prize award. It goes on:

Lady Helen, who is a director of the Karsten Schubert Gallery, whose artist Rachel Whitehead was on the shortlist of four for the prize, was accompanied by her boyfriend, fellow art dealer, Tim Taylor.

This certainly packs in the facts, but has the reader lurching, with its *who* and *whose*. Such Chinese puzzles seem almost deliberate sometimes in diary columns. The style has a long tradition, pioneered in what used to be called the shiny papers, of which *The Tatler* was the leader. The advantage of the *who* clause was that it gave the information in the form of an aside, so that it would not stand out too prominently and irritate readers who knew it already, yet it would satisfy those who did not. Some diarists would flatter their snobbier readers by putting in an *of course*, so that the above item might read:

Lady Helen, who is, of course, a director of the Karsten Schubert Gallery . . .

This style has been so often mocked that few reporters would dare use it now.* But the *who* device is still going strong.

Worst is the *who* clause which is tacked on to a main sentence when it has little or nothing to with it. The following example explains what I have in mind:

The Prince and Princess of Wales attended a gala performance of Verdi's Requiem at the Royal Albert Hall last night. It was given by the London Symphony Chorus to celebrate the Princess's 30th birthday and to benefit the charity Barnardo's. The Requiem is one of the favourite pieces of music of the Princess, who wore a cocktail dress in midnight blue set off with a pearl choker with outsize sapphire pendant. – Extended caption in the *Daily Telegraph*

The Princess's taste in music is one thing, her taste in dress another. It is ridiculous to put them in the same sentence and link them with a *who*. I suppose the writer didn't want to give the fashion note a separate sentence because that might have made it seem just as important as the music, and decided to put it last to show that it wasn't. The result is a good example of anticlimax, or bathos ('an unintentional lapse from the sublime to the absurd or trivial' – *Concise Oxford Dictionary*). If I had been writing that report I think I would have put the last sentence the other way round. Let's try it:

* *Of course* survives in corrections: 'Our cover picture last week was, of course, a portrait of Lord Harris of Greenwich, not Lord Harris of High Cross. We apologise to both parties.' The message is: 'Silly us, we knew this all the time, as we're sure you must have done too.'

> The Prince and Princess of Wales attended a gala performance of Verdi's Requiem at the Albert Hall last night, given by the London Symphony Chorus to celebrate the Princess's 30th birthday and to benefit the charity Barnardo's. The Princess wore a cocktail dress in midnight blue set off with a pearl choker with outsize sapphire pendants. The Requiem is one of her favourite pieces of music.

Not bad. The sequence is logical – the birthday occasion leads on naturally to the Princess putting on her pearls and sapphires, sitting down and listening to the music. And at least we have got shot of that tiresome *who*.

Sometimes we just have to let one in. A blobbed par under the above item tells us:

> Mr Gerald Ronson, who recently completed a prison sentence for his part in the Guinness affair, was presented to the Queen Mother at the Royal Opera House last night.

Mr Ronson's stay in prison has as little to do with the Queen Mother as the Princess's cocktail number with Verdi. But if you *are* going to mention it, where else can you put it?

> Mr Gerald Ronson was presented to the Queen Mother at the Royal Opera House last night. He recently completed a prison sentence for his part in the Guinness affair.

No no! Try again:

> Mr Gerald Ronson recently completed a prison sentence for his part in the Guinness affair. He was presented to the Queen Mother at the Royal Opera House last night.

No no no! Better leave it as it is.

Double conditionals

Almost as tiresome as the double relative (*who . . . which* and so on) is the double conditional, an *if* inside an *if*, as in this item by Pendennis of *The Observer*:

> It would be highly unjust if Norman Lamont were to lose his job should the Tories win yet again in November. Some might consider the Chancellor of the Exchequer should be given at least part of the credit for cutting inflation and bringing down interest rates. But relations are

reported to be cooling between Number 10 and Number 11 even though Lamont landed the top Treasury job because he helped mastermind Major's victory.

The writer of this paragraph knew how awkward it is to have an *if* depending on another *if*, so he tried to get round the second one by using the *should* construction. This transparent ploy, far from rescuing him, actually made matters worse. For *should* is a genteelism. It is associated with the language of commerce ('Should you decide to take up our offer') and with oh-so-nice tea-party hostesses ('Should you wish to make use of the toilet'). Business executives and hostesses are not our immediate concern, and may write and talk as they like; the point is that their language sounds wrong here. It's a pity, too, that there is another sort of *should* in the very next sentence.

There are another two dependent clauses, the second one depending on the first, in the sentence after that, which might perhaps have been avoided, but never mind. Also worth noting, incidentally, is the writer's attempt at 'elegant variation', which we shall be meeting in the next chapter. Norman Lamont becomes 'the Chancellor of the Exchequer' at the second mention, and a bit lower down the chancellorship becomes 'the top Treasury job'. These decorations are not needed. *Observer* readers could have been relied on to know who Lamont was and the nature of his work.

But back to that double conditional. If there had been no other way of putting the idea, then the writer would be excused. But there is:

Cluttered version

It would be highly unjust if Norman Lamont were to lose his job should the Tories win yet again in November. Some might consider the Chancellor of the Exchequer should be given at least part of the credit for cutting inflation and bringing down interest rates. But relations are reported to be cooling between Number 10 and Number 11 even though Lamont landed the top Treasury job because he helped mastermind Major's victory.

Tidied-up version

It would be highly unjust if yet another Tory victory next November were to lose Norman Lamont his job. Some might consider he should be given at least part of the credit for cutting inflation and bringing down interest rates. But relations between Number 10 and Number 11 are reported to be cooling, despite the part Lamont played in masterminding John Major's victory. Indeed, it was because of the help he gave at that crucial time that he got the Chancellorship in the first place.

The tidy version is a dozen words or so longer – a price worth paying for the sake of easier reading.

Art of short sentences

Pendennis was no doubt writing to an immediate deadline, which I am not. And as Hazlitt remarked, writing simple English is hard.

How hard can be seen from the news columns of the old *Daily Telegraph*, where I used to sub, long before it changed to a more relaxed style. The paper enforced an austere, unadorned English among its reporters, partly because there was much less space in those days, partly because simple sentences made for quick reading, and partly because its proprietor thought that frills were frivolous and inappropriate for a paper whose advertising slogan was 'Readable, Reliable, Realistic'.

The result was often dismal. Few of its employees could write attractively in that straitjacket: sentences, maximum 25 words; paragraphs, maximum 50. Its circulation went on rising, but not because of the beauty of its prose.

I would be the last to plead for a return to such mean, pinchbeck ways.

But there have been a few journalists who have been able to manipulate the short and simple sentence with no apparent loss of power. One of

> [At Harrow] I got into my bones the essential structure of the ordinary British sentence – which is a noble thing. – Winston Churchill

its greatest masters in recent times, at least among those who wrote for newspapers, was the late Charles Curran (the MP, not the BBC man). This is how he started a book review for the *Sunday Telegraph* in 1970:

> We must integrate our coloured immigrants. So say the loudspeakers of our race relations industry. But what if the immigrants don't want to be integrated?
>
> This shocking question bubbles up from *The Un-Melting Pot*. It is a study of Bedford. That town has become Britain's Tower of Babel. One in five of its 70,000 inhabitants hails from overseas.
>
> Some are Europeans: Italians, Poles, Latvians, Lithuanians, Ukrainians, Yugoslavs, Hungarians. About 2,500 are from India, mostly Punjabi Sikhs. About 1,000 are Pakistanis. About 2,000 are West Indians. Between them they represent nearly 50 nationalities, including Chinese.
>
> What brings them here? Bedford's brick industry. It is booming,

because of the demand for houses. But full employment enables British workers to stay out of it – and they do.

Hence, capitalism has sent for the immigrants. They have arrived in waves, ever since 1945. John Brown, warden of a technology institute near Bedford, studies each group in detail in this book.

The style is deliberately rhetorical and therefore would not necessarily work in a news story. But there is no doubt that it is extremely effective. It is an object lesson for feature-writers who think that freedom from the constraints of news reporting gives them the right to tease us with long and complex sentences – like the one I quoted from Anne Robinson's column in the *Daily Mirror* (see page 62).

It might be interesting to imagine how Charles Curran would have handled that Robinson item. Here is her version again, and, beside it, what he might well have written:

Robinson

It is difficult to find a concise example of the hopelessness and powerfulness of obsessive love but a quote I spotted this week in an absorbing new biography of author Elizabeth Smart who had four children by the notorious womaniser and poet George Baker and received from him not one iota of financial or emotional support, sums it up. 'Even if he had quintuplets in every village in England', she wrote, 'and sleeps with his mother and the entire US Air Force, I can't help it. I love him.'

Curran

We all know about the hopelessness of falling obsessively in love. Sometimes we hear almost too much about it. Concise examples are hard to find. But I spotted one this week. It comes from an absorbing new biography of the author Elizabeth Smart. Elizabeth Smart had four children by the poet George Baker. He was a notorious womaniser. She got not a penny from him. He gave her no emotional support. Yet she was able to say this of him: 'Even if he had quintuplets in every village in England and sleeps with his mother and the entire US Air Force, I can't help it. I love him.'

That surely sums it up.

The Curran version is slightly longer than the original – 112 words against 90 – but it is easier to read, even, or perhaps specially, in that narrow measure. It has 13 sentences to Anne Robinson's three.

Uncoiling a serpent

For my last example of the serpentine sentence I go back to the news columns. It comes from *The Times*, and we are in Westminster Abbey. The story begins:

> The Trollope Society yesterday claimed victory for its vigorous campaign, backed by the Prime Minister and his wife, to win Anthony Trollope a niche in the overcrowded confines of Poets' Corner in Westminster Abbey.

Then comes the sentence:

> Trollope, who wrote the Barsetshire chronicles and the Palliser novels in his spare time (he had a full-time job with the Post Office, for whom he invented the pillar box), is to be commemorated with the first of 30 plaques in a previously plain south transept window which the dean and chapter of the abbey have agreed can be pressed into service as an annexe for late literary luminaries who cannot be accommodated elsewhere. [The report goes on to discuss the overcrowding in Poets' Corner.]

Broadly speaking, we can divide complex sentences into two sorts. The first and more tedious takes us down various sidestreets, some of them again branching off others, before bringing us back to the main thoroughfare. The second has a simpler structure. It goes round a number of corners while continuing in the same general direction.

The sentence from *The Times* is a mixture of both sorts. It can almost be made into a word-map:

(A) Trollope
    who wrote the Barsetshire chronicles and the Palliser novels in his spare time
        (he had a full-time job with the Post Office
           for whom he invented the pillar box)

(B) is to be commemorated with the first of 30 plaques in a previously plain south transept window
    which
        the dean and chapter of the abbey have agreed
    (c) can be pressed into service as an annexe for late literary luminaries
        who cannot be accommodated elsewhere.

So long as the groups of words are stepping towards the right of the map this sentence is comparatively plain sailing, though terribly clumsy. It is at (B) that we see its real weakness: it has made a huge detour before getting back to the point. After that, except for the small hiccup before (c), it is again easy enough to follow. It could, of course, be straightened out a bit by making two sentences, avoiding the big jump back to (B):

> Trollope wrote the Barsetshire chronicles and the Palliser novels in his spare time (he had a full-time job with the Post Office, for whom he invented the pillar-box). He is to be commemorated with the first of 30 plaques in a previously plain south transept window which the dean and chapter of the abbey have agreed can be pressed into service as an annexe for late literary luminaries who cannot be accommodated elsewhere.

This won't do. It is too bald. It insults readers of *The Times*, who like to be thought of as literate men and women whether they are or not. The idea of the wide detour is that those who don't need reminding who Trollope was can skip rapidly through it and get on with the newsy part. So everyone ought to be happy. But it is still an unwieldy sentence.

It is also somewhat mannered, with its old-fashioned phrases ('literary luminaries', 'pressed into service' and so on). This being so, the author could probably have got away with a mildly joky reference which would bring the detour into the main structure, thus avoiding the serpentine effect, without seeming to talk down to readers. Something like:

> Until now the most visible monument to Trollope has been the pillar-box, which he invented. But it is for his spare-time work as author of the Barsetshire and Palliser novels, rather than for his full-time achievements as an official at the Post Office, that Trollope deserves his place in the Abbey. He is to be commemorated . . . etc.

Though rather precious, this simplifies the paragraph while still instructing the ignorant and matching the style of the piece.

It would be more fun to imagine how a popular paper might have treated the same story, supposing it had decided to run it.

> Prime Minister John Major claimed victory for one of his candidates yesterday. But this one won't be voting for him.
>
> For novelist Anthony Trollope died in 1882. The bookloving premier and his wife Norma have been campaigning long and hard to get him a memorial among the good and the great in Westminster Abbey's Poets' Corner.

Now the Dean and Chapter have agreed to give the go-ahead. But the author of *Barchester Towers*, the hilarious tale of goings-on among the clergy already familiar to millions of TV fans, will not be allowed a statue.

Poets' Corner is so crowded that he will have to make do with a plaque in a stained glass window nearby.

The Victorian scribbler – he wrote 47 novels – specialised in stories of political intrigue and once stood for Parliament himself. Does John Major ever take a leaf out of Trollope's books?

An aide said: 'I doubt it. Unlike the Prime Minister, Trollope never won a seat.'

The *Times* man got his story from the Trollope Society and followed it up by talking to someone at the Abbey. But his imaginary colleague, once the story broke, had to work nearly as hard, if not harder. Without that last phone call his story would have gone straight to the spike.

Even so, something extra might have been needed if it was to avoid that fate. Another call? And with a bit of luck, another quote:

But workaholic Trollope did more than dabble in politics and write novels. That was all done in overtime.

His real job was in the Post Office. He even found a moment to think up a bright new invention which is still in use today. The pillar-box.

Tom Jackson should know all about that. The retired general secretary of the Post Office Workers runs a mail-order bookshop in Ilkley, Yorks.

Handlebar-moustachioed Jackson came out from behind the shelves yesterday to say: 'Tony Trollope is my hero. He should have been in the Abbey years ago.'

Is this version any better or worse than the one in *The Times*? All you can say is that if this would never make *The Times*, its own version would certainly not make the *Express*.

A good example

There *are* some styles of writing, meanwhile, which would do credit to whatever paper they appeared in. The following item is from an opinion column; I will leave you guessing until you come to the end of it what paper it comes from:

William Waldegrave, Health Secretary, is forever boasting about the large number of hospital staff who support his precious privatised hospital Trusts. How does he know?

One way would be to organise a ballot. The Tories are as keen as anything on ballots in trade unions.

They even insisted there should be ballots before council estates could be flogged off to private developers or housing associations.

But when it comes to hospital Trusts, ballots are suddenly out of favour.

The Parkside NHS campaign, which is trying to save the famous St Mary's Hospital Paddington and its associate St Charles from Trust status, have sent me the result of a ballot they held in the hospitals.

Among the staff at the two hospitals, the result was as follows:

For the Trust: 123. Against the Trust: 1,221. Mr Neil Goodwin, chief executive of St Mary's, is not impressed by this 10 to one majority. He points out that only half the staff took part in the ballot.

So why hadn't the authorities organised a ballot in which everyone could vote? 'I don't think it's appropriate,' he said. 'It's a fairly crude way of assessing the views of the staff.'

I asked Mr Goodwin if he thought that a ballot every five years for a new government was a fairly crude way of assessing people's opinions. He did not reply.

Instead, he gave an assurance that NHS patients would still be treated at St Mary's new Trust hospital.

I think the point is this. Tories are very strong supporters of ballots, provided they feel they can win them.

The paper is the *Daily Mirror*, and I am only sorry that my newspaper cutting of it does not carry its author's name. There is only one sentence in the whole 20-sentence piece which could be called at all complicated (the one explaining the Parkside NHS campaign). The others can all be spoken aloud in a single breath, a test worth carrying out on one's own prose from time to time when it seems to be getting a little too convoluted.* The piece progresses in a series of logical steps, one at a time. The sentences are short but not monotonously so, and they *sound* right. This

---

* Like all tests and rules, this one is not inviolable. I have held up William Hazlitt as a good man to know, yet it was he who was responsible for one of the longest sentences in literature. There is no space to quote it here, but it comes from his essay on 'The Feeling of Immortality in Youth' and is (if I counted right) 350 words long, or nearly half a column in a broadsheet newspaper – and it has only one main verb. But since it consists mostly of lists of ideas divided by semi-colons it works perfectly well and we feel as fresh at the end of it as we did at the beginning. I do not recommend imitating it.

is tabloid writing at its best. But apart, possibly, from the colloquialisms *flogged off* and *as keen as anything* there is nothing in it which could not have been read in, say, *The Guardian*; indeed, I sometimes think I could do with more writing like it there. See page 143 for some choice *Guardian* colloquialisms.

6 SOME STORYTELLING TECHNIQUES

Tell me all. Tell me now. - Finnegans Wake

The techniques I shall describe in the first part of this chapter are not exclusive to popular newspapers, but they are most often found in them. The problems are the same as those we have been discussing: how to engage people's attention immediately without crowding the first paragraph with too many facts at once; how to keep the syntax simple and still produce lively copy.

This *Sun* exclusive shows one common way of doing it:

> Gulf war hero Pablo Mason has been given a roasting by the RAF for wrecking his £20 million Tornado jet.
>
> The pilot, whose handlebar moustache became familiar on TV, was carpeted on the day other Gulf fliers received gallantry medals from the Queen.
>
> Last night one shocked RAF colleague said: 'No one doubts that the timing was a deliberate snub to Pablo' . . .
>
> The crash he was blamed for came soon after the 41-year-old squadron leader returned from Saudi Arabia to his base at Laarbruch, Germany.

A old-fashioned broadsheet paper, if it had got the story too, might have started it:

> Squadron Leader Pablo Mason, 41-year-old hero of the Gulf War whose handlebar moustache became familiar on TV during the conflict, has been reprimanded for wrecking his £20 million Tornado jet.

This is not quite so satisfactory. It tries to tell us too much at once.

Instead the *Sun* reporter gives the necessary information bit by bit in the course of his narrative, in descending order of interest; and he does it by the familiar device of a 'The . . .', followed by a further description, at each mention of the man concerned: 'The pilot . . .' – 'The 41-year-old squadron leader'.

This newsman from *The Times* makes use of the same technique in a despatch from San Antonio, Texas:

> Bill Clinton, beset by allegations of marital infidelity, visited this city of the Alamo yesterday. He came not to fight a last stand, but determined to revive a traumatised campaign.
> The Arkansas governor and frontrunner for the Democratic presidential nomination denounced the 'cash for trash' mentality gripping America . . .

He could have started the second par:

> Mr Clinton, governor of Arkansas and frontrunner for the Democratic presidential nomination, denounced (etc.)

but that would have involved using space to repeat the name and then holding us up with a pair of commas. More to the point, it would have been open to the objection we noted in the previous chapter when we were discussing gossip columns: since most if not all readers of *The Times* would know who Bill Clinton was, they would only be irritated by being told so in this direct manner, though they might not at all mind the information being slipped in obliquely. So the 'The' is quite appropriate. But it is rather clumsy here.

So is its use in this *Today* story, reporting the disgrace of a public figure. It starts:

> The career and reputation of one of Britain's most senior law chiefs was in tatters last night after he was brought down by the oldest crime in the book.
> Sir Allan Green, forced to resign from his £82,775-a-year post as Director of Public Prosecutions after allegations of kerb-crawling, had been seen talking to prostitutes . . .

So far so good. Then, two pars and three sentences later, we read:

> Only nine months ago the man in charge of criminal proceedings throughout England and Wales was knighted, on the recommendation of John Major, for his work in upholding the law.

We get the picture. (Lower down we have: 'The dapper former public schoolboy'.) But that phrase *the man in charge of criminal proceedings throughout England and Wales* is too long for the 'the' device – as is the italicized phrase below:

> It was when he got to the bit about sex and drugs that the foundations of Lambeth Palace seemed to quiver.
> Dr George Carey, the 55-year-old Archbishop of Canterbury and 103rd incumbent, was chatting yesterday about his new job over date biscuits and coffee.
> *The feather-ruffling evangelical man of the people* is enthroned on Friday, and was explaining away criticisms of the service . . . – *Daily Express*

Quite a mouthful – much too much to slip in like this after a 'the'.

This gossip item in *Today* also makes use of the device:

> Julia Roberts and Kiefer Sutherland's romance was doomed to failure because of her jealousy, a close friend of the actor claimed yesterday.
> Canadian disc jockey Karin Begin says Sutherland carried on an affair with her while he was preparing to marry the Pretty Woman star.

(I was not quite sure who 'the actor' was, but never mind.) As set in *Today's* narrow column the words *the Pretty Woman star* are eight lines away from Julia Roberts, the person whom (I think) they are identifying. I should like to have known that bit straight away. And I don't think the formula works too well when it is tacked on to the end of the piece as it is here.*

A clip from the *Daily Mirror* does much the same thing:

---

*It *might* have worked if it had merely conveyed an opinion rather than a piece of information - e.g.: 'Canadian disc jockey Karin Begin says Sutherland carried on an affair with her while he was preparing to marry the *tempestuous star*.' (See further examples below.)

A delayed 'the' can also be effective as a surprise or double-take, as in this post-election item:

A tall, gangling, red-bearded figure went to sign on at Coventry's Job Centre on Monday. 'Name?' the clerk asked. 'Nellist', the figure answered. 'First name?' 'Dave.' Titters began to break out in the queue behind. 'And when did you lose your job?' the clerk asked. 'About 1 am Friday morning,' replied the defeated Independent Labour candidate for Coventry South East. - From a diary par in *The Independent*

Pop star Dannii Minogue had something missing from her latest outfit – material. There was plenty of rope, but darn it, not a lot else.

Dannii tied fashion critics up in knots during a song and dance routine at Radio 1's stand at the Clothes Show in Birmingham. She kept warm – just about – by donning a furry hat. And designers reckoned the Home and Away soap star's material loss was really a net gain.

I'm afraid I can't show you the fetching picture which went with this jokey stuff. But wouldn't you say that the phrase *the Home and Away pop star's*, apart from being awkward in itself, was placed rather too low down for style and fit? I would have yanked it up a bit and started the piece:

Pop star Dannii Minogue had something missing from her latest outfit – material. There was plenty of rope, but darn it, not a lot else.

The Home and Away soap sensation tied fashion critics up in knots (etc.).

On second thoughts I might have abandoned the 'the' device and restarted the second par

Dannii, taking a break from her Home and Away soap, tied fashion critics up in knots (etc.)

because I think the 'the' form is used often enough already. And I felt ill at ease with film critic Tom Hutchinson's way of explaining in the *Daily Mail* who Spike Lee was. His piece started:

Spike Lee has gotta have it.

Like the heroine of his first movie, the most successful black filmmaker knows exactly what he wants.

This seems to me a good example of how not to do it. (*The most successful black film maker knows exactly what he wants* sounds like a generalization, or maxim.)

The technique is harder than it looks. You can too easily leave the reader wondering who you're talking about.

From the *Evening Standard*:

The Duchess of York flew to Switzerland today for a New Year skiing holiday. But her first appointment was at the bedside of 10-year-old Lady Gabriella Windsor, badly injured in a skiing accident on Monday.

The daughter of Prince and Princess Michael of Kent . . .

Hang on. What's she got to do with it?

. . . received serious injuries . . .

Oh I see, he must mean Gabriella. Then why not restart it

Lady Gabriella, daughter of Prince and Princess Michael of Kent, . . .

which, though risking annoyance to those who knew already, would have put the matter beyond doubt? The writer's reluctance to repeat the name has misled him into misusing the formula.

Avoid repetition . . .

Repeating names is one thing – there can be nothing against it. Repeating metaphors or emotive words is another. It suggests that the writer may be short of ideas. From an article in *The Times*:

> There has been a sense of loss in Waterloo Place recently, as the Crafts Council has vanished from its old haunt, to be replaced temporarily by the Japan Festival. This month, however, it pops up again, resplendently rehoused in Pentonville Road. Though it is further away from the centre of London than its old haunt, psychologically it does not seem so . . .

This is not workaday prose: there's an attempt at elegance (note the rather classy *resplendently housed*). Its effect is marred by the repetition of the phrase *its old haunt*. One old haunt would have been quite enough. Putting in a second one makes one think either that the writer was too pleased with the phrase and wanted us to see it again – like a child tediously telling grown-ups the same riddle – or that he couldn't think of any other way of describing the Crafts Council's old premises. Either way it's a squelch.

Here is Anthony Burgess on George Orwell's widow, Sonia:

> She was a brief wife and not a good one: she rejected the burdens of fostermotherhood. She became rich, drunk and frequently obstreperous, but her posthumous work on her husband's behalf – though often wrongheaded – was a gesture of belated love.
>
> Orwell, I think remains the best-loved of all 20th-century British writers . . .

It is all very well said, but the grand cadence of the first par with its strong ending, *belated love*, is spoilt by its immediate echo, *best-loved*, in the next sentence. The currency is devalued. The repetition was evidently accidental, since Mr Burgess was writing about two quite different sorts of love, the first private, the second public.

The ear should be able to pick out such unwanted parrotings. Another example, this time from a *Daily Telegraph* columnist:

What on earth is happening to the string quartet? This esoteric and often unapproachable branch of classical music is currently being transformed by the radical and provocative approach to marketing their art adopted by some of the new ensembles.

It was a good column and I wondered why its author didn't think it worth while weeding out the word *approach* which appears so soon after *unapproachable*, an entirely different use. If the use had been the same it wouldn't have mattered – if, say, what he had said was:

. . . This esoteric and often unapproachable branch of classical music is being transformed by some of the new ensembles, who think its unapproachability can be disguised by a bit of marketing.

Not very stylish, but at least it looks as though the repetition was done on purpose, instead of being a meaningless echo.

Overworked reporters may reasonably complain that they have no time for trifles of this sort. My answer to them is that if they have a good stock of words in the first place they should not have to worry. Anyway, repetitions are usually easy to weed out. From the Harare *Herald*:

The Sunningdale councillor, Cllr Benny Chisvo, has advised Harare City Council against allocating residential stands to people who cannot afford to build houses.

Instead, the council should build houses which should be rented out instead of having home ownership schemes, he said.

That short passage has two *insteads*, two *build houses* and two *shoulds*. The second *instead* introduces an explanation of the 'residential stands' of the first paragraph, but is unharmonious and slightly confusing. A *rather than* would have solved the problem. The second par could have read:

Instead, the council should build them for renting out, rather than starting home ownership schemes, he said.

Here is a well-handled item from the *Cambridge Evening News*:

> Dozens of children have been moved out of their school after staff spotted a rat.
>
> Health officials were called into Great Wilbraham Primary School after a cook saw the six-inch rodent scurrying from the building near the kitchen.

At first mention it's a rat, at second it has become a rodent. Shades of Mr Borthrop Trumbull! But you can see why the reporter did it. The effect of the nice strong intro ending with the *rat* would have been spoilt if it had been so closely followed by another *rat* in the very next sentence. And at least we are told the size of the nasty thing.

. . . But don't overdo it!

Take this imaginary fragment:

> Captain Jones, released from his 40-week imprisonment in a Ruritanian jail, spoke yesterday of his terror when armed thugs approached him outside his hotel. 'It was a terrifying experience,' he said.
>
> Captain Jones's hands still shook at the memory of his ordeal. It is not clear whether Ruritanian terrorists had a hand in his capture.
>
> His fellow-officer Major Smith is still incarcerated.

Any writer who was listening to his own words would have wanted to get rid of that *terror* in the first sentence. It diminishes the force of Captain Jones's own statement, making it sound as though the captain was merely echoing something already said. And a good writer would not have used the expression *had a hand in* so soon after that vivid reference to the shaking hands – there are plenty of other ways of saying *played a part in*. He might also have considered altering the word *terrorists* in the second par, coming as it does so soon after Captain Jones's own *terrified*.

All this is reasonable. But inexperienced writers, warned against such examples of repetition, get quite obsessed by its dangers and are haunted by the awful notion that they may have used a word more than once in the same paragraph. A good writer would certainly not have written a pompous word like *incarcerated* in the example above just to avoid the harmless repetition: *imprisonment . . . in prison.*

Elegant variation

The commonest way of avoiding repetition is to use the 'the' device –
not, this time, for giving the reader more facts about someone, but simply
as a form of stylish decoration. This 'elegant variation' is entirely unnecessary. In my schooldays we called it the 'Erstwhile Cantab' style after
the anonymous sports writer who, anxious not to be found repeating the
name of a football forward he had mentioned in the previous sentence,
and noticing from his card that the man had been a Cambridge Blue, put
in 'erstwhile Cantab' instead, and was mocked for it ever after.

Sadly, the habit persists today. When the newspaper proprietor Robert
Maxwell was drowned in 1991 there was much speculation about the cir-

> It is the second-rate writers, those intent rather on expressing them-
> selves prettily than on conveying their meaning clearly, and still more
> those whose notions of style are based on a few misleading rules of
> thumb, that are chiefly open to the allurements of elegant variation. –
> *Fowler's Modern English Usage*

cumstances of his death; it was a long-running story and it naturally
involved much use of Maxwell's name, but some journalists seemed to
have a horror of repeating it. Thus the *Daily Mail*'s industrial reporter
opened one of his stories like this:

> A City analyst exposed Robert Maxwell's crooked methods more than
> a year before the tycoon's empire collapsed.

Fair enough: if he had put

> A City analyst exposed Robert Maxwell's crooked methods more than
> a year before his empire collapsed

it might have left just a tiny doubt as to whose empire *his* was, and he
didn't want the awkward repetition of *Robert Maxwell's . . . Maxwell's
empire* in the same short sentence, though I wouldn't have minded it
myself: at least it would be better than saying *the latter's empire*. But then
the next sentence reads:

> Media expert Brian Sturgess sent a notice to clients with shares in the
> Maxwell Communication Corporation in October last year warning
> that the tycoon was performing 'juggling acts' with company money.

And two pars down:

Mr Sturgess said yesterday that the publisher virtually dictated retractions of his claims.

Mr Maxwell, the tycoon and the publisher are, of course, all the same person, but the writer, having avoided another *Maxwell* by calling him a *tycoon*, couldn't bear to have yet another *tycoon* in his piece so he had to have a *publisher*. Thus *tycoon* is an elegant variation on *Maxwell* and *publisher* an elegant variation on *tycoon*. After that he admits defeat and gives us two more *tycoons* ('the tycoon took exception. . . . The tycoon had just borrowed £2 billion . . .'). In another story immediately below this one, the first par has *Maxwell*, the second *the tycoon*, the third *the publisher* and the fourth *the tycoon* again.

Six tycoons and two publishers in only 17 paragraphs make for monotonous reading, more monotonous, in fact, than the perfectly natural repetition of the name which all this tycoonery was designed to avoid. Nothing would therefore have been lost by substituting *Maxwell* in each case (though I would have allowed myself the first *tycoon*, for the reason I have given).

The famous hostage Terry Waite suffered the same fate after his release. I gave up counting the times I had seen him described as 'the freed hostage' and 'the Church of England envoy' in long articles where it was already perfectly clear who he was. I admired all the more the restraint of Bill Mouland of the *Daily Mail* whose splash story on 30 December 1991 used the name 'Terry Waite' or 'Mr Waite' seven times in the course of his 22-paragraph report – about once every three pars. The elegant variationists would have shuddered at such boldness, but of course it all read beautifully and I wished others had done the same.

The test is simple. Does it add to the information given? If not, don't do it, *please*. Here it plainly adds nothing:

Top author Sir Kingsley Amis was branded a boring woman-hater by the star-studded cast of his new TV blockbuster yesterday.

'Amis is not one of my favourite people,' said actress Sheila Gish, 49, who accused the writer of creating female characters 'thinly, chauvinistically and through a man's eyes.' – *Today*

Since we know already from the first line of the piece that Amis is an author, there is no point in calling him 'the writer' in the next sentence. This is elegant variation at its most inane, for the journalist didn't even have to repeat Amis's name. He could have put 'him'.

His last par starts 'The 69-year-old novelist . . .' and there is half an excuse for this since he hasn't yet told us how old Sir Kingsley is (compare 'the six-inch rodent' on page 81); but he could have avoided telling us yet again what Sir Kingsley's profession was by simply writing '69-year-old Sir Kingsley', or, if he didn't want to start a par with a figure, 'The 69-year-old Sir Kingsley'. (Higher up the column the man playing the film's hero is named as John Thaw, 'the 49-year-old actor'. What was he if he wasn't an actor?)

There must, I think, have been an editorial edict at *Today* at that time telling reporters they should always give people's ages. In the same issue Joanne Dowding was reported as having successfully sued Ginny Griffiths for selling her a lame mare; Mrs Dowding is described down-column as 'the 44-year-old farmer' and Mrs Griffiths as 'the 51-year-old dealer'. Such an edict presents reporters with the chore of having to get the ages in gracefully, without the bald 'Mrs Joanne Dowding, 44, went to demand her money back from dealer Ginny Griffiths, 51 . . .' which is what we did in my early days at the *Daily Telegraph*. I'm not sure which technique I like less.

Anyway, the test is what matters: does it add? The following par from an obituary of a Member of Parliament, William Rees-Davies, failed the test badly:

> In 1982 he was ordered to pay compensation to a family who had rented a 'luxury' Corfu house from the MP, only to discover no water, damp beds, mould in the saucepans and fungus in the kettle.

'The MP'? Now who could that be? Some fellow Parliamentarian, perhaps. No, it is none other than the said Mr Rees-Davies – the 'He' who starts that very sentence. Try 'him'.

'Elegant variation' is perfectly acceptable if it adds flavour to the piece, though it is easily overdone. The invariable formula can become tedious:

> Sexy rock star Prince has fallen for a stunning top model who won his heart when she swanned down the catwalk.
> *The diminutive singer* was knocked out by curvy beauty Francesa Dellora when he saw her modelling . . . – *Daily Mirror*

My next example, also from the *Mirror*, shows the classic popspeak form:

> Smiling Suzanne Mizzi had a smashing time at her 24th birthday party – even though she kissed goodbye to her cake.
> Friends with a taste for fun gave the blonde model an iced confection based on her luscious lips.
> And Suzanne, who's just had cosmetic surgery to give herself the perfect pout, thought their gift looked mouthwatering.
> So it did – until the butterfingered beauty dropped it on the floor at her bash in a London nightspot.

An opening adjective ('Smiling'), the name, then a 'the . . .', then another 'the . . .' all help to build up the picture. The first 'the' is informative, the second decorative. (I would certainly not want to lose 'the butterfingered beauty'.) The form is found time and time again in popular journalism.

The *the* device is, of course, an old trick, at least as old as Shakespeare. Othello speaking:

> And say besides, that in Aleppo once,
> Where a malignant and a turbaned Turk
> Beat a Venetian and traduced the state,
> I took by the throat *the circumcised dog*,
> And smote him – thus.

Today's hacks are not writing poetry, but we use the same device as Shakespeare – often, as he did himself, to show bias or contempt. Descending from the sublime to the prosaic, I offer this *Daily Mirror* news story, ignoring the childish pun (my italics again):

TORY MINISTER ENDS UP WITH EGGAR ON HIS FACE
Apology over 'smear'

Schools Minister Tim Eggar had egg on his face yesterday over his claim that Britain's biggest teachers' union 'subscribes heavily to the Labour Party'.

The accident-prone Minister was forced to apologise to the 181,000-strong National Union of Teachers . . .

And here is columnist Peter Mackay being rude about Richard Ingrams in the London *Evening Standard* (my italics):

Marriage difficulties are no joke for anyone. But Mr Ingrams has a particular reason to be embarrassed by them. He has spent the past 20 years criticising friends who have split from their wives.

The church-organ playing Mr Ingrams's line is simple: it is wrong to split up.

This is not so much the Elegant Variation as the Gratuitous Adjective. It is part of the columnist's (sorry – *Mr Mackay's*) way of doing things. (Would it be acceptable in a *Standard* news story? The answer to such questions is discussed in Chapter 8.)

Listen to the words

We should try to avoid what I call, perhaps unfairly, estate agents' syntax – 'Containing six bedrooms, the property is within convenient reach of

Bristol' and so on, where a dependent phrase is tacked on to the front of a main clause in an inconsequential way. The habit is not confined to estate agents. It is also common among obituarists, as thus: 'Educated at Harrow and Brasenose College, Oxford, he went on to join his father's export business in 1957 . . .' It is a great temptation for obituarists who are trying to avoid their copy turning out as a jerky succession of short sentences, but if too often resorted to it can be irritatingly monotonous. An uncharacteristic example from the *Daily Telegraph* (whose obituaries are usually stylish enough) was its tribute to Marlene Dietrich; the second, fourth, sixth and seventh paragraphs started:

> Celebrated for her roles in *The Blue Angel* and *Destry Rides Again*, she appeared in 50 films between 1923 and 1964 . . .
> Husky-voiced and fair haired, with heavy-lidded eyes, she displayed a cool 'don't care' expression . . .
> Blonde, Teutonic, with high-chiselled cheek-bones, she mesmerised her audiences . . .
> Famed for playing prostitutes in films, her world was never one of convention . . .

Marlene's *Telegraph* obituarist – Hugo Vickers, an excellent biographer – doesn't usually write like this, but the conventions of the craft must have seduced him.

The lesson is: vary the shape of your sentences. If they all sound the same, they may rock the reader to sleep. Your ear is the master in this

---

Of the five senses, the most precious to the writer is the sense of hearing. – Keith Waterhouse

---

matter. For example, we are all (or should be) in favour of the short and simple sentence, as warmly recommended in Chapter 5. But a succession of them, each the same length, can get the reader thirsting for a longer one.

One of the best British newspapers for clear, stylish prose (at least at the time I write this – things may change) is the *Daily Mail*. Here is the beginning of a full-page leader it came out with at the start of the 1992 General Election campaign; it is interesting for its blemishes as well as its virtues. Take no notice of the political message, but listen to the cadences. (The dots are the leader-writer's.)

THAT feels better. Like the longed-for application of ice-pack to fevered brow comes confirmation that April 9 is the day.

What blessed relief to know at last that in just four weeks' time it will all be over bar the voting. The warm-up has been a marathon. Parliament and public have been panting for the race proper. The uncertainty has been killing business confidence.

On one thing at least, then, all the party leaders can agree as the starting pistol is fired:

Punishingly close though the General Election threatens to be, Britain wants it and needs it.

This Parliament is at its last gasp and should be put out of its misery.

Before the Commons chamber falls silent and all MPs who are standing again are reduced to the humbling rank of prospective candidates to fight the gruelling fight on the hustings, let us have the grace to remember some of those who are leaving it for the last time.

Speaker Weatherill, bewigged and benign, who has presided over its braying cacophony like a quizzical flopsy rabbit . . . Bruiser Healey, who threw his intellectual weight around with rumbustious abandon . . . Nigel Lawson, who with the arrogance of a financial grandee dismissed the present recession at its onset as 'a blip' . . . Orator Foot, whose cranky far-Left manifesto for the election of '83 was dubbed the 'longest suicide note in history' . . . Sir Geoffrey, the dormouse with an assassin's knife . . . and the Iron Lady herself . . .

The first four sentences – down to 'marathon' – go swimmingly. The next five begin to pall: they all have roughly the same weight. There is nothing wrong with any one of them in itself, but there is no flow to them, they don't carry us forward. So the sixth and seventh pars ('Before the Commons' and 'Speaker Weatherill' are a welcome change in the pattern. Then in the next par we are ready for another brace of short statements. Variety is the spice.

The following fragment from a review by Hugh Thomas in one of the British quality Sundays is also worth studying (it is about a biography of the author Gerald Brenan):

> Brenan thought originally. He had endless curiosity. He took great trouble. He read very widely in several languages. He loved nature. His interest in poetry and fiction made him value those things pre-eminently. His relationship with Spain was more curious than generally supposed. He lived as a young man alone in a remote village. Later he and his wife, an American poet, Gamel Woolsey, lived in a lovely house with a marvellous garden near Malaga. Later still he lived in a larger house further from the coast (as a father, not as a lover) with Lynda, a young and understanding student who was interested in St John of the Cross.

This is admirably plain and, at first sight, very informative, but there is something obscurely wrong with it. Why does one get pleasure from the chain of short sentences by Charles Curran quoted on page 68, while this similarly patterned sequence by Hugh Thomas leaves one with a sense of discomfort?

I would say it had lost direction at least by the end of the sixth sentence ('. . . value those things pre-eminently'). After that the thoughts become detached from each other, not only syntactically – not only because they are separated by full stops – but because they no longer match: they have a random feel to them. In what sense was Brenan's relationship with Spain curious? Was it because, as we are told in the next sentence, he lived alone in a remote village? Or is that another point altogether?

Anyway, it is with relief that we reach the more generous pastures of the last sentence quoted here. Lord Thomas knows as well as anyone that too many short cadences make dull music, but in this instance he seems to have realized it a few sentences too late.

Perhaps he wasn't listening to himself. One should always do that. The readers, of course, will probably read the piece much too fast to be able to hear it. But if the cadences are right they will be able to read it even quicker.

Feel the width

It is worth bearing in mind, if possible, how one's copy is going to look on the page.

A good clean sentence can be read easily and quickly however long it is. But the narrow columns of the average news page make long sentences seem longer. A single-sentence paragraph of anything more much than 25 lines *looks* daunting.

That is why the leader pages of broadsheet papers tend to carry only six columns, say, rather than eight. The wider measure reduces the column inches taken up by a paragraph of any given length, and lets leader-

> The longest par I ever saw in a popular paper was 300 words and 104 lines (29 cm) long across 8 ems (about 3.5 cm). It was a stream-of-consciousness piece by Jeffrey Bernard in the *Sunday Mirror*, and very rum it looked. A record?

writers elaborate their disclaimers, qualifications, asides and other grace-notes without tiring the eye. Some papers have broad columns for leaders and narrower ones for the Letters to the Editor below them. It makes correspondents think their letters are a decent length and at the same time encourages them to keep them short.

Many popular newspapers print their leader comment in narrow measure like the rest of the paper, but this hardly matters because a good tabloid leader is written in very short sentences anyway.

7 BAD HABITS

Read over your compositions, and whenever you meet with a passage which you think is particularly fine, strike it out. – Samuel Johnson, quoting an Oxford tutor

The advice passed on by Dr Johnson 220 years ago is still sound, and modern newspaper technology makes it easier to follow than it was in the eighteenth century. The 'delete word' and 'delete line' keys are there to hand. It's usually only the bad writers who fall in love with their own words, and can't bear to part with them.

Dump these words

The *Daily Telegraph* is woefully inadequate in reporting most aspects of modern society. – *Daily Mail* editorial

That *woefully* does nothing to strengthen the point being made. It is just an automatic word, which has so often been used to qualify *inadequate* that the writer has put it in without thinking.

Sir Allan, 56, sensationally quit as Director of Public Prosecutions hours after vice cops saw him talking to a young prostitute in London's notorious King's Cross. – *Daily Mirror*

The news was sensational enough without our needing to be told so. More effective to let it speak for itself.

Two of the men who overthrew Mikhail Gorbachev were sensationally dumped from power themselves yesterday. – *Daily Mail*

Sensationally can be dumped. If the writer had meant 'in sensational circumstances' there might have been some point, but that was not what he meant: the circumstances, as it turned out, were not exceptional, only the fact itself.

To put it another way, things do not become dramatic merely by having a dramatic word attached to them.

Oddly enough, if you cut out the intensifier you may often find that the message is made *more* forceful, not less. Try these:

Mr Smith has got it wrong.
Mr Smith has got it wildly wrong.

Do we really think less of Mr Smith after reading the second version than we did after reading the first? On the contrary, most of us would say that the simpler statement carries the greater conviction.

His favourite daughter Ghislane, 29, was visibly shaking with emotion as her father's body arrived in the holy city. – *The Sun*, in Jerusalem for the funeral of Robert Maxwell, newspaper proprietor

Isn't *visibly* unnecessary here? Doesn't it weaken the force and effectiveness of the picture the reporter is trying to put over? What he meant, presumably, was that the daughter was shaking so violently that even the pressmen behind their barrier could see her doing so. But the sentence is certainly stronger without the word. The only trouble might be that without it the readers wouldn't believe the story. How did he know? Was it only hearsay? No, he *saw* it! Hence *visibly* shaking.

Keep it if you insist. But try these:

I fear the Hon Member has made a fool of himself.
I fear the Hon Member has made an utter fool of himself.

No contest here. Delete *utter*! And what about this?

The house was a blazing inferno.

Every inferno blazes. The only excuse for inserting *blazing* would be that the writer thought his readers might not know what an inferno was. That is fair. For those who do know, however, *inferno* is a powerful enough word, all the more powerful for standing starkly by itself; sadly, the more often we put *blazing* in front of it the weaker it gets.

It is surprising how often we can cut the adverb without spoiling the message:

The fines usually average between £50 and £150. – *Today*

Usually can go. There is no such thing as an unusual average. (What the writer meant was that the average fines *varied* between those sums, depending on the magistrate; but *usually average* is a bit of a nonsense.)

The building was completely gutted.

This is pleonastic. (*Pleonasm*: using more words than necessary to convey an idea.) Delete *completely*.

Even her remarks were not her own. They were basically scripted for Rustie [TV cook Rustie Lee] in a document now in the hands of *The Sun*.

Basically is a feeble word. It is so often used in speech by people who aren't quite sure whether they are saying what they mean, or don't know what they mean, that it amounts to hardly more than an 'Er-um' or a clearing of the throat. Were Rustie's remarks someone else's or weren't they? Best do without this word. 'Most of them were scripted' or 'The gist of them was scripted' (whichever was the case) would have made things clearer.

Here are some more pleonasms. Even the best writers can be caught with them from time to time; and any good sub-editor knows how easy it is to save space by going through a careless writer's copy and cutting out the superfluous words.

Most of these were collected by Harold Evans and his researchers, who swore that all of them, believe it or not, came from actual newspapers or periodicals. It is not hard to spot what words can go, but I have put alternatives, or helpful comments, in brackets.

A teacher by occupation (a teacher)
A journalist by trade (a journalist)
Absolute perfection (perfection)
Absolutely unique (unique)
Achieved a new record (achieved a record)
Acres of land (acres)
All-time record (record)
And your past record? (your record?)
Appreciate in value (appreciate)
Chief protagonist (protagonist; see page 117)
Complete monopoly (monopolies are, by definition, complete)
Complete perfection (so is perfection)

Consensus of opinion (consensus)
Falsely (fabricated)
Few in number, small in size (few, small)
Foundered and sank (foundered; if it foundered, it sank)
Funeral obsequies (funeral)
Grateful thanks (thanks)
Have in my possession (possess or, better still, have)
He is prejudiced in advance (he is prejudiced)
He will be 60 in two years' time (in two years)
Hot water heater (water heater; hot water doesn't need heating)
In the interim period between (in the interim between; or just between)
In abeyance for the time being (in abeyance)
Spent his whole life (spent his life)
Still persists (persists)
Strangled to death (strangled)
The true facts (if they are not true they're not facts)
Totally exhausted (exhausted)
Universal panacea (all panaceas are universal)
What are your future prospects? (What are your prospects?)
Whether or not (whether)
Widow of the late Mr Smith (well, he would be)
Young infant, young adolescent (infant, adolescent)

Most of those phrases are not just pleonastic but *tautological* (*tautology*: a phrase which says the same thing twice in different words). They ought really to lean out of the screen and shake you by the hand. Broadcasters, however, are on their own, and have no delete-word keys in front of them. They are particularly vulnerable. A correspondent sent me this list of unnecessary repetitions, most of them 'heard during interviews with cabinet ministers, trade union leaders and the like':

The country of origin which they came from.
You've done this thing before in the past.
Never been previously possible before.
The latest up-to-date information.
The enemy is surrounded on all sides.
His animal studies of lions, giraffes, etc.
They have given a number of donations.
We are part of the environment around us.
He had an individuality all his own.
People certainly do have a nostalgia for things of the past.
It's an individual venture starting up for the first time.
She decapitated the heads of several flowers.

We boiled them in hot water.
Their first debut.
They did not do it formerly so well as they did in the past.
Continue to co-operate together.
The first priority is . . .
We are continually doing that sort of thing all the time.
A continuing plan into the future.
It was diverted elsewhere.
Inaccessible to get to.
A resumption of talks seems set to resume.
Perched above the main factory underneath.
An assortment of different kinds.
He is right on his heels behind him.
We are near several towns and not very far from any of them.
Nocturnal animals that only come out at night.
A post-mortem examination of the dead.
Build this tunnel underground.
On the other hand the alternative view is . . .
A local businesswoman in this area.
If we don't succeed the first time we'll try again a second time.

This next group shows examples of unnecessary additions (usually prepositions*) to verbs which can manage perfectly well on their own:

Ascend up the stairs (ascend them; better, go up or climb them).
Polish up (polish)
Connect up (connect)
Revert back to (revert to)
Meet with (meet)
Meet up (meet)
Meet personally (meet)
Win out (win)
Merge together (merge)
Follow after (follow)

Now for an unassorted collection of phrases burdened with words which are doing no work at all. They should always be cut, preferably by their authors:
He has not written as yet (he has not written yet)
As compared with (compared with)
He arrived on the scene late (he arrived late)
She went out in order to buy a paper (she went out to buy a paper)

* See Glossary.

The firm is engaged in producing bootlaces (the firm is producing boot
   laces)
They are pressing for the imposition of heavier fines (they are pressing
   for heavier fines)
She owed the sum of £500 (she owed £500)
The town of Boston in the county of Lincolnshire (Boston, Lincs)
Petrol filling station (petrol station or filling station)
In the early hours of the morning (in the early hours)
A short space of time (a short time)
On the occasion when (when)
The month of June (June)
In a state of decay (decayed)
No one else except (no one except)
On a regular basis (regularly)
In a cleft stick situation (in a cleft stick)
With a smile on her face (where else?)
He was in bed suffering from a cold (in bed with a cold)

There is a big category of words which might well be cut for space, but
could otherwise be left alone, depending on the context. Some examples:

The offer was flatly rejected. (*Flatly* does tell us something here. There
   are polite rejections.)
He failed to get full satisfaction. (*Full* could go, but he might have got
   partial satisfaction.)
A temporary reprieve. (A great temptation to cut the adjective. But not
   all reprieves are temporary.)
He was asked to repeat his remark again. (*Repeat again* looks like an
   obvious tautology; but he may have repeated it twice already.)
The book was reprinted again. (As above. 'The first reprint' would
   mean the book was printed again. This means the second or subse-
   quent reprint.)
He opened the bonnet in an effort to find what was wrong. (*In an
   effort* could go, but it does carry a hint that he'll fail.)
Vitally necessary. (*Vitally* is probably unnecessary here, and the phrase
   is certainly overworked. It should be reserved for situations which
   really are matters of life and death.)
Uncommonly strange. (Some things *are* stranger than others.)

There is no need (unless, as I say, space is very tight) to overprune. If
we take out *all* superfluities the tree can look bare. Phrases like *utterly
destroyed* and *absolutely exhausted* can always be shortened. They may,
on the other hand, give just that little extra emphasis which shows that

---

Professor Strunk's advice

William Strunk Jr, in his famous handbook *The Elements of Style* (later known as Strunk and White), wrote: 'A sentence should contain no unnecessary words, a paragraph no unnecessary sentences', and he is often quoted, but without his qualifying remark: 'This requires not that the writer make all his sentences short, or that he avoid all detail and treat his subjects only in outline, but that every word tell.'

---

the writer cares about the subject. Once again, context is all. A viewy, informally written feature can bear more 'unnecessary' decoration than a news story in a serious paper. (I shall have more to say on such matters in Chapter 8).

Automatic doublets

Beware the pair of words that stay together only because they have become used to each other. One of them is wasting the paper's space and the reader's time.

> Lord Palumbo's track record on fund-raising foundations is a matter of record. – *Sunday Telegraph*

What is the difference between a record and a track record? The metaphor came, of course, from athletics, but *track record* came to be used so often and so perfunctorily that it lost any edge it might have had. (Lord Palumbo's record on fund-raising foundations is well known.)

> When the membership of the Liberal Democrats elected him [Mr Paddy Ashdown] their leader in 1988 instead of the astute, if temperamental, Mr Alan Beith it represented a significant seismic shift.

This was written at a time when plain shifts were already hard to find. They were all seismic. Best not to use the word at all unless you think the shift in question really has changed the face of the earth. Since the election of Mr Ashdown might have changed the face of the Liberal Democrats, there was some excuse for it here, but not much.

Other automatic doublets that come to mind:

- *Shelf life*. This phrase from the retail world was smart when it first came out but is surely past its best. (*Life* will usually do just as well.) But occasionally it can come in useful when there really is a call for it:

Fashions have a short shelf life in America. – Peregrine Worsthorne, *Sunday Telegraph*

This being a shopping metaphor and fashions being associated with shopping, we can buy it here.

● *Sea change.* Cliché-mongers seem to think all changes are sea changes. But they are not necessarily the same thing. Originally (as in Ariel's song in *The Tempest*) a sea change was a slow change, a gradual metamorphosis.

Reports of a sea change in the Libyan leadership. – Colin Brown, *The Independent*

This is the correct use. The writer meant that Colonel Gaddafi was beginning to alter his policies, not that other leaders were beginning to replace him, which is what the sentence would have meant without the word *sea*:

Reports of a sea change in the Libyan leadership. (The leaders are behaving differently.)	Reports of a change in the Libyan leadership. (The leaders are being replaced by others.)

But the expression has been used too often – often enough for most readers to have forgotten what it meant, if indeed they ever knew. It should be treated with care.

● *Ground rules* (rules); *role model* (model). *Ground rules* is from the world of sport and *role model* ('One of the basic technical expressions of feminism' – Kenneth Minogue) of the sociologists; but since most readers have probably forgotten this they will have become meaningless to them and it is pointless to use them.

● *Hit-list.*

Some books on Waterstone's hit-list are being priced at less than Dillon's 25 per cent discounts. – *Daily Telegraph*

Here the writer is talking about a list of books being sold for less than the publishers' prices. But a *hit-list* is a list of potential victims. He meant 'list', but produced an automatic doublet.

Mixed metaphors

We use metaphors – words or expression which describe one thing in terms of another – all the time, often without thinking. All the automatic doublets above are metaphors.

The trouble with mixed metaphors is that they can too easily get in the way of each other. Here is Robin Oakley writing in *The Times*:

> John Major's honeymoon with the public continues. Some within his party, however, have brushed the last traces of confetti out of their suitcases.

So far so good. The writer has taken the tired old *honeymoon* metaphor and brought it to life again. But then he goes on:

> In part it is simple pique over loss of privilege and table placing. There is a sense of affront on the right that others too are being invited to dish out the pencils and exercise books. But there is growing alarm among the staff officers of the No Turning Back group and the foot soldiers of the 92 Group . . .

No sooner have we taken in the pleasing image of the wedding party than we are back in school; in the next sentence we are in the Army. The changes of scene are too rapid, and tend to cancel each other out.

Writers who overload their copy with explicit metaphors of this sort are in danger of irritating the readers. Much the same effect can often be seen in television documentaries when words and picture don't match, as

> Incompatible metaphors: a sure sign that the writer is not interested in what he is saying. – George Orwell

in an account, say, of the economic problems of a Caribbean island accompanied by pictures of bathing belles: the belles, however charming, simply get in the way. Another example:

> It is this promise that led him [Mitterrand] to the last-ditch initiative being considered by the Security Council yesterday – the six-point plan which thrust a mixture of hope, uneasiness and exasperation into the cocktail of pre-war tension that has swept the world this week. – Suzanne Lowry, *Daily Telegraph*

The idea of thrusting a mixture into a sweeping cocktail at the last ditch is hard to envisage. An attempt at painting a vivid picture has ended up as a confusing daub. (At least the *mixture* wasn't *heady* – another automatic doublet.)

Here's a ripe one from the economics correspondent of *The Times*:

The 'serious fault lines' in the exchange-rate mechanism that the prime minister says will have to be addressed before sterling rejoins are likely to be put under intense pressure as currency trading returns to full swing.

City journalists, like sports journalists, are prone to metaphor, and why not? But that writer hadn't given herself time to think.

The great juggernaut of war, unleashed on Thursday, rumbles on. – Paddy Ashdown in *The Observer*

Juggernauts certainly rumble; but it is the dogs of war, not the juggernauts, that are unleashed. Again the picture is confused. And here is a splendid mixed metaphor from the *Daily Mail*:

Foreign minister David Levy said that for the first time Israel was in a war situation. The next step, he said, was not in their hands.

Metaphors should never be dragged in where they don't suit the structure of the sentence, as in this example, also from the *Daily Mail*, about the Honours List:

In the first such list compiled under his [Mr Major's] supervision, politics takes a back seat to his other great passions – sport and music.

Takes a back seat to just doesn't work. If the writer really wanted to insist on the metaphor, he could easily have said: '. . . he gives politics a back seat, reserving the best ones for his other great passions . . .'

Some metaphors are simply inappropriate to the context. I once heard Ian Trethowan saying on Radio 4 that the great thing about Charles Hill, the Radio Doctor, was that he was 'on the same wavelength as his listeners'. Well, of course he was, wasn't he?

Told that his horse required a fast pace, Grasso-Caprioli kicked on out of the stalls . . . cleverly poaching a few extra lengths on the descent into the straight, when the other six riders were all jockeying for position. – *Amateur Rider*

This pulls the reader up short, as it were. The original meaning of *jockeying* had little to do with jockeys, more to do with tricksters. Best not to use it about actual jockeys.

> Some [Palestinians in the occupied territories] are housed in tents. –
> Letter in *The Times*

If *housed* still means anything at all, it means something different from
this. The correspondent wasn't thinking. 'Some are living in tents' or
'have been put in tents', depending on what he really wanted to say,
would have met the case. *Housed* conjures just the wrong picture.

Our language has a splendid store of images, bigger than any to be
found in other languages. The moral of all this is: don't reach idly for the
shelves and take down the nearest bunch of metaphors that come to
hand. There are plenty of better ones in the cupboard.

'Literally'

Literal, to quote the *Concise Oxford Dictionary*, means 'Taking words in
their usual or primary sense without metaphor or allegory'. Metaphors,
by definition, can never be literal. It therefore makes no sense to say, for
example, that such-and-such an idea 'literally beggars belief'. *Literally* in
this context is an entirely meaningless intensifier, and can be cut. (So can
entirely in the sentence I have just written.)

This does not mean that *literally* should never be used:

> If Saddam will simply flee, he can keep his tools and wait. He can liter-
> ally get away with murder. – Barbara Amiel in the *Sunday Times*

That is a correct and effective use of the word. Miss Amiel has neatly
taken a well-worn metaphor and brought it back to its 'primary sense',
where it suits her purpose well. We must also allow (some of us reluctantly, in view of the horrid pun) the following from the *AA Magazine*:

> There was a time when vast tracts of [South Wales] were black, the
> grass was ash-grey and the air was laced with liberal doses of smog.
> Nowhere was this more true than at Ebbw Vale. Ebbw Vale was the
> pits . . . literally.

Noun-strings conceal vagueness

Noun-stringing is a virulent and rapidly spreading disease. Here is an
example from the *Daily Telegraph*:

> [The owners of Tobacco Dock, a shopping complex] have refused to
> freeze rents in response to low customer levels.

Low customer levels is of course pure businessese. It should have no place in a national paper. All we see in the mind's eye when we read this inelegant phrase is a graph in a company report, rather than shopkeepers looking up and down an empty shopping mall, which is where the story's interest really lies. The sentence could easily have been adjusted by the use of another verb or two:

> The owners have refused to freeze shopkeepers' rents, although there are not enough customers to pay for them.

Admittedly, *in response to low customer levels* is nice and succinct – my version is five words longer – and we do know what it means. But it doesn't exactly stir the mind.

The habit of avoiding verbs, (or 'high verb avoidance level', as I suppose our *Telegraph* writer would put it) comes to us originally from Germany by way of the United States, where spokesmen prefer to talk of the *capsule splashdown location* rather than 'where the capsule has landed' – or 'is about to land', it is not clear which. That is the trouble with these clumps of nouns without verbs: succinct they may be, but they are not always too precise.

> A spokesman for British Telecom said the company was upgrading its customer complaints process to provide better service. – *Sunday Correspondent*, 24 October 1990.

Upgrading its customer complaints process sounds as though something is being done, but does not tell us what. More money, more staff, more courses in politeness? Noun-strings conceal vagueness. If the answer is not known, why not say 'finding better ways of dealing with customers' complaints'? That would at least be clear and honest.

A *Daily Telegraph* leader writer wrote during the Gulf War of:

> the limitations of surveillance photography and damage assessment techniques.

Again the meaning is clear, but we cannot be sure that *techniques* goes with *surveillance photography* as well as with *damage assessment*, in which case these last two noun-strings would really be clumsy adjectival phrases.* But those six nouns, five of them derived from Latin or Greek, ring like a knell.

The next sentence in the same leader reads:

---

* See Glossary under Adjective and Phrase.

In the days to come, the absence of conspicuous successes may further feed the media, and thus public, impatience, or even induce pessimism.

The media impatience is awkward enough (some would hardly call it English), but is made more awkward still by the insertion of another phrase between *media* and *impatience*. And the necessary comma after *media* momentarily suggests that *media* must be a noun, which, after all, it usually is. What's wrong with the good old possessive?

. . . may further feed the media's, and thus the public's, impatience . . .

That takes up no more than a whisker of extra space, and makes everything clear. But some journalists seem deliberately to avoid genitives, as though there were something unsmart about them.

Professor Carter said that he thought the guide would help to raise British education standards. – *The Times*

Would it not have been more natural, and nearer the English that most of us know and use, to say 'the standards of British education'? But there seems also to be a fear of prepositions such as *of* and *in*:

Mrs Bottomley . . . is to be co-chairman of the Women's National Commission, which tries to ensure women's viewpoints are given proper weight before Whitehall decisions are reached. – *Daily Mail*

The writer manages to avoid saying *women viewpoints*, but then has to put *Whitehall decisions*. Why not 'before decisions are reached in Whitehall'? It would only take up three more letter-spaces, but how much stronger it would be!

Here is the deputy registrar of Nottingham University, reported in the *Independent on Sunday*:

We want to broaden our entry base and to do that we need to change our course structure and change our applicant profile . . . As student financial pressure bites, individuals will need to take different routes.

This is terrible. Does *broaden our entry base* mean 'attract more candidates' or 'attract a wider variety of people'? Presumably the former, because the latter must be what is meant by *change our applicant profile*. It takes a bit of puzzling out. As for *student financial pressure*, it is obvious from the word *bites* that the deputy registrar has given no thought to what *pressure* is. He is just turning out words, like a cement mixer. But he couldn't get himself to say 'Now that students are going to have less money', because that would not have accorded with the dignity of his office.

Lower down the column the reporter herself uses the expression *students' mobility* ('There will be practical constraints to students' mobility') which is not very elegant, but better than *student mobility*. 'Students will find it hard to move' might have been better still.

Educationists, oddly enough, are among the worst noun-stringers. The journalist who reported the near-nonsense above was not to blame, since she was only quoting him. But it is dangerously easy for journalists to fall into the same kind of language as that used by their contacts, like the *Daily Telegraph* leader writer quoted on page 101 who, understandably perhaps, had been hypnotized by too many military briefings. And here is someone who seems to have caught the style of the secretariat in Brussels:

> The Commission will not put a figure for food aid in front of ministers when they meet in Luxembourg. Instead, it will use previous Soviet import figures to show that total food import needs are between $8bn and $9bn. – *Independent on Sunday*

The noun-string *food import needs* has an official feel about it. There is a lot to be said for conveying the flavour of an organization by quoting from its pronouncements, so that the reader can see the language in which it clothes (or hides) its ideas. But it's not good to find such language spilling over into the journalist's own copy. It suggests that he or she may even think in the same way, which is not what we want from a newspaper.

The following is from a report about plans for a new building in London designed by Sir Norman Foster:

> Containing more than 200,000 sq ft of offices, the building would be clad in steel and a mixture of clear and opaque glass. – *Daily Telegraph*

That particular form of sentence is easily recognizable. Is it not characteristic of the style of estate agents? A dependent clause *(Containing . . . offices)* is stuck rather awkwardly on to the front of the sentence's main statement, though the two parts are about different things.

It would be more natural to put something like this:

> The building's cladding would be of steel and a mixture of clear and opaque glass. Inside, there would be room for 200,000 sq ft of offices.

There is nothing grammatically wrong with the original version. But by slipping into the dialect of the estate agents the writer unwittingly gives a faint impression – quite unjustified here – that he is somehow to be identified with them.

Here is part of a letter to *The Times*:

> . . . This is the object of the national curriculum tests and if it can be attained by parent effort rather than teacher effort, so much the better.

The repetition of the noun-string suggests that this correspondent is actually proud of it. His letter would have been read with more pleasure, and would have been more effective, if he had written '. . . if it can be attained by the efforts of parents, rather than teachers, so much the better'. Perhaps he had been reading too many public notices like those in National Trust properties:

VISITOR CAR PARK

or even been tempted by the newspaper ads selling croquet sets, anoraks and so on, headed

READER OFFER

One would have thought it not beyond the paper's typographical resources (typography resources?) to have found a way of fitting in an extra word:

OFFER TO READERS

After all, no one *says* 'reader offer', surely? Have the officers of the National Trust ever *heard* any tourists telling their spouses that they were 'popping back to the visitor car park'?

The German language manages these things by running a whole daisy chain of nouns together to make a single word, as in

Damenlederhandschuhfabrikationsniederlage,

a depot of the maker of leather gloves for ladies, and very neat too. But we are writing English, not German. And the German technique would not work in the following instance from the *Daily Telegraph*:

> But collectively the impact of directives on alcohol, tobacco, car and food advertising as well as data protection and telemarketing which come into effect in 1993, would damage free speech, competition, jobs and the unification of Europe, as well as industry profits, according to the council.

One is reminded again of Hazlitt's advice: 'Not to throw words together in any combination we please, but to follow and avail ourselves of the true idiom of the language.' Those four nouns *alcohol, tobacco, car* and *food* are all being press-ganged into duty as adjectives; and until we get to the word *advertising* we are not quite sure what they are up to. Noun-strings can confuse.

The whole sentence is in a tangle and it is hard to know where to start unpicking it. In defence of the journalist who wrote it, one has to remember that it is probably the result of her having had to explain in only an inch of type the thrust of a long and wordy document, itself badly written and infested with sub-sections.

But I can think of no defence for this caption from a local paper, about pupils who set up business delivering flowers to each other:

> Love's young dream? Helen Jackson is offered a rose by Jonathan Evans as the 16-year-old Barton Court, Canterbury, entrepreneurs prepare for a Valentine's Day enterprise.

It is the entrepreneurs, of course, not Barton Court, who are 16 years old. How irritating, though, is that intrusive 'Barton Court, Canterbury', commas and all! And it was quite unnecessary. What would have been wrong with 'the 16-year-old entrepreneurs from Barton Court, Canterbury'? It is natural to speak and write of 'a London man' or 'a Faversham woman', but some journalists almost seem to think that putting the place-name first is the invariably 'correct' way of doing things. When Samuel Taylor Coleridge was in the middle of composing *Kubla Khan* he was interrupted, he wrote afterwards, by 'a person on business from Porlock'. He did not write 'a Porlock, Somerset, person'.

Another example, from the world of education again:

> The *Independent* recommended that a new national quality authority be created to inspect, advise and audit the performance of schools, taking over both local authority advice and inspection and HMI. – *The Independent.*

Quality authority is, of course, an ill-sounding phrase, but there is also a slight smell of ambiguity about it, because *quality* can also be used as an adjective meaning 'high-class', as in *the quality press* or *a quality product.* Perhaps we are being told that the proposed national authority is going to be a good one? No, this time the word is being used as a noun: it is the thing the authority will be monitoring, not a description of what the authority will be – and it's the quality, by the way, not the authority (I think) that will be national. Better to undo this rather tiresome little knot of words and start again:

The *Independent* recommended a new body to monitor national quality; it would inspect, advise, etc.

But we are not out of trouble yet. *Both local authority advice and inspection and HMI* could do with some sorting out. *Local authority* here is not a noun-phrase,* which it normally is, but an adjectival phrase, describing the inspection as well as the advice, but not HMI, which is the second part of the 'both'. It is all a bit of a muddle. The following, I should have thought, would be clearer – and might remind readers that we are talking about people, not just about abstractions:

. . . it would inspect the schools, advise them and monitor their performance, taking over not only from the local authorities' inspectors and advisers but also from HMI.

(Better still, 'from Her Majesty's Inspectorate', if it hasn't been spelt out already.)

Of course, the meaning of the original version takes only a second or two to decipher, but why should the *reader* have to do the work? (After too much of this sort of thing the reader will give up bothering anyway.)

From a newspaper advertisement put out by the National Union of Teachers:

[Parents] should have the right to enough teachers and support staff to meet their children's needs.

Carelessly read, *support* might look like a verb. Why not 'supporting staff'?

From *The Independent on Sunday*, in a piece about a forthcoming conference on the environment:

Four sets of talks will take place: rising car usage will be high on the agenda.

This is crisp enough, but again we seem to be presented with a graph. *Usage* is, in any case, the wrong word here: it means 'custom' or 'way of using'. The phrase should properly have been *rising car use*, which is not very attractive to say the least. The sentence could have been humanized a little, and the emphasis improved, with the minimum of change:

High on the agenda will be people's increasing use of cars.

* See Glossary.

From a news item in *The Independent*:

The latest Department of Education figures show that the take-up of
the scheme fell slightly last year.

You can guess what happened. The reporter had written 'The latest DES
figures' but the sub, no doubt warned against the use of too many initials
in copy, dutifully spelled out 'DES', thus turning *Department of
Education* into an ugly adjective. Better to have altered it to:

Latest figures from the Department of Education show . . .

The take-up of the scheme fell slightly is Civil Service talk. Once more we
find it hard to blame the reporter, who has doubtless been up to his ears
in such talk. But the *natural* way of putting it would have been:

Latest figures from the Department of Education and Science show
that slightly fewer pupils joined the scheme last year.

That, incidentally, comes out just three words longer than the Civil
Service version. If it makes a line, let's ditch the DES. While we are at it,
we might as well start the sentence with the part that matters:

Slightly fewer pupils joined the scheme last year, according to the latest
Government figures.

Of course, it would be absurd to suggest that noun-adjectives are always
to be avoided, or are usually wrong. The language could not do without
them. I have just used one myself (*Government figures*). There is no
quicker or more convenient way of saying *furniture van* or *London bus* or
health service. Indeed, if we try to substitute the equivalent adjective we
may find ourselves saying something different: a *health service* may not be
a healthy service; a *fur coat* is supposed to be made of fur, a furry coat
not necessarily. But using the noun instead of the adjective is often pointless.

For a better authority than mine on this subject, I appeal to Sir Ernest
Gowers. The noun-adjective, he says in *Fowler's Modern English Usage*, is
useful in its proper place, but it

is now running riot and corrupting the language in two ways. It is
throwing serviceable adjectives on to the scrapheap; why, for instance,
should we speak of an *enemy attack*, a *luxury hotel*, a *novelty number*,
an *England eleven*, when we have the adjectives *hostile, luxurious, novel*
and *English*?

What is worse, it is making us forget that to link two words together with *of* may be clearer and more graceful; . . . to forget, for instance, that though *nursery school* is a legitimate use of the noun-adjective, *nursery school provision* is an ugly and obscure way of saying *provision of nursery schools*; that if *a large vehicle fleet* were translated into either *a large fleet of vehicles* or *a fleet of large vehicles* an ambiguity would be removed.

Gowers wrote that in 1965, and the tendency he deplored has gathered pace since then. Some of his examples are not well chosen. An enemy attack is certainly hostile, but a hostile attack may come from an angry friend; and a novelty number belongs to a certain genre which can't be described in any other way, and may not even be particularly novel. But his general argument stands. Many journalists, particularly in the quality press, use noun-strings because they seem neat and economical, which is praiseworthy in itself. Too often, as I have shown, they end up as the opposite – merely flabby.

Noun-strings in headlines

These are often quite unavoidable, and we should not be too severe on them, except when they need decoding or are open to more than one interpretation. The classic – I never met anyone who actually saw it, but it is supposed to have been authentic – was

OYSTER BARS JAM PROBE

which has been calculated to mean at least three possible things. I did see this in *The Independent*:

POLICE CHECK ON NANNIES URGED TO PREVENT ABUSE

At first you might think the police are checking on the nannies who are being urged to prevent the abuse. But try mending it (in 45 letter-spaces or less). Conversely, at first I thought this one in the *Daily Telegraph* was a four-noun heading, and wondered what it meant:

SCHOOL REPORTS DEBTOR PARENTS

till I realized that REPORTS was a verb, and nothing to do with end-of-term assessments.

Since the mid-1980s, for a complex of reasons, daily and weekly newspaper designers had been allowed by their editors to give more and more space to display, both of pictures and of type, and this gave the subs a chance to make their headlines more expansive, less ambiguous. The downside was a danger of dullness. *The Independent* in 1992 carried this headline over a thoughtful article by William Rees-Mogg:

G7 FACES QUESTIONS OF FUNDAMENTAL INTEREST

which surely qualified for one of those Most Boring Headline competitions that journalists like to hold from time to time.

By chance, it was under Rees-Mogg's editorship some 25 years earlier that *The Times* had pioneered a policy of long and explicit headlines; it was said that these usually told one enough to make it unnecessary to read the articles below them. One of them, if I have remembered right, was

FEW CHANGES IN LOCAL GOVERNMENT ELECTION RESULTS*

The policy was abandoned later.

None of these considerations applies to the British tabloid press, whose headlines may often be one-word expressions of editorial opinion. (See under 'Screamers' in Chapter 9.) Meanwhile no British national paper that I can think of goes so far as to follow the French headline formula as seen in *Le Monde*, which nearly always requires a verb. The International *Herald Tribune* is also noted for its chatty headings. (Examples: 'That Strike on the Israelis Nearly Saved Bandarbush' and 'After This Court Ruling, Abortion Debate Will Shift to the Streets.')

More space-wasters

Noun-strings often save space, but at the cost of clarity and style. Meanwhile there are other ways of keeping things short and crisp. Here is an example of space wasted:

She also urged employers to adopt a more flexible approach to taking on mothers, encouraging job-sharing and flexi-time. – *Daily Mail*

---

*This is in the Cockburn tradition. Claud Cockburn's famous 'Small Earthquake in Chile: Not Many Dead', which he devised when subbing for *The Times*, was, of course, a spoof. The example above is genuine.

Adopt a more flexible approach to taking on mothers is a clumsy way of saying 'make it easier for mothers to take jobs'.

The test is the same here as it is for noun-strings. Is it natural? Is it precise? Can it be said – to quote Hazlitt again – to be part of 'the true idiom of the language'? If it fails on only one of these counts, a better way of putting it should be found.

The climate is changing with regard to child care. – Spokesperson on *Woman's Hour*, Radio 4

In terms of Sweden and Great Britain there's a big difference. – The same

Loose prepositional phrases like *with regard to* and *in terms of* usually try to connect two things which won't stick together properly. In the first instance the speaker didn't quite know how to attach the 'climate' metaphor to its subject, child care, so she reached for a 'with regard to', rather like a carpenter botching up a loose chair-leg with a couple of nails. She could have said 'The climate of child care is changing'. But there is something wrong with this too. What does it mean exactly? 'Attitudes towards child care are changing.' Yes, but whose attitudes? Local government's, social workers', foster parents'? The speaker may have known, but not the listeners. Time and again if you look at a *with regard to* you will find a lack of thought somewhere. She should have abandoned the climate idea altogether. Then she would have had to think about what she meant.

'In terms of' in the above example is comparatively harmless. The speaker wanted to say something about Sweden and Britain but hadn't decided how to put it, so she tacked this phrase on the front of her sentence to give herself time. It can take less attractive forms:

American English has greater currency than British English in terms of the international leisure and media markets.

This was said by the head of International House, 'the largest private British institution for marketing English', according to Mary Kenny, who quoted him in the *Daily Telegraph*. I somehow hope International House has not got any larger since then – in fact I wouldn't mind its total disappearance if this is the sort of English it markets.

In terms of can become a bad habit with even quite experienced speakers when they get too lazy to think through what they are saying. Repeated too often, it eventually becomes highly irritating. In writing, needless to say, it is inexcusable.

Over comes into much the same class as *with regard to*. Example:

Angry Labour MPs last night hit out over a cash payment to disgraced law chief Sir Allan Green. – *Daily Mirror*

Hit out over is a clumsy way of saying 'condemned'. Or, if you like, 'angrily condemned'. *Hit* suggests a target, but since the writer hadn't a target in mind at the time of writing, he had to cobble up the idea with an *over*.

Another example, from a local paper this time:

ROW OVER AWARD
Former Wealden District Council leader Herbert Smith has hit back at criticism over a £50,000 planning compensation award he received.

Mr Smith defended the payout which followed planning confusion, and this week accused critic Cllr Mike Skinner of electioneering.

The award was negotiated by Wealden officers after councillors ignored the advice of planning officers over Mr Smith's application to build a house in Ninfield . . .

There are three *overs* here. The one in the headline is fair enough, but the other two tell us far too little about what is going on. It turns out to be a rather complicated running story, hard to explain quickly (note that the reporter has had to use a *followed* and an *after*) in which the elected representatives, ignoring professional advice, gave Mr Smith planning permission to build a house and were overruled by Whitehall, but Mr Smith got something from the council for his out-of-pocket expenses, which some people thought wrong. Readers coming to the story for the first time might not know all this, though, and would wonder what the critics said, and what the 'advice over Mr Smith's application' had been. Nor, after three pars, do we yet know how Mr Smith defended himself, though this is the new part of the story (the rest is recap).

It was a tricky one I admit. The *overs* don't help, though. They might have been avoided like this (leaving the headline as it is). Alternative version on the right:

ROW OVER AWARD
Former Wealden District Council leader Herbert Smith has hit back at criticism over a £50,000 planning compensation award he received.

Mr Smith defended the payout

ROW OVER AWARD
Former Wealden District Council leader Herbert Smith, who was awarded £50,000 compensation by the Council when the Government turned down his application to build a house in

which followed planning confusion, and this week accused critic Cllr Mike Skinner of electioneering.

The award was negotiated by Wealden officers after councillors ignored the advice of planning officers over Mr Smith's application to build a house in Ninfield.
. . .

Ninfield, hit back at his critics this week.

He accused LibDem Cllr Mike Skinner of 'electioneering' and said: 'My application was approved by the full council' (etc.).

Wealden planning officers had been against Mr Smith's application but the council had ignored their advice . . .

The alternative version does have a rather long 'who' clause in its first sentence (not always easy to avoid, as we discussed in Chapter 5), but at least it tells us what it's all about. And we have also managed to do without the unhelpful clause: 'which followed planning confusion.'

Idle Words

If you find yourself using expressions like these,

1 owing to the fact that	8 for a period of time
2 with respect to	9 in the final analysis
3 on the subject of	10 in present circumstances
4 despite the fact that	11 in the current climate
5 the question of	12 in the event of
6 on a limited basis	13 I have to say that
7 as far as . . . is concerned	14 As a result of

you must immediately ask yourself whether there is something wrong, otherwise you would surely have used a shorter form:

1 because	8 for a time
2 about	9 in the end
3 about	10 at the moment
4 although	11 as things are
5 –	12 if . . .
6 ?	13 –
7 As to	14 because

If the shorter form fails to meet the case, dismantle the sentence and start again. I put a dash against (5) and (13) because they can be left out altogether without changing the sense of whatever is being written, and a question mark against (6) because it might mean so many things – 'not very often', 'on a low budget', 'so long as few people know about it', etc.

Basis is indeed a footling word. Here is an example:

> He was getting reports from a variety of sources on a weekly basis, and occasionally he was briefed by senior diplomats in Britain and America. – James Dalrymple in the *Sunday Times*, about hostage John McCarthy's father, Pat

On a weekly basis is not only wordy but also imprecise. Did it mean Mr McCarthy was hearing from all his sources each week, or from at least one of them each week? Was he 'getting weekly reports' or 'getting reports weekly'? Apart from being irritatingly vague, *on a weekly [or daily or monthly] basis* is pompous enough to remind one of the terrible

> Over a period of 18 years . . . I have been going into schools on a far greater basis. – College lecturer on Radio 4, in support of his belief that standards of English have been rising

Mr Trumbull whom, you will remember, we met in Chapter 1. It can hardly be used seriously now. It can, however, occasionally come in handy for comic effect, which is all it is good for:

> He was unable to keep more than two or three of the Ten Commandments on a regular basis.

I forget the source of this nice remark. *The Times*'s Diary column also used the phrase in a properly sarcastic way with an item about a competition among printers to produce a book in less than 12 hours:

> It would be churlish to point out that broadsheet newspapers, which contain at least as many words as the average modern novel, meet even tougher deadlines on a daily basis.

But what sounds right in a diary is not necessarily right in a news story.

Sorry, wrong word

Mrs Malaprop is, of course, the 'weather-beaten old she-dragon' in Sheridan's *The Rivals* who prides herself on her 'nice derangement of epitaphs'. The occasional malapropism is still to be found in modern journalism, though none as absurd as hers. Commoner ones include:

Alibi for *excuse*. An alibi is a claim, or a proof, that someone was somewhere else at a particular time, usually when a crime has been committed. It is so often used in the wrong way, particularly in speech, that the meaning *excuse* will soon be in the dictionaries. Indeed the *Concise Oxford Dictionary* already includes this definition, marking it 'disputed use'. Meanwhile, since there is at present no substitute for *alibi* in its proper sense, it is a pity to use it in the wrong one.

Around for *round*. American English prefers *around*, but English English makes a distinction. A detective *looks around* an empty house but walks *round* the outside of the house and *turns round* when he hears a noise behind him. American usage has gained rapid ground here, though. This is a pity, since it can lead to ambiguity:

> Steel fencing has now been put up around the commando-style course to stop it being used. – *The Sun*

The writer meant *round* the course, i.e. on its perimeter, not here and there on the course. But this is right:

> She hopes to leave the hospital *around* Christmas time.

Born and *borne*. *Borne* is part of the verb *bear* and means carried (past participle) or gave birth to. 'She had *borne* her infant long ago and could not remember when it was *born*. She died after a difficult illness bravely *borne*.' Ignorant writers used to leave the 'e' off *borne*. Now they are more likely to put an unwanted 'e' on *born*, by much the same process which persuades them to leave out too many apostrophes where they would once have put too many in. (See Chapter 9 on punctuation.)

Complimentary for *complementary*. A complement is 'one of a pair', not a kind remark. So a complementary copy is a copy which goes with or adds to an earlier copy. A complimentary copy is one which comes with the sender's compliments.

Contemporary. This has two meanings: 'of the same time or period' and 'modern, up-to-date'. It should therefore not be used where there might be doubt as to which sense is meant. If you tell me you hate contemporary architecture I understand what you are saying, but not if you describe a performance of *Julius Caesar* in contemporary dress. Contemporary with now, or with Shakespeare, or with the ancient Romans?

> The books were chosen, according to Mortimer J. Adler, chairman of Encyclopaedia Britannica, for their contemporary significance. – *The Independent*

What can he mean? Did those old books reflect the spirit of their time, or are they relevant today despite their age? Mr Adler is then quoted as saying:

> They are . . . essentially timeless and universal, not confined to interests or circumstances that change from time to time and from place to place.

So he means 'contemporary with now' but also 'contemporary with then', and indeed contemporary with any time you care to mention, which is rather pointless. Perhaps he, or the reporter, should have chosen another phrase.

Depreciate for *deprecate*. The first means 'lose value', or, if it has an object, 'undervalue' or 'belittle'. To *deprecate* something, on the other hand, is to disapprove of it, or plead against it. Modest people are self-deprecatory. 'Self-depreciatory' is unidiomatic: you can't say it's wrong, but it's just not used.

Discreet and *discrete*. An old chestnut. *Discrete* means distinct or separate, a word seldom needed. *Discreet* is the word for people who can keep secrets.

Disinterested. This does not imply 'lack of interest', but simply that a person is not biased one way or the other. The right word here for 'not caring' could be *indifferent*; but since this, too, at one time carried the same meaning as *disinterested*, and is sometimes still used in this sense, *uninterested* or *not interested* would be better.

Ex-patriate. A distressingly common mistake. It should, of course, be *expatriate*, no hyphen. Why distressing? Well, it certainly makes no difference to the reader's understanding of what is meant. But it does show ignorance.

> The 8,000-strong ex-pat French subscribers to *Paris Match* in London. – *Daily Telegraph*

Wrong. *Ex* means a number of things: *former* (ex-lover, ex-policeman), with hyphen; *out* or *thoroughly* or *away from* (exclude, exasperate, exonerate), without hyphen. There are other meanings, but the only one with a hyphen is the first. People who put the hyphen in *ex-pat* are thinking, not of someone who is living *outside* their native country, but of someone who is *no longer* there, a former patriate; but there is no such word as 'patriate' in the dictionaries. Some writers therefore spell the word *ex-patriot*, but of course there are plenty of expatriates who are still deeply patriotic.

In a decade or two from the time I am writing this, I dare say none of this will matter: people will have forgotten. But it will go on mattering to journalists so long as they have readers who know which is the correct form. Why upset them?

Flaunt for *flout*. To flaunt something is to display something in an ostentatious way; to flout it is to show contempt for it.

Forego, forgo. The first means to go before, the second to go without.

Hoard for *horde*. A simple misspelling. The first is a stockpile, the second a rabble.

> The farmers did not want hoards of sightseers invading their fields. – Letter to the *Daily Telegraph*, about corn circles

For 'hoards' read 'hordes'.

Hung for *hanged*. Pheasants are hung; people (in some countries) are hanged.

Implicit, explicit. An implicit message is one that is *not* spelt out but is clear from the context and language. An explicit one *is* spelt out.

Indite for *indict*. To indite something is to put it into words, write it up. *Indict* means, of course, 'formally accuse'.

Infer for *imply*. A common error. You *infer* something from evidence: for example, from the fact that a friend is late, that the traffic is bad. You *imply* your annoyance by looking pointedly at your watch.

Mitigate for *militate*. *Mitigate* means 'relax or cause to relax the severity of' (a court sentence, for instance, or the wrath of an opponent).

> Editors are looking for examples of journalistic skill, which is likely to mitigate against essay pieces. – *The Guardian*, announcing a writing prize

The editors meant *militate*. Mrs Malaprop would have been in with a chance.

Normative. This word is of interest only to statisticians or to those writing about statistics. Anyone else who uses it almost certainly means *normal*, and is being pretentious.

Off the record. Someone who talks off the record doesn't want what they say to be used. If they* don't mind its being used but want their name kept out of it, their remarks are *unattributable.*

> A senior spokesman for *The Times*, who could not bring himself to go on the record, speaks of the need for change, and a mutual agreement between [Philip] Howard and Simon Jenkins, editor of *The Times*. – Peterborough, *Daily Telegraph*

If the spokesman really was off the record, his view should not have been cited. The confusion arises from the expression *go on record as saying*, which means that the speaker *does* expect his name to be used. Failure to understand the above can lead to recriminations.

Some colleagues I know refuse to listen to people who offer titbits of news or gossip 'off the record'. Confidential information can be useful but it can also be embarrassing, particularly when the item comes from two sources, the one off the record, the other on. If you use it, whoever was off the record thinks you have betrayed them. Then again, the 'off the record' formula can be used by politicians and others to muzzle journalists. It is easy to be so flattered by the great man's confidences that you forget why he's offering them.

Plausible. Means either of two things: convincing (of an argument) and deceitful (of a rogue). Make sure the readers know which you have in mind.

Principle for *principal.* The college principal is a man of principle. And the principal, not the principle, is what careful investors add the interest to.

Protagonist. There can only be one of these at a time, so you can't say 'Both the protagonists lost their tempers'. Originally a *protagonist* was the principal character in a play. Now it generally means a *champion*, but we can do with both words. To speak of a protagonist implies that there is a contest, but a champion could be merely the leader of a pressure group, or just someone's best friend. So let us use *protagonist* in its proper sense.

Replace. This not is so much a malapropism, more a word that needs to be used with care.

> Ideally . . . I would like to see the box pews replaced. – Article in the *Sunday Telegraph* about Christ Church, Spitalfields, an eighteenth-century church in London

Does he mean that he wants the pews put back, or taken away and something else put there instead? A rich field for misunderstandings here. In this case it's the context – the author admits to being

---

* See Chapter 11 for the use of *they* in this context.

'a fanatical purist' – that tells us which; but readers may not have time to go puzzling out contexts.

Simplistic for *simple*. Almost opposite meanings. A simple problem is an uncomplicated one. A simplistic person is someone who thinks a problem is simple, or makes it sound simple, when it is not – takes a simplistic view of it.

> Which brings us, I suspect, to the real crunch in this otherwise simplistic matter of fairness versus unfairness. – Ian Aitken in *The Guardian*, about proportional representation

This is slightly puzzling. Mr Aitken does not explain who is being simplistic. I am pretty sure he meant 'simple' here.

Straight for *strait*. The first means direct or uncrooked, the second means narrow, as in the Straits of Dover. A headline in *The Independent* read:

MR SWAGGART LEAVES THE STRAIGHT
AND NARROW AGAIN

This was about an evangelist who had succumbed to the flesh. At first I thought *straight* was a pun and that the man had become a gay *(straight* being a popular word for a heterosexual). But it was only a malapropism. 'Strait is the gate, and narrow is the way, that leadeth unto life' is one of the sayings of Jesus, in the King James's Bible. A person who is in a bad way is in desperate straits, not straights. Puritans tend to be straitlaced, and mentally ill persons may be put into straitjackets.

Substitute. Means to put something else in place of something. Not the same as *replace* (but see above). The following is confusing:

> The PM [wants] a return to the pre-war-style regional railways while Treasury Minister Francis Maude and Trade Minister John Redwood view the plan as merely substituting one large public monopoly with smaller ones.

It's the smaller ones that the PM wants to substitute, not the large one. The writer meant 'replacing'.

Usage for *use*. Another bit of pretentiousness. *Usage* means custom, or else the *manner* of use. So you can say: 'With careful usage this machine will last for years', though 'use' would do just as well. What you can't say is: 'This machine will stand years of usage.' (What sort of usage?)

Ambiguities

Even the best writers need sub-editors. From a report in *The Times*: '

> Count Nikolai Tolstoy failed yesterday in a High Court claim that he is no longer liable to pay more than £2 million in damages and costs won by the Conservative peer Lord Aldington in a 1989 libel award.

This seems to mean that though the Count might be liable to pay £2 million he would not be liable to pay anything more than that. Such a thought would not occur to the reporter, who knew the story and couldn't imagine anyone reading it differently. A good sub would have altered it to '. . . no longer liable to pay £2 million or more' etc.

Which, who, whom and so on refer to what's just gone before them so it is unwise to write, shall we say:

> They were the parents of nine children who could look back on a life lived to the full

unless you really mean that it was the children who were feeling nostalgic.

Than can be tricky. A man who said he appreciated his dinner better than his wife might be accused of being an uncaring husband when all he meant was that he ate better than she. Misunderstandings can be avoided if another verb is brought in:

> I enjoy my dinner better than my wife does.

For ambiguities arising from the use of *because* with a negative, see pages 148–9; for a warning about the placing of *before*, page 58; and about punctuating *which* and *while*, page 150.

8 THE PERSONAL TOUCH: QUESTIONS OF STYLE

Comment is free but facts are sacred. – C. P. Scott

Every journalist learns this maxim by the great owner-editor of the old *Manchester Guardian* (later retitled, Scott would have been sorry to hear, *The Guardian*).

The first Lord Camrose, who owned the *Daily Telegraph*, believed that comment should be confined to the leaders and the features pages, leaving the unadorned facts to the news columns. He even had different editors for the two parts of the paper, with himself as the link between them – there was no joint news/features conference.

Though I know of no other newspaper that went as far as Camrose did, editors still subscribe to his principles, theoretically at any rate. Clause Three of the British newspapers' voluntary Code of Conduct says: 'Newspapers, whilst free to be partisan, should distinguish clearly between comment, conjecture and fact.'

Yet the logic of such a division is much less apparent now than it was in the time of Camrose or Scott.

We realize, as they chose not to, that there is hardly such a thing as an unadorned fact: that its impact on the reader must depend on how the writer sees it, and on how he or she relates it to the other facts available. If truth were absolute we'd need far fewer newspapers.

'Facts,' the late James Cameron – one of the finest journalists of his time – once said to me, 'are boring. It's what you make of them that matters.' A *Daily Express* colleague used sometimes to get things wrong; when this was pointed out to him he would be indignant. 'Every fact in that story is true,' he would say. And indeed it was. But the piece was still wrong.

Scott (who died in 1932) and Lord Camrose (died 1954) were pre-television men. Television made readers think differently. It is not surprising that more and more news stories were being given personal bylines at about the time TV was becoming generally available. Viewers could see the person who was reading the news. The newscasters may have had little say in what news was chosen for them to read out, but this didn't prevent them from becoming national personalities in a way radio news readers never really were.

By comparison, a newspaper report bylined 'From Our Own Correspondent' or 'Standard Reporter' seemed all too anonymous. The

---

Small adjustments to the vocabulary can be enough to turn a story round. Juries know this. Say a pensioner is in court for allegedly kicking a dog. In the prosecution's account he is described as 'an old man', in the defence's 'an elderly gentleman'. Both accounts are *factually* true, but each puts quite a different complexion on the character of the defendant. (I take this analogy from Randolph Quirk.) Tabloid papers do it all the time, but more crudely than this, with liberal sprinklings of adjectives. ('The accident-prone Minister.')

---

theory had been that an unnamed byline gave an impartial authority to the news: it was The Paper that was telling it. But now readers wanted to know *who* was telling it.

Writer and reader could then tacitly agree that a news item was, after all, a personal account. Once this was mutually understood, it opened the way to a more relaxed kind of reporting, so that today there is sometimes little difference between the style of a news report and that of a feature.

The approach oblique

It was Scott's *Guardian*, oddly enough, that led here. While colleagues on other papers were still in the habit of filing more or less deadpan (or supposedly deadpan) reports, the *Guardian* man would trot round the subject like a skittish pony pretending he wasn't ready to be saddled. (Or, as a distinguished *Telegraph* features editor and former *Manchester Guardian* sub, the late Ralph Thackeray, would have put it, 'He'd taxi up and down the runway before taking off.') One *Guardian* man, reporting a contentious conference of the National Union of Students, began his news story:

As the Good Book tells us, if a house be divided against itself, that house cannot stand.

That was in about 1970. We mocked him for it, but envied him too. Sometimes the subs, much to his annoyance, would cut these pleasing frills. Most of us would not even have attempted them, unless we were doing a colour piece. It was said that you had to read several paragraphs before you discovered what a *Guardian* story was about. (The headline, probably a more or less outrageous pun, wouldn't tell you.)

Nowadays a news item in the *Sunday Telegraph* or *Sunday Times* may well start in this way – indeed, if it weren't for the strapline saying NEWS across the top of the page you might mistake it for a feature.

Here's an item from another Sunday heavy:

Blood and feathers. Sinewy carcasses shredded by lead shot and spiralling downwards to find the soft mouths of dogs. An astounding landscape of greys and greens and browns, broken stones and heather, open to the elements.

Then the voices. Voices less accented than enamelled, that make the skin crawl with irritation and simple chauvinism. Voices complacent, proprietorial, vowels flattened and stretched by centuries of self-satisfaction, languid with the pride of ownership. Listen to them dispense their orders and listen as their servants respond with feudal honorifics.

Those, you'll be surprised to know, are the first two paragraphs of a *news story*. They come from *The Observer*, and the heading is

KILL OFF THIS INGLORIOUS HANGOVER OF FEUDALISM

which is the sort of comment-by-headline we are all used to in the tabloid press (SAVE THIS DONKEY!) (WHAT A BRUTE) but wouldn't until recently have expected to find in a serious newspaper. It certainly makes a bit of a nonsense of that voluntary Code of Conduct.

The paper's real mistake was in putting the piece at the top of a page headed NEWS. The only newsy thing about it was that it appeared in the week after the grouse-shooting season had started; but an annual date is not news, though it could make a nice peg for a personal opinion piece like this one.

Anyway, it's a good example of the confusion between news and not-news. Incidentally, Sunday newspaper editors would be excused if they encouraged such confusion. It's not always easy to get enough hard news to fill the columns on a Saturday, yet market research suggests that readers read newspapers for news, or what they conceive to be news. Since, however, many readers haven't considered the difference between a news item and a feature, a NEWS strap comes in handy . . .

Much more interesting than that painfully overwritten *Observer* piece are the genuine news items which have been written as though they were features, like that old *Guardian* report about the students' conference I mentioned on page 121 – or this more recent report in the *Sunday Telegraph* about clergy stipends:

> The ability of the lilies of the field to grow without toiling or spinning has long encouraged Christians to think little of tomorrow, because 'tomorrow will be anxious for itself'. But unlike Church of England parish priests, the lilies have never had to pay electricity bills or be responsible for the upkeep of crumbling medieval buildings. If they did, they might share the widespread concern about the Church's finances.

That was the first par. It gracefully breaks the rules we defined in Chapter 4 – begin at the beginning, first things first, tell 'em what's happening.

So does this news item in the *Sunday Times*:

> It was a familiar spectacle. Diego Maradona, the world's greatest football player, was in tears. But this time it was not on account of losing the World Cup. He was on his way to prison.

Only at the end of the second paragraph do we learn what has happened: Maradona has been arrested for being in possession of drugs.

The Guardian's news columns carry on the tradition:

> Black flags on lamp-posts lined sections of the route, soldiers patrolled the gardens of local houses, graffiti on a crumbling tower block urged 'stiff all paras.'
> The funeral procession of Patricia Black, the 18-year-old woman blown up in St Albans, Hertfordshire, by the bomb she was handling, wound its way down from a bleak housing estate in Lenadoon to West Belfast's Milltown cemetery yesterday, with a relatively low-key security presence.

The copybook way of handling this would have been to transpose those first two paragraphs. The news, after all, is in the second; the opening par has colour but no definition. We know from the headline that this is the funeral of an IRA activist. But whose funeral? It leaves us to guess. The transposition would read perfectly well:

> The funeral procession of Patricia Black, the 18-year-old woman blown up in St Albans, Hertfordshire, by the bomb she was handling, wound its way down from a bleak housing estate in Lenadoon to West Belfast's Milltown cemetery yesterday, with a relatively low-key security presence.

Black flags on lamp-posts lined sections of the route, soldiers patrolled the gardens of local houses, graffiti on a crumbling tower block urged 'stiff all paras.'

The Daily Telegraph's much briefer agency account was in the old style. It began:

Patricia Black, 18, the IRA bomber who blew herself up at St Albans two weeks ago, was buried in Belfast yesterday without any paramilitary trappings after her family objected to an IRA funeral.

Both styles flourish, sometimes in neighbouring columns of the same newspaper. A basement story on the front page of *The Independent*, reporting conditions in Yugoslavia during the 1991–1993 civil war, begins:

Tourism in what used to be called Yugoslavia is not exactly booming. So perhaps the advertisement from the Belgrade Tourist Board was not surprising. 'One-day sightseeing tour of Vukovar,' it said.

The first paragraph of the report immediately above it reads:

Senior Labour figures yesterday scorned Paddy Ashdown's call for a non-socialist regrouping on the centre-left to oppose the Conservatives, while Mr Ashdown emphasised that his move was not 'anti-Tory'.

The Ashdown story is in the old style, the Yugoslav in the new, and they could hardly be more different.

It is not a question of which is 'right'. That depends on the expectations of the readers. If they are after the immediate facts they will be irritated by a leisurely opening. But if they have heard the news already, perhaps on TV, a straight intro will be too bald.

The Guardian's man in Belfast may well have been right to decide that an atmospheric scene-setter was a better come-on than the rather detailed information ('St Albans, Hertfordshire', etc.) that he gave in his second par. And the *Sunday Telegraph* reader with no train to catch has time to consider the lilies over breakfast. The point of that story – 'widespread concern about the Church's finances', which a daily colleague might have started with – could wait for a sentence or two.

Don't mix styles

We must give the readers what they want. At the same time, they must be in no doubt what we are giving them. Here is an instructive example.

This news story from *The Times* looks at first sight like a straight report:

> *By Melinda Wittstock, Media Correspondent*
> The BBC is to force the independent programme maker that wins
> the contract to produce *Question Time* to abide by rules its own pro-
> ducers have often ignored at their peril. Come September, the BBC
> current affairs flagship must include more women panellists, after
> months of criticism that male politicians dominate.

But it turns out to be neither one thing nor the other, running aground
in the middle of the first sentence. We wonder what's going on. What are
the 'rules' about women panellists, who made them, and what 'peril'
awaited the producers who ignored them? The next sentence makes it
clear that the writer is thinking more in terms of a feature than of a news
item: it starts 'Come September', an informal phrase. This second sentence does throw some light on the mystery, but who made the 'criticism'
it speaks of – the governors, the director general, the viewers?

The point the piece is making would be welcome in a feature, where
there might be room to expand on it, but not here, where it is just a bit
of a mess. Note the clumsy noun-clause *the independent programme maker
that wins the contract to produce Question Time* stuck in the middle of a
complex sentence, and the bad case of 'theism' in the sentence after it (*the
BBC current affairs flagship*).

Perhaps I am being unfair to that *Times* journalist. She was trying to
inject something of her personality into a news story; it so happened that
the attempt went wrong, but who should blame her for trying? After all,
others are doing it.

The answer is that there is a time and a place for everything. (See
below under **Consistency in style**.)

Ego trips

Regular columnists with familiar bylines – familiar, anyway, to the readers of their own newspapers – can do very much as they like. They have
fools' licences. Edward Pearce's commentary column on the leader page
of *The Guardian* the week after the 1992 General Election started:

> Forgive me if this column has an air of preoccupation. But at least as
> much as the contestants, I have been physically wrapped up in the elec-
> tion. Recent *Guardian* columns have been produced in hotel bedrooms
> in such places as the Wheatsheaf, Sandbach, conveniently placed on a
> route of 2,238 miles between Finchley and Huntingdon by way of

Cardiff and Edinburgh, with stops off in Cheltenham, Chester-le-Street, Clitheroe and Birmingham.

The journey . . . was not one to be missed . . . [and so on].

It is not until we reach the third par that we discover Mr Pearce's purpose, which is to discuss the fallibility of the pre-election opinion polls and his own prescience in such matters. Another journalist, trying the same thing, might make the readers splutter with impatience. But these readers have come to the column because they want to know what Ed Pearce has been up to. He is the black-and-white equivalent of the television personality. It's *him* they're listening to as much as to what he's saying.

There is an obvious danger. It is too easy a step from such chattiness to the tedium of the facetious after-dinner speech. Simon Hoggart, a first-class journalist most of the time, fell into the trap with this piece in *The Observer Magazine*:

I leave this space in *The Observer Magazine* next week and will turn up instead in the newspaper itself. From our magazine eyrie on the second floor we can watch all the people who work on the newspaper proper scurry around in their atrium below. A Cabinet reshuffle in Turkey, a hi-jacking in Surinam, and off they dart, hither and yon.

Up here we tend, by comparison, to be reflective, eschewing the quotidian round of news, the gallimaufry of mere events, as we ruminate peaceably on the deeper, more powerful currents which flow beneath life's choppy, spume-flecked surface.

Had you visited us here, after lunch, say, you might, on occasion, have been deluded by the closed eyes and the soft, rhythmic breathing into thinking that I was asleep. In fact, this was merely a device to discourage the attentions of colleagues who might otherwise have disturbed the strong tidal pulses of my intellect. . . .

I suppose you could call this sort of thing meta-journalism: journalists writing about being journalists. The meta-novel – the novel about a novelist writing a novel – has been established for many years and it is hardly surprising to find the genre adapting itself to the Sunday press. It is certainly fun to write. You can bring out some of the lovely old words (*gallimaufry*, *spume-flecked*) which would only be ridiculed if they appeared in a serious feature, overwriting being out of fashion except among the tabloids. Here they can be allowed because everyone realizes you are using them ironically.

Of course it's pure self-indulgence, and the cult of the personality encourages it. I have before me an article by the distinguished columnist Maureen Freely in the review section of *The Independent on Sunday*. Its

900 words include 36 'I's and 23 'me's or 'my's. The author refers to herself every 15 words, on average. Here's how she starts:

> How much longer am I going to have to put a brave face on things? Never has it been clearer that I don't control my own life. I used to think that I had an edge if I kept myself informed, but every time I open up a paper I find another safe assumption destroyed . . .

(Seven 'I's already.) The thrust of the piece was that life tended to get on top of Ms Freely sometimes and how she longed to be allowed a tantrum or two as children are. In other words, it was in the tradition made popular by that veteran columnist Katherine Whitehorn of *The Observer*. Ms Whitehorn, whose column first appeared in 1960, made her name by writing about the small things of domestic life and everyone loved her because she told us that she could be just as inefficient and hopeless as the rest of us: journalism with an identifiable human face.

Such writing has had a big influence on the features and magazine pages of the British press. But it is also part of the larger movement which we have been discussing.

The trend towards the personalized account is not found just in the soft centres of the Sunday newspapers. It is also found in the best kind of reportage. Compare those two stories from the Gulf War, both from the same issue of *Today*, from which I quoted in Chapter 3: one came from a briefing, the other from the field. The man in the field didn't know as much as his colleague in Riyadh, but it was a much better report, because it was about what he himself saw.

An unknown freelance hawking his feature articles round the newspapers knows that he is unlikely to get anywhere much with a piece on, say, 'The Future of Lloyd's'. If he can offer something under the heading 'My Brush with Lloyd's' he can be pretty sure that some features editor is going to read it – and even like it. But not, or almost certainly not, if it turns out to be a mere ego trip. It's only a few who can start a piece: 'A funny thing happened to me on my way to the word-processor . . .'

Alan Coren, of *The Times*, tried to show that he could be one of the few with this piece in his usual corner of the leader page which appeared in the summer of 1992. I reproduce its opening sentences, not as an example to imitate, but as an extreme instance of egocentric meta-journalism:

> It is only fair to warn those of you about to embark on today's farrago that very little will come of it. You will disembark, I fear, complaining of an absolutely bloody ghastly trip, the silly fool not only took the long way round, he kept getting lost, and God knows where he dropped me, the middle of nowhere. I shall almost certainly write a

strong letter to Hackney Scribblage Office. I do not pay good money to . . .

I know all this because I myself have just embarked upon it, as you can see, and I have to tell you that conditions up ahead are extremely murky. Visibility is down to less than 50 words. (etc.)

There is no headline: only a strap ('. . . *and moreover*') and then the byline, writ large. (The cult of the personality finally arrived when newspapers began to print the columnist's name – Miles Kington, Bernard Levin – instead of a headline, and in the same type as the headline would have been; William Hickey of the *Daily Express* was an early example, but that was a *nom-de-plume*.)

Humorous exaggeration

Tabloid journalists (but not, it must be stressed, the really good ones) make their points by piling on ever more evocative adjectives (see Chapter 3). Ego-tripping columnists make theirs with a different sort of exaggeration.

This is how Peter Watson of *The Observer* started off a piece critical of estate agents:

I must begin this week by apologising for my appearance. If I look a little, well, *déshabillé*, my fine features caked with mud and my silk suit all but ruined by the oil-droppings from a London bus lane, it is simply because I have just spent some considerable time rolling around on the ground.

No, it wasn't an argument with Mr Bruno* (a very decent chap, I hasten to say). I had merely read, in the *Financial Times* no less, a short account of a speech by Sir Gordon Borrie, Director-General of Fair Trading, to the National Association of Estate Agents. The image of the 'profession', he said, was 'improving'.

I tell you, I laughed so much that I was on the ground for two whole days and nights.

Mr Watson was making the point that the idea of estate agency being a profession, with a rising reputation at that, was ludicrous. He may very well have been right; but he took more than 100 words to say it. He is following two traditions.

The first comes from P. G. Wodehouse, who was not only funny but also a tremendous stylist. Wodehouse was a great man for the pic-

*Frank Bruno: a well-known pugilist of the time.

turesque overstatement. His characters were hardly ever startled: they were more likely to 'leap six inches into the air, like a nymph surprised while bathing'. Wodehouse, however, would have been able to get through Mr Watson's business in 20 words rather than 100.

The other tradition is that of the Bash Street Kids in the children's comic, where Sir's false teeth go whizzing across the classroom and embed themselves in the fat boy's backside.

> Brevity is the soul of wit. – Shakespeare

Much to be preferred to Mr Watson's long, long joke, in my view, was the quiet swipe with which the late Arthur Marshall used to be able to cut someone down to size, probably in brackets. Or the way Rebecca West could fell a man with a couple of words.*

Facetiousness

The Wodehouse tradition – or perhaps I should call it the sub-Wodehouse tradition, since so few can do these things as well as he did – persists in many places, not just in the heavy Sundays. It is often to be found in the specialist and trade press, as well as in the tabloids. One of the popular national Sundays carried a piece about the film star Elizabeth Taylor which said that she had

> a weight problem that allows the most negligent of dieters to look resolute in comparison

and of her seventh husband that he

> looks like a cross between a bouncer from Stringfellows and half the people who played First Division football for Manchester United in the early Seventies.

Reading such ponderous stuff makes one realize that Wodehouse has something to answer for. I forget who wrote that piece. I do remember that the heading was GONE FOR A BURTON, but I could have guessed that anyway.

The best similes or comparisons, like the best puns, look as though they have come of their own accord. They should never be strained after,

---

*Both West and Marshall have appeared in collections of their work. Try *Rebecca West: a Celebration* (Penguin, 1977). Arthur Marshall's last collection was *Sunny Side Up* (Hamish Hamilton, 1987). Marshall is leisurely and his syntax is involved, but his apparent scattiness is designed, and he never just wastes words.

like this one by the tennis correspondent of *The Independent* about Martina Navratilova at Wimbledon in 1992:

> Granmartina, as my Australian friend Alan Trengrove described her, enriched her 20th visit to the All England Club with a performance only marginally short of producing an upset. She failed chiefly as a consequence of approaches as cramped as the French roads to the Channel ports.

You can almost hear the ticking of the writer's mind. Martina's approaches were terribly cramped, so cramped that they lost her the match. How to convey how cramped they were? As cramped as . . .? Got it! There's a lorry-drivers' blockade in France at the moment. Nice topical reference!

It's all much too contrived. Note also the Erstwhile Cantab touch.* We can't talk about Wimbledon, so boring, so we have to call it something else ('the All England Club'). And perhaps we can find another name for la Navratilova . . .

Sports writing

Sports writers used often to be accused of tortuous writing of this sort (*propelled the sphere* for *kicked the ball* and so on), but there is less of it now among them, so that the following, also from *The Independent*, has an old-fashioned feel to it (it's about bad temper on the cricket field):

> There might be some justification for the contempt that several England players have for Pakistan's idea of etiquette this summer (a mood, incidentally, that was there before Old Trafford) but you only have to go back to the 1987 tours to Pakistan and New Zealand (when England more than fitted the definition of wingeing Poms) to realise that when it comes to occupying the high moral ground, England are in precious little danger of contracting vertigo.

This almost needs a translation. ('Pakistan's idea of etiquette' = *they were rude*; 'more than fitted the definition of wingeing Poms' = *England complained too much*; 'when it comes to . . . vertigo' = *we're as bad as the rest of them*.)

However, Sportspeak has always tended to be more old-fashioned than the other parts of the paper it appears in. Sportswriters need an emotive vocabulary to convey the passions they are reporting on. Their subject favours the high style. Ian Wooldridge of the *Daily Mail*, a paper notable

*See page 82.

at the time for good plain English, opened an article on bad sportsman-
ship thus:

> It is rarely in the nature of this column to seek out mitigating evidence
> to excuse deplorable behaviour in sport, but a Christmas gift of price-
> less entertainment impels me to admit that nothing much has changed
> down the years.

Rarely in the nature . . . mitigating evidence . . . impels me to admit . . .
What do these phrases remind us of? Do they not recall (for those of us
old enough to remember them) the old *Times* fourth leaders which were
flourishing 40 years ago and seemed out of date even then, where no one
ever thought, they always *deemed*?

Trade press humour

It is in the trade press, meanwhile, that the facetious/circumlocutionary
style flourishes best. This piece about pub quizzes comes from the *AA
Magazine* (motoring journals are a rich field):

> No sooner had I walked into the snug of the Kentish Yeoman than
> one of the regulars asked me if I could list the seven dwarfs, what were
> the real names of the Magnificent Seven, and what was the difference
> between a duck.
> As I trawled the darker recesses of my brain for a suitably witty,
> incisive reply, another demanded to know in what year the Riley
> Pathfinder first appeared, the name of the winner of the 1983 Paris-
> Dakar rally and who Suzie Hunt married, after she and James were no
> longer a serious item.
> There was to be no respite – not even time for Marie, the world's
> most patient landlady, to slip me a drink. My inquisitors were joined
> by a third Magnus Magnusson wannabee. He demanded an instant
> reply to the poser 'How many moons does Mars have?' (etc.)

Notice how hardly anything can be said straight. People don't try to
think, they trawl the darker recesses of their brains. They can't ask anything more than once: after that they demand to know, or they demand
an instant reply to their posers. (The phrase *no longer a serious item*,
meaning a broken marriage, is typical of this circumlocutionary technique.) Except for the modish *wannabee*, this could almost have been
Wodehouse's Mr Mulliner talking in the famous bar parlour of the
Angler's Rest.

The style is temptingly easy. Too easy. I suggest it should be resisted – unless, of course, one is sure that one is writing for an editor and a readership that like this particular genre. The following further examples of it are all taken from the Winter 1991 issue of *Esquire*, a magazine that favoured the mode at the time.

> Let's face it, we need another Chardonnay and Cabernet Sauvignon like we need electrocuting.

> You wake at dawn with your head pounding . . . You can't think straight and your memory has gone AWOL.

> . . . the *Mirror*'s man, Monty Fresco, snapped him [Vinny Jones the footballer] doing Test-Your-Strength on Paul Gascoigne's balls while the referee's back was turned, in a picture that overnight propelled Vinny into the forefront of modern football folklore.

> I used to procure them [wild geese] free inside expensive plastic bags from – well, no, my lips are sealed.

The first three examples show the slightly desperate similes or metaphors characteristic of such writing. The fourth comes from a well-handled piece by Matthew Fort about how to cook the Christmas goose, and specializes in a judicious choice* of cliché and a careful mixture of the 'literary' and the colloquial; I offer a further taste of it:

> . . . the fat that so liberally lards the breast of the domestic goose has turned to muscle on the bosom of its wild cousin. For my money, a young wild goose is an even better mouthful than the domestic chappie, but it needs careful cooking, and should be carved very thinly to spare the teeth of the elderly and infirm.

It struck me that this showed a firm grasp of the medium and reminded me that there are good and bad ways of doing everything.

A much less successful attempt at the same style was to be found, also during 1991, in the London *Evening Standard's* column 'Mr Pepys opines'. Examples:

> Why don't revolving doors say which way they should be pushed? Mr Pepys, assisted by the debonair literary agent Hilary Rubinstein, finally gained entrance to Kensington Place Restaurant last week after heaving mightily at the circular door.

> That's quite enough from *The Sunday Times* about championing the quality of life in London . . .

---

* This style is infectious. *Specializes in a judicious choice* is a good specimen of it, I have just realized.

Why are upper-class women so ghastly to look at . . .? That was the topic at a private dinner party Mr Pepys attended the other evening. Do you have any views? Mr Pepys will publish his conclusions in due course.

Here the mixture is not so happy, and expressions like *attended* (for *was at*) and *gained entrance to* (for *got into*) sound merely pompous and twittish among the ordinary banter of *That's quite enough* and *so ghastly*. And, of course, they are nowhere near the beautifully direct seventeenth-

> Proper words in proper places make the true definition of a style. –
> Jonathan Swift

century style of the diarist whose name the columnist has borrowed. You can see why he does it: he wants to show that the old-fashioned verbiage is only put on, like fancy dress, so he mixes some modern talk with it.

Consistency in style

The trouble with the 'Mr Pepys' column was that its author hadn't quite sorted out in his mind (if it was a he) what tone of voice he was supposed to be talking in. Yet this surely is what style is really all about.

Unfortunately the very word *style* can be about four different things:

1 *Stylishness* or polish – an elegant way of writing ('He writes with such style');
2 *House style* (names, titles etc.) as laid down in newspapers' style books, which also advise on
3 *Correctness* – avoiding solecisms, bad grammar and so forth;
4 *Manner* of writing – a neutral use of the word, with no necessary connection with what might or might not be correct.

People often confuse one or more of these. At the moment I am concerned only with the last.

An inconsistent style like that of Mr Pepys in the *Standard* is bound to annoy at least some of the readers, whether those who think it too pompous on the one hand or, on the other, those who dislike it for its colloquialisms.

An item in another breezy column, this time in *The Guardian*, makes the same kind of mistake:

News of Tom Mather. He's the chap whom I wrote about who'd achieved 300 court appearances in his attempt to assert his rights in an enormously complicated family feud over his late brother's will.

That *whom* strikes a jarring note and spoils the effect. The rest of the column is supposed to sound like the columnist chatting away to a few chums, who have never heard the word *whom* uttered in their lives.

A story on the front page of the *Sunday Times* started:

> The court of President François Mitterrand has always been full of beautiful women, leading to much conjecture. But the rumour mills were working overtime last week after he appointed the glamorous Edith Cresson as France's first woman prime minister.
> The cool patriarch and the outspoken redhead formed a close bond 25 years ago, when she was licking stamps in his secretariat.

It is not hard to spot the odd man out here. That previous example from *The Guardian* was to do with grammar; this one is to do with clichés. *The rumour mills were working overtime* would have been quite acceptable to the editor of the *AA Magazine*, say, with its penchant for sub-Wodehousian circumlocution, as quoted a few pages back (*I trawled the darker recesses of my brain* etc.). But its jokiness is not consistent with the language of those opening paragraphs (*the cool patriarch, his secretariat*); the two things are, so to speak, at different ends of the same corridor.

You may ask why I feel able to commend Matthew Fort's efforts in *Esquire*, with his mixture of the formal and the informal, while being so severe on Mr Pepys and the *Sunday Times*. I shall have more to say about such matters in a minute (see under **The virtue of surprise**, page 138). Meanwhile we can partly answer the question by asking ourselves how style is acquired in the first place.

You and the reader: who do you think you're talking to?

All (or nearly all) writing is a transaction between the writer and the reader.* If the writer's idea of what the words mean is different from the reader's, there can be no effective communication and the deal is off.

Obviously, therefore, journalists must have someone in mind while they are writing – someone with whom they are trying to communicate. It might be a news editor or a features editor or it might be Aunt Jobiska; or it might be a composite figure, for whom the editor or the aunt is a sort of stand-in: the readership or audience aimed at. But it shouldn't be no one at all.

We need have no patience with the journalists who declare smugly that

---

* There are obvious exceptions. The poet A. E. Housman called poetry 'a morbid secretion, like a pearl in an oyster' – it had to be written whether anyone read it or not. Diarists may write for posterity, but more often for themselves, either to prop up a bad memory or simply to get things off their chests. So do some novelists. Journalists, on the other hand, are telling people things – after all, that's what they're for.

they write to please themselves. People who aim to please themselves will end up by pleasing no one. I am also suspicious of people who, when asked why they have decided to go in or journalism, say they 'want to write'. Write what? Who for? And, more to the point, who to?

Such people remind me a little of those ads in the personal columns: 'Public school man, own car, available for interesting occupation, anything legal considered, what have you?' Few would bother to answer such an advertisement.

Once you have an audience in mind, then you can decide in what tone of voice you want to address them. And it is only when you have arrived at a consistently identifiable tone of voice, which they can recognize and understand, that you can be said to have achieved a style.

Some writers can't help stamping their personalities on everything they write, just as good singers' voices have a personal quality independent of technique. So much the better.

But the audience comes before the style. And the subject comes before

---

I am not yet so lost in lexicography as to forget that words are the daughters of earth, and that things are the sons of heaven.
 – Dr Johnson (sound as usual, apart from the touch of sexism)

---

the words; this sounds like a truism, and I would hesitate to offer it if I hadn't known so many people who thought of words as creatures with lives of their own, independent of the contexts they are being used in – who is writing them, who reading them, and what the subject is.

'Mr Pepys' failed to find a style; the *AA Magazine* had one; the *Sunday Times* writer just quoted did not.

This writer also had a style and knew who he was talking to:

There's news for all those who would sneer at the Grand Prix tail-enders. Those who secretly believe that, with a bit of practice, even they could tour round that far off Mansell's pace.

The news is, chaps, that you couldn't. Not now, and probably not ever. Now, I don't claim to be super fit, but I do train. And I've never had a stamina problem in any kind of racing car. After four laps in Karl Wendlinger's March, I could not manage any more without resting my head on something.

That was Mark Hale, well in control, writing in *Fast Lane*, a mag for motor-racing fanatics. A good piece. And this writer had a style too:

In connection with your obituary of Lord Havers, it is frequently overlooked that the Law Officers not only advise the government of the day in England and Wales but that they also have responsibility for doing so in Northern Ireland. This is a most demanding duty involving much travelling.

In the Heath government of the 1970s Sir Michael Havers (as he then was) was Solicitor General from 1972 to 1974 and, together with the Attorney, was assiduous in his duties in extremely difficult circumstances. I well recall the skilled yet practical advice which ministers then received, and I formed a lasting admiration for his abilities . . .

The obituarist, as you may guess, is an elder statesman, a former junior minister in the Conservative government, and his words appeared on the obituary page of *The Times*. Elsewhere, even in the same paper, such

> People think that I can teach them style. What stuff it all is! Have something to say, and say it as clearly as you can. That is the only secret of style. – Matthew Arnold

phrases as *it is frequently overlooked that* and *was assiduous in his duties* would have been thought unnecessarily pompous and old-fashioned. Here they are perfectly suitable. We may not talk or write like that ourselves (heaven forbid, I hear you say), but we recognize the style and the personality that goes with it. More about this fragment in a minute.

The following two excerpts are from quite different newspapers but are in the same clearly identifiable style:

1   **HOUSE OF SECRETS WHERE TIME STOOD STILL**
The death of a 103-year-old descendant of Anne Boleyn has finally let the modern world through the doors of a mid-Wales country mansion to marvel at room after room of treasures shielded from time.

The modern world's representatives are Sotheby's antiques experts, who believe the possessions of the late Mrs Josephine Murray will raise £500,000. In an atmosphere of awe, they are now carefully cataloguing and valuing the contents of Penpont, a magnificent pile yesterday hidden behind a screen of trees dappled in bright autumn sunshine . . .

Early in the nineteenth century, an imposing classical colonnade was erected along the front of the three-storey house. As decades turned into centuries, Penpont filled up with rare paintings, exquisite furniture, glistening silverware, ceramics and even ukuleles and castanets.

2   **THE ROMANCE OF RAIL!**
                Just the ticket to recall those
                 dreamy days of steam
Turn back the clock to revel in the romance of the steam era by making a nostalgic rail journey through some of Britain's best countryside.

The aroma of steam and the rhythmic beat of the carriage wheels will bring back memories of the wonderful days of steam.

The second excerpt comes from a popular local evening, the *Oxford Star*. It is a good specimen of automatic nostalgia and illustrates incidentally the dangers of reaching for the nearest cliché when you should be paying attention to what you're writing about.* The article about the country house seems to have been designed for much the same sort of market, though the nostalgia is of a slightly different kind and reminds one, with

> Style is the dress of thoughts. – Lord Chesterfield

its timeless treasures and its dapply trees, of popular romances. It comes from *The Observer*, a classy Sunday for the discriminating reader, and I was so surprised at seeing it that I thought it must have got there by some strange computer error.

The *Observer* piece also told us that the Penpont estate was of 2-500 acres and that

> Lost in the lush, undulating country, studded with ancient woods and copses, are 12 farms and numerous cottages. Near at hand, a walled garden the size of many a town park lures the visitor through the maze of paths.
> Like the contents of the house, those acres are steeped in history.

The picture caption reads 'Sotheby's director, Richard Allen, upon a Queen Anne chair, evaluates items in Mrs Murray's tapestry-clad bedroom'. That little word *upon* tells us much: it has, like the rest of the piece, a bogus period look. Mrs Murray's chairs may be genuine, but the language is only repro.

Whatever you may think of those two bits of writing, you must admit that they are consistent, both with themselves and with each other. Both are evidently aimed at people who have no knowledge of the subjects being written about. The Oxford man would not have dared make that mistake about the wheels if he had been writing for an informed readership, and the *Observer* man would not have told us that Sotheby's experts were '*carefully* cataloguing and valuing the contents' (how else would they catalogue them?) if he thought we knew anything about antiques.

The style was right for a popular local evening paper, wrong for a Sunday heavy.

* The 'rhythmic beat of the carriage wheels' is one thing the trippers down memory lane *won't* hear. As the writer makes clear later in the piece, the steam excursion will be running on modern track, which has continuous welded rails.

The virtue of surprise

None of those last three examples – from *The Times*, from *Oxford Star* and from *The Observer* – could by any stretch be called 'good' writing. The item about Lord Havers uses many words of the kind listed in Chapter 1 – words not worth using if shorter, simpler words can be found for the job. However, this is not the only reason for its weakness.

Alan Watkins, *The Observer's* very experienced political correspondent, uses a great many mandarin expressions. I pick three fragments at random:

> No party, we were confidently informed, had ever won an election by promising to increase taxes . . .
>
> Where, I inquired afterwards, was he or she about whom I had been forewarned? . . .
>
> I would not mind at all if a third party attended our talk.

He could have written *told* instead of *informed* and *asked* rather than *inquired* and he need not have taken so much trouble to avoid ending a sentence with a preposition (*about whom I had been forewarned*).

So what makes Alan Watkins 'good' and that obituary notice 'not so good'? Two things.

First, Watkins always has something original to say. The piece about Lord Havers doesn't say anything very much, except that he was a reliable chap, something which could be applied to many people less distinguished than he was.

But then Havers's obituarist goes on to tell us:

> His company on the journeys to Northern Ireland was always looked forward to. It was enlivened by his encyclopaedic knowledge of the brothels of Alexandria, knowledge I hasten to add not gained from personal experience, but rather from having to extricate his sailors back to his ship during the war.

When he does have something to say about the dead man, we stop minding about the mandarin argot. We happily put up with stock expressions like *encyclopaedic knowledge* and *I hasten to add* for the sake of a nice little personal story.

Again, much of the country-house piece I have just quoted from could have been about almost any other country house. The author could probably have written it with his eyes shut. (I'm not saying his eyes *were* shut, only that it reads that way.) A bad artist does the same. He settles down to paint, say, a mountain, but can't get it right, because he is thinking of his own preconception of what a mountain ought to be like instead of looking at the one in front of him.

Second, the language of the 'not so good' examples carries no surprises. Though it contains a great many polysyllables, when you come to

> Many wise men through the centuries, from Aristotle to Sir Winston Churchill, have emphasised the importance of using very simple words . . . But one that is long and unusual should not be rejected merely on that account if it is more apt in meaning. If we were asked whether there was any difference between *woolly* and *flocculent* we should probably say no . . . But Sir Winston, in the first volume of his *Second World War*, uses *flocculent* instead of *woolly* to describe the mental processes of certain people, and so conveys to his readers just that extra ounce of contempt that we feel *flocculent* to contain . . .
>
> – Sir Ernest Gowers

look at it again it really has a very restricted vocabulary. The Alan Watkinses, on the other hand, give us the whole range.

General rules about 'good' writing can be tedious. Mention any rule and you can usually find some notable writer who breaks it. Here's one, though: 'good' writers vary the length of their words just as they vary the length of their sentences. As I've already made clear, a piece of prose with almost nothing but Latinate words in it would be intolerable, but so would a piece with nothing but words derived from Middle English or Anglo-Saxon. And it helps if you can enliven the copy with an occasional touch of the unexpected, so long as it's not too out of character. You have to do a sort of balancing act between the need for consistency on the one hand and for variety on the other.

Has the writer succeeded here?

> When the Olympic flame comes ashore at Empuries in Catalonia next Tuesday, starting the run-up to the Games, it will be a neat piece of symbolism – Greek encountering Greek.
>
> About Olympia and its Grecian nature there is no problem, but some may not realise – or recall – that Empuries, on the Costa Brava, was also a substantial ancient Greek foundation, one step further on from Greek Marseilles. With red rock, green pines, grey ruins and crisp blue sea, this former trading city makes a joy of archaeological excursion. As it happens, it was also where the Romans, bristling with weapons, entered Spain to start the Second Punic War – in which, in the end, they thoroughly duffed up the Carthaginians.

All is in a good straight well-mannered literary prose (the paper is the *Sunday Telegraph*) till we get to the last line and the expression *duffed up*. That belongs to quite a different vocabulary (*EastEnders*?) and you might think it had no business here.

My own feeling is that it's doing a good job. Weren't we getting just a little impatient with all that ancient history? (And why 'Greek *encountering* Greek'?) A touch of the colloquial comes as a welcome change.

One might say the same of the word *ta-ra* in this fragment from a 'Personal View' in the *Daily Telegraph*, about people who lost money with Lloyd's of London:

> I am perfectly aware of what the facts are and what the mood is. Not only do I qualify as a stricken Name, but I have been turning up assiduously at recent gatherings of Names, stricken or otherwise. Few things concentrate the mind as having to say an unexpected ta-ra to a six-figure sum.

Both these examples of the unexpected work all right because the general tone of the piece has been established by the time we get to them. (The second, by Tom Stacey, owes something to P. G. Wodehouse.)

And of course it also works the other way round:

> When John Major finally made it from Brixton to 10 Downing Street, he vowed to create a more classless society in Britain . . .
> Some people may scoff at honours, but life-long effort or commitment should be recognised, as should great achievement and courage. – Leader in the *Daily Star*

A scattering of polysyllables like *commitment* and *achievement* in a tabloid leader are all the more effective because of their rarity.

But to repeat: it's the subject, not the words, that matters. If you've got the subject the words should come (though with luck there will be time to refine them later), and all the quicker for the wide reading you've been doing. The analogy with painting still holds. A landscape artist may reasonably squeeze a tube onto a palette saying 'I think I'll paint this mountain blue' and a writer may do the verbal equivalent – but not if the said writer is a journalist. The journalist says 'Let's see, what colour is this mountain?' and *then* chooses a tube to match it.

The temptations of space

One reason for the more leisurely styles we have been discussing is, of course, the rapid increase in the size of newspapers and journals in the 1980s. There was more space to fill. It is true that the designers grabbed a major share of the newly acquired acres, but the words also multiplied, while the ideas didn't, or not always.

Perhaps we should listen to Saul Bellow when he writes:

A Japanese sage – I forget his name – told his disciples: 'Write as short as you can.' Sydney Smith, an English clergyman and wit of the last century, also spoke out for brevity. 'Short views, for God's sake, short views!' he said. And Miss Ferguson, a lively spinster who was my composition teacher in Chicago some 60 years ago, would dance before the class, clasp her hands and chant (her music borrowed from Handel's Hallelujah Chorus):
                                Be
                            speci-
                            fic!
Miss Ferguson would not put up with redundancy, prolixity, periphrasis, or bombast.

The writer who cares for his readers, says Bellow, must assure them immediately that reading him will be worth their while:

Such a writer will trouble no one with his own vanities, will make no unnecessary gestures, indulge himself in no mannerisms, waste no reader's time. He will write as short as he can.

The temptation was obvious. If I've got a nice lot of room I can tell the story at my own pace, can't I? Such thinking is insidious. It forgets that though the wordage may have become more generous the readers' patience has not.

First-person leaders

The tradition of writing leaders in the first person is fairly new, and is thought to have been started by Peregrine Worsthorne when he was editor of the *Sunday Telegraph* in the 1980s. The great J. L. Garvin of *The Observer* wrote signed leader-pagers when he was editor there, but there was also an unsigned leader, probably his as well.

The objection to the signed leader is that if you abandon the editorial 'we' you immediately diminish its impact: this is no longer a great organ thundering, but one man at his desk.

Here is an example (from a local paper) of a leader which has used the 'I' form:

So British Gas chairman Robert Evans is under fire for picking up a £1,252 a week pay rise, taking his salary to £435,000.

Now I have to say that this is a bit excessive, particularly when so many people face redundancy and bleak times.

It is true that you have to reward people well at the top – but this is going a bit far.

The editor has written 'Now I have to say that' to give his opinions a personal flavour, but in the event this merely reads like a pointless piece of throat-clearing. The leader would be much crisper without it. While we are at it, let's tidy it up a bit:

(*Untrimmed version*)	(*Tidy version*)
So British Gas chairman Robert Evans is under fire for picking up a £1,252 a week pay rise, taking his salary to £435,000.	British Gas chairman Robert Evans is under fire for picking up a £1,252 a week pay rise, taking his salary to £435,000.
Now I have to say that this is a bit excessive, particularly when so many people face redundancy and bleak times.	It is true that you have to reward people well at the top.
It is true that you have to reward people well at the top – but this is going a bit far. (63 words)	But at a time when so many people face redundancy and a shortage of cash, this is surely a bit excessive. (55 words)

We have got rid of the repetition – *a bit excessive/going a bit far* – and we have dispensed with the idle little word *So* at the start. It should not have been there in any case, for a sentence starting *So* is generally understood as introducing an idea the writer disagrees with. *So* would have been appropriate if the leader had started, say, like this:

So the chairman of British Gas thinks he is worth an annual £435,000 of the customers' money [or whatever].

But the editor was *agreeing* with Robert Evans's critics, which meant that *So* got him off on the wrong foot. (Perhaps he had been reading too much of Ernest J. Thribb, the teenage poet of *Private Eye*, whose doggerel always began with a *So*.)*

The best examples of the short, chatty leader are to be found in *The Sun* and the *Daily Mirror*. They do not use 'I', but they seem to be talking directly to the reader.

* We have also changed 'bleak times' – an echo from two Dickens novels, *Hard Times* and *Bleak House* – so as to avoid the slightly unfortunate repetition of 'times' in the same sentence.

The Guardian has been firming up its tradition of informally styled leaders, and we must expect this trend to spread. At the time of writing, *The Guardian* still doesn't sound like the man in the street – more like a progressive university don relaxing over a glass of something – but the conversational tone is emphasized by the liberal use of elisions:

> Only three weeks ago, with buoyant confidence, Labour offered a better managed, more efficient Britain. Last night it was hard put to offer a decently managed, tolerably efficient leadership election. *That's* in no sense fatal . . . The trouble, of course, is that the process *doesn't* fit the need. Labour needs – or thinks it needs – John Smith. *That's* what MPs, by their endorsement yesterday, clearly signal. [My italics.]

The style is not consistent. A leader about the Conservatives' Citizen's Charter is headed THE SEVENTH TIME AROUND and we know the editor wants to show that he is up with the fashion from his use of *around*, an import from the United States, rather than the native *round*. But at the end of that same leader we read that

> a few spitting images now would do scant harm

and with that old-fashioned *scant* (rather than the more idiomatic *little*) we are back in Manchester with C. P. Scott. And *The Guardian* has not, at the time of writing, taken to starting the last par of its leaders 'Seriously folks', the pop equivalent of our old friend 'This much is certain'.

Meanwhile *The Guardian's* diarist sets the pace by sprinkling his copy with highly informal exclamations such as *wham* and *eeek*. I look forward to seeing these expressions in *The Guardian's* leaders in due course.

9 PUNCTUATION

Bad punctuation is a wrecker. As my examples will show, many a newspaper paragraph has ended in the ditch because its punctuation marks needed attention. Here is a quick service manual.

Easy on the commas

The comma is the most used, and the most misused, of all the punctuation marks. Its main function, of course, is to break up sentences into conveniently handled parcels, but it is all too easy to overdo it.

> The chancelleries did not conspire to get rid of Mrs Thatcher, only to see another nationalist brute arise. – Charles Moore in the *Spectator*, in a reflective article about Mr Boris Yeltsin

The comma after 'Thatcher' may have been put there to make an awkward sentence a bit easier. Sometimes commas can help in this way. More often they don't, and this one is no help at all. In fact it actually makes matters worse, because it inclines us to think that the first part of the sentence ('The chancelleries did not conspire to get rid of Mrs Thatcher') is a statement of fact, whereas the fact which Mr Moore is trying to convey is that they *did* conspire. That comma had no business there, and should have been sent packing, thus:

> The Chancelleries did not conspire to get rid of Mrs Thatcher only to see another nationalist brute arise.

The comma in the next example was almost certainly put in for the same reason:

Edna Lumb's paintings of mills and machinery and some of her other observations of British industrial life, go on show tomorrow. – *Daily Telegraph*

The subject of the sentence is 17 words long and the rest only four, so the comma is there to tell us 'You've got to the end of the subject, now here's the verb'. But again it doesn't really work: it is still a rather clumsy sentence. The only solution is to punctuate it so that the reader will expect a comma there *anyway*, by slipping in an extra comma after 'machinery':

Edna Lumb's paintings of mills and machinery, and some of her other observations of British industrial life, go on show tomorrow.

Another example, this time from the tabloid press:

The heiress who claimed a Kennedy raped her, repeated the allegation on prime-time TV yesterday – as her cleared attacker watched. – *Daily Star*

Putting a comma after 'raped her' doesn't make things better.

Some writers and sub-editors spatter the copy with commas. They think this will make the message clearer to readers. In practice it often does no more than slow them down a little.

We have been taught that the comma is there to indicate a pause. Yet the commonest kind of comma-spattering is the kind that asks for a pause where in ordinary speech we wouldn't pause at all:

There is, therefore, no legal barrier in either international or domestic law to prosecuting war criminals simply because their crimes were committed long ago. – Louis Blom-Cooper in *The Guardian*

The commas on either side of 'therefore' are not wrong, but they are unnecessary. They merely hold things up. Would we pause at 'therefore' if we were *saying* this sentence?

Commas between adjectives*

Many people have the mistaken idea that commas are always needed to separate adjectives from each other. I am not sure where it came from. Perhaps it was started by pedantic elementary school teachers some time before the Second World War and has somehow stuck. Take the following example:

* For parts of speech see Glossary.

Hundreds of white doves and balloons were released into the warm, evening sky. – *Times* reporter at Elizabeth Taylor's eighth wedding

Another example:

What were once beautiful, half-timbered cottages now have rusting, corrugated-iron roofs. – Graham Turner, *Daily Mail*

All these commas are wrong. *The Times* is saying that the evening sky was warm. Mr Turner is complaining about half-timbered cottages that are beautiful and corrugated-iron roofs that have gone rusty. In each case, then, the first word is describing the second two words. One has only to compare:

a charming, Irish lady

with:

a charming, Irishwoman

to see the point. It is obviously as unnecessary – indeed, as absurd – to put a comma between 'charming' and 'Irish lady' as it is to put one between 'charming' and 'Irishwoman'. But people will do it. I came across this:

Hanna urged him to persuade a large, black, ex-prisoner called Trevor Hercules that prison pie was both nourishing and tasty. – Nancy Banks-Smith, *The Guardian*

Here we have a prisoner who is not only large but also black, and not only black but also, it would seem, ex. Both those commas should go. And I read somewhere of

a big-boned, chestnut horse.

Again, we're talking about a chestnut horse that is big-boned, not a horse that is big-boned and chestnut.

The largest example I ever saw of this popular error was on a 10-metre advertisement hoarding:

Peugeot 106: The surprisingly big, small car.

Perhaps the copy-writers thought the comma would make us pause on 'big', but it was just as likely to make us concentrate on 'small'. I am sure they congratulated each other on getting the punctuation 'correct', but how wrong they were.

Sir Robert Cook and Patrick Cormack have published glossy, coffee table books . . . – Julian Critchley in *The Author*

This is almost as silly as writing 'a bright, night light'.
Your ear should tell you whether to put a comma between adjectives:

There has been far too much lengthy, over-elaborate advice from so-called curriculum experts. – Assistant teachers' spokesman quoted in the *Daily Mail*

Here the comma separates two distinct ideas and is doing a good job. The comma is also right in this fragment from a *Guardian* law report:

Lawyers experienced in medical negligence are scathing about Department of Health proposals last month for a quick, cheap arbitration procedure . . .

We would certainly look for a comma where three adjectives have an 'and' among them:

A full, perfect and sufficient sacrifice. – *Book of Common Prayer*

We need the comma after 'full'. But compulsive comma-spatterers would be amazed to find how often they can be done without:

Anyway back to Miss [Glenda] Jackson, who being a simple woman of good robust working-class blood has obviously meekly accepted the received wisdom of Hampstead. – Julie Burchill, *The Spectator*

Your spatterer will itch to put commas after 'anyway', 'who', 'good', 'robust' and 'blood':

Anyway, back to Miss Jackson, who, being a simple woman of good, robust, working-class blood, has obviously accepted etc.

None of them is needed. I sometimes think of rogue commas as 'printer's commas'. The old printers seem to have really loved them. John Milton's poetry suffered from a positive dandruff of them, put in by half-educated seventeenth-century compositors; some of them can be found even today in modern editions of his works. More than 200 years after Milton, in Anthony Trollope's time, comma-mad printers were still at it. See what they did to this sentence from Trollope's *The Way We Live Now*:

> Roger was not at all disposed to quarrel with Mr Crumb, because the victim of Crumb's heroism had been his own cousin.

That comma spoils the whole point of the sentence. With it, Trollope seems to be telling us why Roger didn't want to quarrel. Take it away, and we realize that Roger wouldn't want to quarrel *although* Mr Crumb had beat up his cousin: a different story altogether:

> Roger was not at all disposed to quarrel with Mr Crumb because the victim of Crumb's heroism had been his own cousin.

Commas to the rescue

Of course there *are* times when the odd comma is needed to help prop up a wobbly sentence or keep a wandering one on-course, as in the following ever-so-slightly pretentious fragment from *The Times* about the Scilly Isles:

> Parking myself on a bench dedicated to Gloggy Mellor, I made a mental inventory of a few of my favourite things about these islands; soft, reasonable voices spilling out of fields and cottages, shirt-sleeved men and women in cotton frocks pushing prams and trailing goofy dogs . . .

It is not clear how many people are wearing the frocks or whether the men as well as the women are pushing prams. A comma after 'men' and perhaps another after 'frocks' could have brought things into focus. But then the sentence would have sounded terribly jerky. Better to change the words ('Men in shirt-sleeves and women in cotton frocks' would have helped) than to call on more commas.

And there are times when the presence of a comma really is vital, because leaving it out would confuse the reader or alter the sense:

> Neil Kinnock should not be tempted to bask in the afterglow of his party's performance at the Walton by-election because the issues raised for the Labour Party will not go away.

That was the first sentence of a *Daily Express* leader. It badly needs a comma after 'by-election':

Neil Kinnock should not be tempted to bask in the afterglow of his party's performance at the Walton by-election, because the issues raised for the Labour Party will not go away.

Now all is immediately clear. Compare the example from Trollope above, of which this is the converse: Trollope's sentence made no sense *with* a comma, this one is ambiguous *without* one. 'Because' sentences can be tricky.

I don't wear wigs because I feel I have to go out and convince people that I can look different. – Actress Carol Royle, quoted in the *Daily Telegraph*

When we begin that sentence we expect Miss Royle to be explaining why she doesn't wear wigs. It's only the lack of a comma that makes it clear that she *does* wear wigs (but not because she wants to look different).

Commas before 'and' or 'but'

Some old-fashioned teachers used to insist on these. ('He seemed to be asleep, and/but I could not wake him.') They are usually unnecessary, as this one after 'asleep' certainly is. But watch the sense; an extra comma would have come in useful in the following paragraph from the *Observer* business section:

The Reichmanns have been caught in a classic squeeze. They have insufficient trading income to service their debts and their ambitious projects, which include the World Financial Centre, are declining in value.

It looks as though the brothers haven't enough trading income to service their debts and their ambitious projects. But then we get to 'are declining' at the end of the sentence and realize we've been misrouted: the 'ambitious projects' are the start of a new statement altogether. The missing signpost is, of course, a comma after 'debts':

They have insufficient income to service their debts, and their ambitious projects . . . are declining in value.

'While' and 'which'

Sentences with 'while' or 'which' in them often cry out for a comma:

> Mrs Thatcher hated being seen in glasses while any photographer whose paper published a picture of a bespectacled President Kennedy faced dismissal from the White House Press Corps. – Peterborough, *Daily Telegraph*

Until we get past the word 'photographer' we think we are being told about the occasions on which Mrs T didn't want to be seen in glasses. A comma after 'glasses' would have given us a clue as to where the sentence was going.

> The Churches which once insisted that marriage should come before babies have become 'non-judgmental'. – Mary Kenny, *Daily Telegraph*

As it stands this sentence implies that not all the Churches have become non-judgmental, only the ones that used to insist on marriage before babies. We read it as meaning 'those Churches which'. Only the context tells us that this must be wrong. So the reader has to supply a mental comma, as it were, after 'Churches' and again after 'babies':

> The Churches, which once insisted that marriage should come before babies, have become 'non-judgmental'.

But readers should not have to sub-edit the copy as they go along.

A general rule

It is hard to make rules about commas, because there will always be exceptions. But one rule that can usually be followed is:

> *If a dependent clause or phrase in the middle of a sentence has a comma in front of it, it should have one after it too. And vice versa: if there is a comma after it, there should be one before it.*

The best way of illustrating this is to show the rule being broken, as here:

> The authority and effectiveness of the UN having once proved successful in relation to Iraq's brutal invasion of Kuwait, will have an enhanced prestige and authority for tackling other tragic disputes. – The Right Rev Richard Harries, in *The Observer*

This is worth looking at in detail. The bishop's sentence has three parts:

1 The authority and effectiveness of the UN	
2 will have an enhanced prestige and authority for tackling other disputes	(the main statement)
3 having once proved successful in relation to Iraq's brutal invasion of Kuwait	(the subsidiary statement)

But because there is no comma after (1) it looks as though (1) and (3) go together, so that the sentence has only *two* parts:

1 The authority and effectiveness of the UN having once proved successful in relation to Iraq's brutal invasion of Kuwait (i.e. now that the UN has been effective in the matter of Kuwait)	(the subsidiary statement)
2 will have etc.	(the main statement)

This won't do, because (2) is the main part of the sentence, but it has no subject. *What* will have . . .? The sentence sounds all wrong. To get round the annoyance, all we need is another comma, thus:

> The authority and effectiveness of the UN, having once proved successful in relation to Iraq's brutal invasion of Kuwait, will have an enhanced prestige etc.

I go into this sentence at some length only to show how important the rule is, and how tiresome it can be for the reader when someone fails to observe it.

Incidentally, if you have a list of things itemized by commas, remember to close them with a final comma. This fragment, from a review in the *Sunday Telegraph* about George Orwell, explains:

> His imagined life at St Cyprian's, his career as an enforcer of an alien culture on a subject people, his descent into the underworld of the workless and vagrant confirmed an attitude to the world which tried to find articulation through left-wing politics, . . . (Anthony Burgess)

Everything up to 'vagrant' is the subject of Mr Burgess's sentence. Without the vital comma before 'confirmed' we stumble on to the verb before we are ready for it. (I would have marked the end of the subject by inserting an 'all' before 'confirmed'; it would have made a helpful signpost.)

Commas in names and dates

A similar rule, though not so crucial, applies to names and dates:

> She left New College, Oxford, years ago.
> *not*
> She left New College, Oxford years ago.

> In June, 1989, she left Oxford for ever.
> *not*
> In June, 1989 she left Oxford for ever.

In the second example no commas are needed, but if you have one of them then you must have the other as well.

The question of when to put commas between people's names and their descriptions needs some care:

> The former prime minister, Edward Heath, was heckled by Thatcherite Young Conservatives yesterday . . . – *The Guardian*

> The publisher, Christopher Sinclair-Stevenson, still thinks he can squeeze another biography out of Evelyn Waugh. – *The Guardian* again

Edward Heath's commas make him seem as though he were the *only* former prime minister, Christopher Sinclair-Stevenson's as though there were no publishers but him. It would have been all right to put 'Edward Heath, the former prime minister, was heckled' or 'Former prime minister Edward Heath was heckled', which is better still, because it is read more quickly.

So the rule here is:

The poet, John Keats, wrote an Ode . . .	*Wrong*. There are other poets.
John Keats, the poet, wrote an Ode . . .	*OK*. The John Keats we're talking about is the one who's a poet. (This form can sometimes be patronizing, or facetious.)
The poet John Keats wrote an Ode . . .	*Good*. Here's a poet: that poet.

Another example:

> Veteran comedy star, George Burns, who had a problem with his

throat, didn't like the advice he received from a doctor who told him to give up smoking. So he sought a second opinion. From a doctor who smoked. – *The Sun*

Delete the comma after 'star'.

A 'rule' to ignore

A certain amount of pedantry attaches to the use of the comma. Much of it can be ignored. For instance, teachers used to say that it was wrong to join two finite* sentences – that is, sentences with a main verb* in them – with a comma. This is simply not true, though some people still believe it.

He was asleep, his eyes were closed, he could not see me.

That sentence has nothing wrong with it, though it contains three main verbs. But it would be inelegant, and look wrong, to do the same with disparate ideas, ideas which don't follow each other logically:

He was asleep, the cost of living was up again.

Nothing less than a full stop is called for here.

Colon(:) or semi(;)?

The context should tell you whether to use a semicolon rather than a comma.

The idea of compensating passengers for inconvenience is sound enough; although it would obviously be a great deal better if trains ran so consistently to time that such provision was unnecessary. – Leader, *Liverpool Daily Post*

With a semicolon after 'enough', readers may think that the sentence is starting afresh and that 'although' refers forward instead of back: 'although it would be better, it might be better still . . .' (etc.). That semicolon should have been a comma.

Pedants have made one or two rules for semi-colons, but these are so often broken by good writers that we need not bother with them. All that needs to be remembered is that the semi-colon makes a rather bigger

* See Glossary.

pause than a comma does; and the only rule about colons that matters is that what goes after them should always be an explanation, or one or more examples, of what has gone before them:

> One thing I would ask: please don't come here tomorrow.

That is what they are for; so it is foolish to use them instead of semi-colons, since the reader may then be misled into thinking you are about to explain or exemplify something when you are not.

Conversely, it is a serious misuse of the semi-colon to put it instead of a colon, as in my earlier quotation from *The Times*:

> I made a mental inventory of a few of my favourite things about these islands; soft, reasonable voices (etc.)

If ever a colon was needed, it is after 'islands'.

This sentence from *The Economist* shows the right use of both marks:

> Neo-Nazis in Germany; anti-Semitism in Poland; parties surging in Austria and Switzerland; a former imperial grand wizard of the Ku Klux Klan running as a Republican for the governorship of Louisiana: from the Urals to the Ozarks, it seems, the scum is rising.

The writer uses semis to tick off items on a long list, and a colon to explain what they have in common. Popular papers, which hardly ever carry semi-colons, would have used full stops.

Full stops

Don't listen to those who say that a full stop 'has to end a sentence' and that a sentence 'must have a verb in it'. Pedants have told us that this rule is invariable. Not so. Indeed, I have just broken it.

But we must distinguish. There are two kinds of verbless sentences:

1 The kind in which the verb is *understood*, as above: '[This is] not so.' Nothing wrong with that.
2 The kind which are not really sentences at all, but strips of words which have been fenced off from their neighbours to give them emphasis:

> He says he is flying to the moon on Wednesday. Which is not a practical idea. When you come to think of it.

I would never try to ban this second kind, but it nearly always turns out to be too slick. Anyone can do it to give his or her copy a spurious sense of urgency or toughness, the strong-silent-man effect. Here is Linda Lee-Potter doing the wise-guy act in the *Daily Mail*:

> I'm amazed at all the fuss and surprise caused by the fact that the Labour Party organised a lush £500-a-ticket bash. Since I've never met a Labour politician yet who preferred a bacon butty to a brochette de poisson or a pint of Guinness to a glass of Dom Pérignon.

Why cut the sentence in two? Miss Lee-Potter was obviously aiming for the conversational style, yet no one uses 'since' like this in conversation. Could it have been because she thought readers of the *Daily Mail* couldn't manage sentences of more than 25 words? Surely not. However, if I had been subbing her piece I would have been tempted to delete the 'since' to make a couple of proper sentences out of it – or restarted: 'Have you ever met a Labour politician who . . .?' etc.

There is something wrong with this fragment from a thoughtful Christmastide leader in *The Independent*:

> Examine more closely the motives [that actuate people] at Christmas. All the apparent indictments of Christmas turn out to be in its favour.
>
> Because people really do act from the best of motives at this time of year, and more so than at other times.

Almost illiterate, isn't it? And so easy to put right by substituting 'For' for 'Because' at the start of that new par.

The next fragment is from a more informal piece under Catherine Bennett's byline in *The Guardian*. She has been interviewing the author of a new biography about George Orwell:

> 'The great thing about biographies of dead people is that you know how it ends,' Michael Shelden says, laughing joyfully. 'The guy dies! So there is that sensation of knowing where you're headed which you cannot know in your own life.'
>
> Unless you're a flourishing literary biographer, in which case there's a fair chance you're heading for another literary life, and a handsome advance.

There's a worrying feeling that the last sentence has been cut off in its prime. Again, the solution is easy. Start it

> Unless, of course, you're a flourishing literary biographer . . .

There still isn't a verb, but now we don't expect one.

In the following example, from a leader in the *Sussex Express*, the editor has also tried the technique, but with limited success. The subject is Sunday trading:

> . . . Even Prime Minister John Major has refused to condemn the shops. Unlike shadow home secretary Roy Hattersley who appeared to be speaking for the minority rather than the majority when he condemned the government for allowing this to happen.
>
> Another piece of predictable Hattersley political talk.
>
> This matter will only be resolved when the law is changed. Or in the New Year when customers decide whether to shop on Sundays or not. If the response is poor the major stores won't bother. We shall see.

This is certainly snappy and brisk. The trouble is that the second, third and fifth sentences ('Unlike . . .', 'Another piece . . .', 'Or in the New Year . . .') sound like afterthoughts, or contributions from the chap at the other end of the bar. One can almost hear another swig being taken at each full stop.

The *Sussex Express* deliberately adopts a conversational style, which is no bad thing. I don't suppose its editor really wrote his leaders in the pub. But if they sound like pub talk, why should anyone read them? They can hear such talk any day of the week.

One columnist who could wield a punchy full stop, and do it with style, was Jean Rook of the *Daily Express*. Here is an example:

> Those who have sat in Dr Anthony Clare's Radio 4 Psychiatrist's Chair claim he's more probing than a dentist. That he peels the great and famous like onions. That he can see into anyone's soul through the holes in their vests . . .

But here the reader *understands* – supplies mentally – the missing words 'they claim' at the start of those last two sentences, and the whole thing goes swimmingly.

Full stops are also used well in this fragment from a *Daily Mail* leader:

> Many Labour authorities are still run like old-style Soviet truck factories. Indifferent to productivity. Wasteful. Inefficient. Third-rate.

Each full stop is a fist banged on the rostrum. We find the same trick in an advertisement for a fax machine, comparing its results with those of an unnamed, inferior rival:

The one on the left is from a conventional fax machine. Already it's begun to turn yellow. To fade. To curl up. To crinkle.

But the gross over-use of the verbless sentence by advertising copywriters should have warned us against it by now. You know the sort of thing:

Our body-panels are rust-proofed. Not just once. Not just twice. But four times. Which is good for your business. And for ours.

British Rail was among the firms whose advertising agencies were still keen on this technique in 1991:

Peterborough York, Newcastle and Berwick must have passed us by at some point.

Because you arrive at your destination, three hours fifty-nine minutes after you left King's Cross.

But here it seems to have gone off the rails. The second sentence has come to a full stop before it has arrived: as in the example from *The Independent* above, the reader expects a main verb to follow – particularly since in this case the designer has put a whole centimetre of leading between the two pars – but we never get one. (Did I not say that 'because' sentences could be tricky?)

Full-stop-spattering is, if anything, more irritating than comma-spattering. Talking of commas, an assiduous sub-editor would have taken out that comma after 'destination' above and put it after 'Peterborough'. Fussy? No. Commas are like children in the kitchen: welcome when they're helping, a pest when they're not.

Dots . . .

. . . are useful for leading the reader on to a following item, or on from a preceding one, a handy device. More commonly, of course, they show that something is left out of a quote; and it is a matter of judgement how conscientious one should be in indicating such gaps. In reporting what someone has said live they can usually be dispensed with so long as the sense is kept. But when written material is being transcribed it is best if possible to put them in if you are cutting from the middle of a sentence.

Popular papers are more likely to give them quite a different role: for dramatic effect, like this . . .

Blundering council bosses sent a poll tax demand for £209 to . . . a pigeon. – *Daily Mirror* splash intro

And some pops, including the *The Sun* (but not the *Mirror*, which uses the more traditional colons), have them separating the two parts of a double caption:

Thrilled . . . Diana

Susanna . . . 'faulty heart'

John Smith . . . told of sex at Holiday Inn

This is not nearly as satisfactory as colons or double-deckers, both of which *The Sun*, inconsistently, has used too, as thus:

SUSANNA
Faulty heart

. . . And dashes

Whether to put dashes or brackets round a digression is usually a matter of taste. Again, the popular press is different. When it does digress in the middle of a sentence – which is seldom – it prefers dashes. But it needs the dash all the time – to say to the reader: 'Wait for it!', as the dots do in the *Mirror* intro above.

Examples:

Britain's biggest building society told brickie Martin Williams to close his account – because his shoes were dirty. – *The Sun*

Police with loud hailers joined a helicopter squad to talk a man off a roof – only to discover he was a ROOFER. – *Daily Mirror*

Those dashes are there instead of commas, but they could go almost any-where. The *Mirror's* story could equally (and more effectively?) have started:

Police with loud hailers joined a helicopter squad to talk a man off a roof, only to discover that he was – a roofer.

This use of the dash is not recommended for those trying to get their work into the broadsheet press.

(Brackets) and [brackets]

Round brackets for something you want to say en passant: an aside, a digression, a 'by the way' – something which is not part of the argument but doesn't fit anywhere else. Square brackets for quoted material when a word is not in the quote but is needed for the sense:

Mr Baker said: 'I am in two minds about the [dog] licences.'

If a digression is a long one and looks as though it is getting out of hand, thus distracting the reader from the main thrust, brackets may not be enough and other devices may be needed, perhaps a small rejig. The following example is from Nigella Lawson's column in the *Evening Standard*. (Ignore the square brackets, which, of course, merely mark my own interpolations.)

At no stage has he [Salman Rushdie] made any attempt to deny the sincerity of the reaction to the book [*The Satanic Verses*], at least among Moslems.
(I think we may all feel a little more suspicious about the rage the novel has incited among those whose beliefs have not been besmirched by the book, especially when they haven't even bothered to read it.) But realising that passages may offend – however deep the offence – is not the same as accepting the fact that a man has been condemned to death.

I am pretty sure that it wasn't Miss Lawson's idea to start a paragraph with a bracketed sentence, a silly thing to do – the equivalent of an after-dinner speaker who drives his listeners to near-madness by starting: 'Before I say what I have to say, I want to say something quite different . . .' or words to that effect. It is more likely that she didn't make any paragraph marks at all, and that they were left to a hard-pressed sub who put them in any old where. My point, however, is that the digression is too long to be supported by brackets. By the time we get to the closing bracket we may even have forgotten that the sentence opened with one. (Of course, such long parentheses are easily absorbed by the readers of belles-lettres in their fireside chairs.)

Screamers!

It used to be said that exclamation marks, or screamers in the trade, should always be used after exclamatory sentences, as in 'What a mess!' or

How jocund did they drive their team afield!
How bowed the woods beneath their mighty stroke!

(Gray's *Elegy*)

Fowler's Modern English Usage confirmed this rule in its second edition in 1965. Nowadays they are often left off; and if I were sub-editing an opinion column and found such a sentence without one, I would be inclined to leave it like that:

The Chancellor says things are getting better. How naive of him.

The Chancellor foresees an improvement. What an optimist.

Sometimes the sentence is long enough for us to have forgotten by the end of it that it ever needed a screamer:

How fitting it is that he [Terry Waite] left Lebanon yesterday with Thomas Sutherland, one of the two Americans he was trying to free when he was himself taken hostage 1,763 days before. – Leaderette in *Daily Mirror*

A screamer here would be slightly absurd. And it is interesting to see what happens if you put an exclamation mark at the end of this characteristic paragraph by Auberon Waugh in the *Sunday Telegraph*:

What most impressed me in Japan, apart from the beauty and charm of the young women, was the extraordinary politeness. This combination of high intelligence with exquisite manners created an atmosphere where everybody seemed wholly concerned to say whatever would make the visitor happiest. How different from the general comportment of so many young Brits.

A screamer would have altered Mr Waugh's tone of voice and made him sound more indignant than he really wanted to sound, his technique being deliberately off-hand.

A classic example

I am not saying that screamers can't on occasions be highly effective, as in this chilling passage from *Jane Eyre*, when Jane discovers that there is a madwoman in the house:

The moon . . . looked in on me through the unveiled panes, her glorious gaze roused me. Awakening in the dead of night, I opened my eyes on her disk – silver-white and crystal-clear. It was beautiful, but too solemn; I half rose, and stretched my arm to draw the curtain.

Good God! What a cry!

The night – its silence – its rest, were rent in twain by a savage, a sharp, a shrilly sound that ran from end to end of Thornfield Hall.

Those must surely be two of the most dramatic exclamation marks in literature.

Screamers used to be used a great deal, too, not to mark an exclamation like Jane Eyre's, but merely to indicate strong emotion:

The man was a beast!

They are less used in this way now, and this is very much in accordance with current practice among good writers, who believe that a strong statement, if the words are properly chosen, should be able to make its own impact without having to draw attention to itself with an unnecessary punctuation mark.

We still use them in our letters, perhaps to show that we are being nice and friendly, but in newspaper writing they are best used sparingly, except in headlines in the popular press:

COO!

(Splash heading in *The Sun*, over a story about a pigeon which had been sent a poll tax demand.)

COPYCAT!
PUSHY'S AT
IT AGAIN

(A popular paper's reference to Princess Michael of Kent, who had been accused of plagiarism.)

GOTCHA!

(Another *Sun* splash, after the sinking of the Argentine cruiser *Belgrano* in the Falklands war.)

That last example, widely criticised at the time and in fact pulled out in later editions, was an exception. The screamer is hardly ever found over serious copy. Take this *Sunday Mirror* splash:

EATEN ALIVE!
Docs save boy's face
from stomach of
savage pet dog

If the heading EATEN ALIVE had referred to, say, a case of cannibalism in Woking, we can be sure there would have been no screamer. Screamers tend to trivialize.

To test this, guess what these two headings might be about:

DISASTER
DISASTER!

The first could be about a serious mining accident. The subject of the second is more likely to be the MCC's early collapse at Lord's.

I am told that it was Oscar Wilde, though I must confess to not having checked, who said that using an exclamation mark was like laughing at one's own joke.

> BR guarantee to get you to White Hart Lane on Saturday if you leave Blackpool on Wednesday! – Cartoon caption in sports pages of the *Daily Express*

Does the screamer make this crack any funnier?

And what is the function of the screamer in this front-page story from the *Faversham Times*?

HIGH-VOLT RESCUE

A brave Faversham fireman risked a 500-volt shock to save at least one of Hypurr's nine lives on Thursday. But the rescue almost had an unhappy ending when the kitten escaped his grasp and fell 20ft to the ground!

Did the reporter, knowing that he or she had a weak story, add the exclamation mark to pep it up? If so, it didn't work. Or was it ironical?

Indeed, I sometimes feel that the only cast-iron excuse for screamers (apart from actual exclamations, or shouted commands) is when they are being used ironically, as they are by Maureen Freely in a book review in the *Independent on Sunday*:

> It is after orgasm that our hero runs into trouble. Apparently he loses interest in women after he has had them! This means he is incapable of mature relationships with the opposite sex! Then one day he meets his match . . .

It is typical of the trend, I suggest, that Ms Freely could successfully use them here to knock an idea down, though their original function would have been to hype it up. Screamers are not what they were.

Question marks?

The same principle applies to question marks as it did to screamers: if the sentence is so long that the reader will have forgotten it was a question, the mark can safely be left off. From a letter to the *Daily Telegraph* from the Archbishop of York:

> To make the matter crystal clear may I explain, once again, that what I have been criticising is the notion that God deliberately prepares unending torments for some people as a punishment for wrongs done or lack of belief during their time on earth.

The wordy archbishop should by rights have put a question mark at the end of all that – he was, you remember, asking a question ('may I explain?') – but it really turns out to be a statement rather than a question; in fact a query might even be slightly tiresome here, introducing a hint of truculence not necessarily part of the writer's character. So we needn't be pedantic about it.

Italics

I once worked for an editor who banned italics altogether, except in foreign words and the names of plays or books. Using them for emphasis, he said, was a sign of inadequacy: the order of the sentence should be enough to show which the important words were.

I saw his argument, but it was too austere a ruling. The emphatic italic has its uses. It gives a piece a more conversational tone, as if one could almost hear the writer banging the desk as they say the word. Columnists may resort to it freely (but not too freely, unless they want to sound like Indignant of Wimbledon); feature writers with discretion; news writers, I should have thought, never, except in the popular press.

Foreign words

What foreign words should be in italics? Some of the best authorities, from John Dryden in the seventeenth century down to Eric Partridge and H. W. Fowler in the twentieth, have mocked people who used a great many foreign expressions, the idea being that our own language is rich enough without the need for such posturing, as they see it. Journalists should certainly be careful with them if they want to avoid a reputation for snobbery. Some writers have done well out of the genre (the sort of writer who would want *genre* in italics). We have all read this kind of thing in the Sunday supplements:

Sipping my *café rechauffé* (but, it must be confessed, not too *rechauffé*) outside the *estaminet* in the *place*, I spotted the diminutive figure of *la patronne*. '*Ca va?*' I called across the *pavé*. It was then that I saw that she was *enceinte*. For me, it was a *coup de foudre* . . .

The only possible answer to that, I suppose, is *chacun à son goût*. But a good rule to follow is: Don't use a foreign word if (as in the above examples) there is an English equivalent. In other words, don't bring them in for effect. Obviously it would be foolish to bar them. There is no quick way of saying *mutatis mutandis* or *quid pro quo* (though the popular press seems to manage without these two useful little phrases). But as often as not it will be found that if there does turn out to be no equivalent, the word or words can easily go in ordinary Roman type. For instance, to italicize the untranslatable Greek word 'moussaka' would be absurdly affected. The same goes for 'chateau', which is the French for a French mansion.

Apart from that, it's a matter for judgement whether a foreign word has become familiar enough to claim naturalization. I would put 'rapprochement' in Roman but give the italics to *bêtise*.

Others may disagree. Here is a short list showing some of my own preferences; those who think I have not got enough italics may be proved wrong in a few years.

à la carte	démodé
à la mode	*donné(e)*
angst	*double entendre*
arrière pensée	*embarras de richesse*
art nouveau	en passant
belles-lettres	ennui
bête noire	*entre nous*
bêtise	frappé
concierge	hors de combat
déshabillé	hors d'oeuvres
déclassé	*idée fixe*
décolletage	*idée reçue*
décolleté	*jolie laide*

lebensraum	rapprochement
mutatis mutandis	realpolitik
noblesse oblige	schadenfreude
nomenklatura	status quo
nouvelle cuisine	tour de force
plus ça change	*verboten*
pons asinorum	v infra, v supra
porte cochère	yang
quid pro quo	yin

Proper names in roman, not italic, e.g. Bundestag, Quai d'Orsay, Reichstag, Taoiseach, etc.

Accents

As soon as a word becomes part of the language and can shed its italics, it can generally be stripped of its accents as well, if any. Years and years ago they took the accents off 'hotel' and 'depot' then, rather later, off 'debut' and 'detente'. Now hardly anyone asks for an accent on 'regime' or 'elite'. The only obvious exceptions are words whose spellings look odd or misleading without them, such as 'café' and 'fiancé'.

Hyphens

The question of when to hyphenate – and when to join two words to make one – has probably started as many arguments among sub-editors as any other point of style. Dictionaries differ. The best article I know on this subject is in *Fowler's Modern English Usage* (second edition 1965, revised 1983). It takes three pages of double-column small-print type. I strongly recommend it.

The general trend (deplored by some) is to hyphenate pairs of words which used to be separate; and to make single words out of pairs which used to be hyphenated. (The old sparking plugs became sparking-plugs then sparkplugs.) But house style must decide whether to put 'a beautifully timed stroke' or 'a beautifully-timed stroke'.

Here, meanwhile, are some hyphens which are wrong by any criterion:

1 That stroke was beautifully-timed.
2 She is, of course, much-liked. (*Sunday Telegraph*, about the former politician Shirley Williams. The statement was true, the hyphen is superfluous.)
3 Unless I have ill-judged the portents . . . (Political commentator in *The Times*.)

4 The service can ill-afford to lose his expertise. (*Today*.)
5 It was not until he was 38-years-old that he discovered that his 'mother' Ethel . . . was really his grandmother. (*Daily Express*, about a film actor.)

But these are all right:

The much-liked Shirley Williams.
The portents were ill-judged. (Hyphen optional.)
The 38-year-old Jack Nicholson. (Hyphens essential.)

So are these:

He went through the don't-call-us-we'll-call-you routine.

And this:

There will be no dramatic gesture like an interest-rates reduction, nor entry to the European narrow band for sterling. – *The Guardian*, looking forward to a Tory Party conference

– though it would have been better if the writer had put 'a reduction in interest rates', gaining just a little elegance for the price of two extra letter-spaces. (See my remarks on noun-strings in Chapter 7.) But at least the hyphen is a help here.

The principle should by now be obvious. Words may need to be joined by hyphens when together they make up a descriptive phrase which would look awkward without them. Thus in the sentence

She made an off-the-cuff speech

'off-the-cuff' is an adjective describing the speech, but

Her speech was off the cuff

has no adjectives in it and needs no hyphens. The following sentence is from a piece in *The Times* about Hardwick Hall in Derbyshire:

Designed in the late 16th-century for Bess of Hardwick, the house contains outstanding furniture, tapestries, and needlework.

I offer no prizes for spotting the error. The sentence, incidentally, was

written by a journalist, not an estate agent, despite its language. It shouts
for a re-write:

> The house was designed in the late 16th century for Bess of Hardwick.
> Its furniture, tapestries and needlework are outstanding.

Note that we also have got rid of the unwanted comma after 'tapestries'.

Hyphens are useful for avoiding ambiguities. Without one a *child-killer*
becomes an under-age murderer.

They are pretty well essential when their absence would change the
meaning of a word, as in

re-form (form again)	reform (change)
re-creation (making again)	recreation (amusement)
re-count (count again)	recount (tell)
re-act (play it again)	react (respond)
re-serve (serve up again)	reserve (keep)

They are also expected when a *re-* is followed by another 'e' as in *re-enact, re-establish, re-enter* and so on, also in *co-opt*, but dictionaries differ over whether to put one in *co-operation*.

I end with a curiosity:

> Anne immersed herself in work, making long trips which brought her
> into ever-decreasing contact with her husband. – John Parker in the
> *Daily Mail*

The hyphen in 'ever-decreasing' is certainly helpful. But this is an own-goal sentence. It reminds one of the building that soared to a comparatively low height, or the cricketer who amassed very few runs.

Apostrophes

Successive generations of schoolteachers spent so much time talking
about the importance of the apostrophe that many of their pupils, feeling
bullied, put them in wherever they could. Hence the 'grocer's apostrophe',
as in *apple's, potato's* and *pear's*, still seen on stalls. Brighter pupils, realizing that the apostrophe is meant mainly for possessives (William's
book), dutifully inserted them in *her's, their's* and *it's*, forms still to be
found, not so much in newspapers but occasionally in advertising copy.

Now, however, the pendulum has swung. Young writers have heard so

much about the horrors of the grocer's apostrophe – largely from Mr
Keith Waterhouse, but from others as well – that they hardly dare put
one anywhere. Some, too, have been persuaded by progressively minded
teachers that small points of punctuation matter less than the grand cre-
ative sweep, and that worrying about such things can even inhibit their
flow of ideas. Anyway, the result has been that we now see a whole lot of
mistakes like this:

> Parents rights should include limits on class sizes for their children.
>   – National Union of Teachers, newspaper advertisement

The rights of parents, I need hardly say, are parents' rights, with apostrophe.

The other function of the apostrophe is to indicate an elision, that is, a
vowel missed out as in speech: *isn't, don't,* for *is not, do not; it's* for *it is.*
Not long ago these informalities were considered quite improper except
inside quotation marks, when what somewhat actually said was being
reported. There are still sub-editors who insist that such shortenings
should be banned from book reviews, leaderpage articles and the like,
which they think require a more dignified tone. But there are not many
who take this view.

Journalism, as I pointed out in Chapter 1, uses a language closer to the
spoken word than other kinds of writing do, and this trend has acceler-
ated in recent years. It is therefore only natural to reproduce the accepted
forms of speech.*

In general, a *do not* instead of a *don't* can look absurdly affected in a
signed feature, but too many recurrences of *it's* and *there's* may strike a
note of overfamiliarity and so alienate readers: there is a danger that they
might begin to say under their breaths: 'This is all very nice and chatty of
her, but I hardly know her.'

Possessive apostrophes

In fourteenth-century English *the king's men* would have been spelt *the
kinges men*; the apostrophe stands for the missing 'e'. It also happens to
be useful for distinguishing *kings*, meaning more than one monarch, and
king's, meaning *of* the one king. But *kings'*, meaning *of the kings*, has no
such history: the apostrophe is just there for the sense. With singular
words ending in 's', repeat the 's' after the apostrophe: *St James's Square,
King Charles's statue, his mistress's eyebrow* and so on. The clue is the
way it's said.

---

* See Chapter 10 for apostrophes in quoted speech.

The Jones' house is correct only if the family in question is called Jone. The proper form is *the Joneses' house*, which may look a little odd but if it sounds right it's right.

Capital letters

When to write 'Archbishop' and when 'archbishop' may be purely a question of house style, where all that matters is consistency. But the capital can also be effective for the purpose of irony. The harmless remark:

Jane, a one-parent mother, is interested in women's rights

can be turned into something vaguely contemptuous simply by a change of case:

Jane, a One-Parent Mother, is interested in Women's Rights.

It's a fairly cheap trick, and it doesn't work when read out loud.

10 'QUOTES'

Uses and abuses

The trouble with quotation marks (inverted commas) is that they can be used in many different ways – I make it at least six – and it is therefore important that the writer and the reader should agree, at each instance, exactly what they are for. To explain what I mean, I categorize their main uses here:

1 To show that the word or sentence is someone else's, not the author's: to introduce a quote. The commonest and most obviously legitimate use. Very handy, too, in headlines:

> Anger of 'Scapegoat' Jail Boss – *Daily Express*
> Julie 'Had Three Lovers on Night of Murder' – *The Sun*

The papers aren't saying the prison governor *was* a scapegoat, or that Julie really did have all those lovers.

> Ministers have gone out of their way to denounce 'trendy' teaching methods. – *Daily Mail*

Without the quotes, the reporter would have seemed to be identifying himself with the ministers: it's their word, not his.

2 To distance the writer from what is being talked about:

> . . . The second reason, which emphasises again the otherness of this side of Oxford from the 'ancient seat of learning', is the appallingly high level of illiteracy . . . – Christine Hardyment in the *Daily Telegraph*

Ms Hardyment is uneasy with the description of the city as an ancient seat of learning. Perhaps she thinks it is too fulsome, or perhaps she knows it is a cliché and doesn't really want to be associated with it for this reason. It is hard to tell which.

3 To cast doubt:

> The forthcoming 'biography' of Jesus Christ . . . – Amit Roy in the *Sunday Telegraph*

Mr Roy's quotes suggest that this is not going to be a proper biography.

> That gifted actor Derek 'Mr Sitcom' Nimmo was one of several 'celebrities' who traipsed along to Westminster Cathedral to bed down in a cardboard box as part of National Sleepout week. – Peterborough, *Daily Telegraph*

The 'nickname' quotation-marks really come in class (1). But the quotes round 'celebrities' are a pure sneer, easily done – so easily, in fact, that there is a temptation to use this device too often.

> Mr Ingrams sits in a rats' nest, but it is one he created himself. Ian Hislop was anointed 'editor' of *Private Eye* for one overwhelming reason: he represented no threat to Richard Ingrams.

The above comes from a long and malicious piece by Peter McKay in the *Evening Standard*. The quotes round *editor* are near-libellous. Cheap stuff, this.

4 To offer an unspoken apology for using a cliché or a slang expression. An old device:

> Even *The Water Babies*, a rather 'slushy' children's book, contains propaganda against the employment of boy climbers by chimney sweeps. – David Daiches, *Literature and Society*, 1938

Dr Daiches seems to have been ashamed of 'slushy', presumably because he thought it too informal for a work of criticism. But there is also a hint of *distancing* here: people may call the book slushy, he is saying, but look at the propaganda in it.

> Two teenage joyriders were yesterday cursed to live forever with the torment of having killed a 10-month-old baby . . . The 'hotters' goaded police into chasing them through the streets of Newcastle, Britain's car crime capital. – *Daily Mirror*

'Hotters' was a new term at the time, and the quotes were needed.

5 To show that the word is being used in a special or unusual sense:

> Will there now be conflict between the 'ultras' (or, if you prefer it, 'irreconcilables'), who have been scandalised by the circumstances of Mrs Thatcher's downfall, and the party proper, which has reverted . . . to a more traditional 'one nation' Conservatism? The irreconcilables are to be found in the ranks of government . . .
> – Julian Critchley, *The Observer*

Once Mr Critchley has made it clear that he is using 'irreconcilables' in a narrow sense to do with internal party differences, he can leave the quotes off next time, as he does here.

But the quotes round 'one nation' are of a different sort:

6 To show that the writer is using a verbal shorthand to define something which would take too many words to explain properly. Here is a graceless example by Sir Charles Wintour, writing in *The Times* about another newspaper:

> The business section looks promising, with some useful 'trend' type articles and readable charts . . .

One expects something a bit more stylish from a former editor of the *Evening Standard*.

We should never use quotes as an excuse for laziness or because we haven't the space, or the expertise, to say what we mean.

Which function?

Faced with all these different possible applications, readers will only get irritated if they are not sure what the quotation marks are being used for. In the next example, do they come in class (1) (taking someone else's words) or class (4) (apologizing for a cliché)?:

> Police have set up an undercover operation, codenamed Taurus, to identify those 'pulling the strings' behind the rackets. – *Daily Mail*

Perhaps this was an expression which the police used when talking to the reporter, but perhaps again it was a term in general use among policemen, or perhaps the reporter thought it was a bit of a cliché and had better go in quotes. Who could tell?

> Sir John is one of many urging the Government to 'grasp the nettle'. – Front page lead in *The Times*

Was this a phrase used by Sir John and his fellow-urgers, or is this just the reporter excusing himself for a colloquialism (or a cliché)? Here is another little puzzle, this time from the columns of the *Daily Telegraph*:

> As a young reporter on the *Daily Telegraph* it was from Boothby that I got my first 'scoop'.

This could come into classes (2), (3), (4) or even (5). The writer doesn't want us to think this is his sort of word. Or it wasn't really a scoop, people only said it was. Or he thinks it's a slang expression. Or he wants to make it plain that he's talking Fleet Street lingo. Whatever the answer, all the quotation marks do is to make him look strangely like an amateur who doesn't know his craft. And there seems to be no point in quoting 'no man's land' in the following:

> At the moment, Mr Major is in a kind of 'no man's land'. He is trying to argue his case both ways. – Paddy Ashdown in the *Daily Mail*

Why should Mr Ashdown be frightened of the phrase? How much more telling the idea would have been if he had cut out the hesitation and written:

> At the moment Mr Major is in no man's land. He is trying to argue his case both ways.

There is nothing wrong with the expression, but by putting it in quotation marks the writer makes it seem as though he thinks there is. And a wrong word doesn't become the right one just by the magic device of having quotes put round it.

Another example of quotes which seem quite unnecessary:

> As John Major wrangles with ministers over social reform schemes, like his Citizens' Charter, debate smoulders on whether an ancient institution, the House of Lords, should be 'reformed' out of existence and into an elected chamber. One prevalent assumption is that the Upper Chamber is 'undemocratic' because it is unelected, another is that it is an anachronism, standing in the way of greater political and social liberty. – *Daily Telegraph* columnist

Presumably the columnist put 'reformed' in inverted commas because the reformers didn't want to reform the Lords so much as annihilate them, and 'undemocratic' because he didn't think it mattered whether they were undemocratic or not. In that case he should certainly have put 'an achronism' in quotes too, and, while he was at it, 'political and social liberty'. If we were to quote everything we disagreed with in this way, our copy would be infested with a plague of inverted commas. This sort of thing only brings them into disrepute; and it is an uncertain way of conveying one's feelings.

Here is an instance of quotation marks being used for two quite different purposes in the same sentence:

> Lebrecht revels in 'outing' Karajan as an 'unrepentant Nazi'. – Book review in the *Independent on Sunday*

The first is class (5), the second class (1). Both are unexceptionable; but too many quotation marks look bad on the page.

In the next example, the first is in class (1) and the other two in class (5):

> Up to two or three years ago the [Manchester City] council received just 'one or two' requests from the public alarmed about commuter 'rat-running' through side streets. There are now 300 requests a year. Publicity over early 'traffic calming' measures, governing speed restriction proposals and the increasing volume and speed of traffic through once-quiet residential areas, have all contributed to increasing concern, says David Blackburn, assistant city engineer. – *The Guardian*

That last long sentence carries signs of having been written in haste, but at least the expressions 'rat-running' and 'traffic calming' are explained. It is the unexplained quote that should be avoided. Too often it makes writers look as though they are merely fumbling. In general, quotes should be taken off unfamiliar phrases as soon as reasonably possible, and if the writer has any doubt whether they should be used in a particular instance, the answer is probably no. The only experienced writer I can think of who sprinkles them broadside through his copy is Michael Wharton in his 'Peter Simple' column, first in the *Daily* and later in the *Sunday Telegraph*. But he uses them to point up the absurdities of cliché and jargon, of which he is a master. He is a special case.

Finally, when using class (1) quotes – that is, quotes to introduce someone else's words – try if possible to make sure that the readers know where the quote came from.

> Mr Harvey Proctor, Mrs Gorman's predecessor as MP for Billericay, called as witness by Mr Mudd, denied that he had 'flagrantly' breached Parliamentary rules by approving a brochure advertising dinners at the House of Commons to American tourists.

. . . He denied it was a 'flagrant breach' of Parliamentary procedures. He saw nothing wrong with Parliament being used as a tourist attraction, although he would not go so far as 'payment and turnstiles at the door'.

In the above hilarious case (reported here, from agency, in the *Daily Telegraph*) we must assume that the words 'flagrant breach' and 'payment and turnstiles at the door' were uttered by Mr Mudd and denied by his witness, but we can't be sure that they hadn't originated from the prosecution. This is not too serious. But it is odd that 'breach' is quoted the second time the phrase comes up, but not the first. If we are to take the quotes at their face value, on the first occasion Mr Proctor is not denying that there was a breach, only that it was flagrant; on the second, he denies that there was any breach at all. That might well matter.

In this second example, from a report about dog certificates, the quotation-marks are pretty well meaningless:

Last night it emerged that Mr [Kenneth] Baker had been forced by police, after a 'furious row', to retreat from a plan to make the force responsible for issuing the certificates.

Who said there had been a furious row? The police? Mr Baker? A spokesman from the Home Office? There may well have been a particular difficulty here, owing to the notoriously unhelpful practice of some Home Office press officers up to that time, of asking for opinions (or 'facts') to be aired but insisting that they should never be attributed to the Home Office; the reader would then be forced to the conclusion that the opinions were those of the reporter. Unfortunately this intolerable state of affairs is not much improved by the use of unattributed quotes.

Quoted speech

Obviously it is often impossible when interviewing people, or getting statements from them by telephone, to transcribe exactly what they have said – not because one's shorthand is rusty, but because most people talk too much and there is not the space. So of course they have to be edited; and there are pitfalls here. Take this example. The Royal Agricultural Society of England, patron Prince Charles, has produced a report with which the Prince doesn't entirely agree:

A press conference had been scheduled for tomorrow morning but was put back until the afternoon at the request of the Prince. 'He wanted the RASE council to debate it before the press got it. I don't know why,' an official said.

As it stands, the quote sounds slightly hostile to the Prince: 'I don't know why' is only a hair's breadth away from 'I can't think why'. But supposing the conversation had really gone something like:

Official: Hello there. I'm afraid our press conference the day after tomorrow has been changed. It'll be at three o'clock now.
Journalist (smelling something): No problem. Isn't the report ready yet?
Official: Oh yes, but the Prince wanted the council to debate it before the press got it.
Journalist: Really, why?
Official: I'm afraid I don't know.

To report all this verbatim would be a tedious waste of space, so the journalist shortened it, but in doing so gave the official's remark a colour which had not been there before.

I'm not saying this is what actually happened on that occasion, but that such things often do. If that was an actual quote, fair enough. If it wasn't, and I was right about the way the conversation went, the only fair way out would have been to close the quotes and start again:

'He wanted the RASE council to debate it before the press got it,' an official said. He did not know why.

Here is a quote from a neighbour of hostage Terry Waite, talking in the local pub soon after Waite's release:

'Terry always had a cheery word for everyone around here. He is a great local figure and it will be wonderful to see him again.' (Quoted in the *Daily Mirror*)

If you say this out loud you realize that the second sentence just isn't how people talk. It's somehow stilted. But of course you can guess the problem: it was boiled down from a longish conversation. How to make it sound natural?

That *and* surely strikes a wrong note. Three short sentences would have brought the quote nearer to real life. It's a small matter, but it makes a difference:

'Terry always had a cheery word for everyone around here. He's a great local figure. It will be wonderful to see him again.'

Even if the neighbour didn't say this all in one go – the reader can imagine the gaps at the full stops – each sentence seems authentic. And we have given him a *he's* instead of a *he is*. For quotes should, if possible, look like quotes.

> Mr Schneider, who also demanded an inquiry, said: 'I have seen a recent photograph of Gilbert. He does not look like me at all.
>
> 'It is so worrying that on the basis of a hazy description our lives could be put at risk.' – From the Brighton *Argus*, about an alleged wrongful arrest

I bet Mr Schneider said 'I've', 'doesn't' and 'it's'. But the second paragraph looks very literary. (Anyone actually talking would have put it the other way round: 'It's so worrying that our lives could be put at risk on the basis of a hazy description.') I suspect that he never *said* this at all and that it was a written statement, in which case the reporter ought probably to have made it clear that this was so: 'Mr So-and-So said in a statement . . .' It seems to me that people like to know these things; they help build trust between a paper and its readers.

In the days when I used to go to ministerial press conferences it was noticeable that the first question, however inane, was always put by the man or woman from the *Daily Express*. The reason emerged later when the quote appeared in the paper as 'The Minister said to me . . .', giving the impression that this was a personal interview. The reporter had to get in a question, didn't he? No need to say that the quote was addressed to 50 other people too . . . The practice was regarded by colleagues as a bit of a joke, but it wasn't really honest. It was also probably quite obvious to any *Express* readers who also read another paper.

As everyone knows who has done interviews on tape, once the words are on paper they don't always *read* like natural speech, though they may have been accurately transcribed. There is a temptation to alter them so as to make them sound natural. I should not have thought that there was anything wrong in doing this; you might even find yourself being thanked by the interviewee. (Many a Member of Parliament has had cause to be grateful to *Hansard's Official Report*, for this reason.)

People who are not used to talking to the press are often apt to carry on in a pompously artificial way. Court witnesses can be similarly afflicted, like this one in a rather seedy sex-abuse case who was quoted by *The Sun* as saying in Leicester Crown Court:

> 'I became accustomed to the gifts I was receiving,'

whereas if he had been among friends he would almost certainly have said:

'I got used to the presents I was getting.'

Here, of course, you do have to quote the actual words, however strained they seem – likewise this police statement about a boy who had been kept in the house by his mother all his life:

'Mother and son were taken to Addlestone police station as it was deemed necessary to remove them from the conditions prevailing in the house.'

The form of words should be kept: we all realize that police spokesmen talk like that. Nor should we alter bad grammar:

'I don't know whether my daughter suffered at the hands of this madman. From the first day it has haunted me what she went through.' – *Daily Telegraph* report

This sounds like a genuine quote, and all the better for it.
The quotes below also sound absolutely authentic – except for one thing:

Police launched a major investigation today after a man was found dying outside a block of flats . . .
    Neighbours were mystified by the incident. Reginald Pearce said: 'At night time it's difficult to hear anything other than the traffic and people coming out of clubs. I heard nothing unusual last night.'
    Graham Stubbs said: 'We saw two drunken kids about midnight but did not take any notice. It makes you think when something like this happens.' – Brighton *Evening Argus*

Only a police witness would have said '*did not* take any notice'.
    Finally, it's wise to resist the temptation to make up a quote, however heavily your news editor ('Well what would she have said?') may be leaning on you to produce one – if only, though not only, because you can so easily get caught. *The Sun* came badly unstuck when it needed a quote from a Falklands War widow whose husband had been given a posthumous VC; unfortunately she was not available at the time of going to press, but *The Sun* went ahead with the following report, which got it a deserved rebuke from the old Press Council:

VC's widow Marica McKay fought back her tears last night and said: 'I'm so proud of Ian, his name will remain a legend in the history books forever' . . . Hugging her children at their home in Rotherham, Yorkshire, she said: 'I'm proud of Ian's Victoria Cross . . . but I'd change all the medals in the world to have him back.'

It was the *Daily Mirror* that spotted the fraud – it knew the quote was made up because on the night in question Mrs McKay wasn't in Rotherham but in London as the guest of the *Mirror*.* And the *Daily Mail* made a fool of itself when it quoted Benny Hill's sorrow at the death of fellow-comedian Frankie Howerd, unaware that Benny had died before Frankie and the news of his death had been delayed. (The quote had apparently been provided by Benny's manager, also under the impression that he was still alive.)

Making up quotes without naming the source ('Another local farmer said . . .') is obviously safer, but where's the fun in it? Any fool can cheat.

A colleague's story about air travel incorporated a witty quote introduced by the words 'A passenger quipped . . .'. Later he confided that the passenger in question was himself. It was reluctantly agreed that since it was an actual quote this was within the rules.

---

*The full story of this affair is told in *Lies, Damned Lies and Some Exclusives* (Chatto, 1984) by Henry Porter, who rightly asks whether the words 'his name will remain a legend in the history books forever' would have been the likely response of a grieving widow.

11 GRAMMAR

Correct grammar and syntax are of no importance so long as one makes one's meaning clear. – George Orwell, *Politics and the English Language*

Orwell was a great man for overstatement. Anyone who took this remark seriously would soon be in trouble. Consider these two sentences:

The Prime Minister believes Britain will have nothing to be ashamed of in digging in its heels.	Prime Minister he think Britain won't have nothing to be ashamed of when her dig in her heels.

Both mean exactly the same thing, both are equally clear, but if the London *Evening Standard*, from which the left-hand version came, decided to carry the right-hand version instead its offices would be flooded with angry letters.

Why would the readers be so upset? A lot of their protests, I suggest, would be not so much about the grammar itself but about the *manners* that went with it. Unconventional grammar is like unconventional dress. People may find it offensive. Dungarees clothe the body just as effectively as evening dress does, but you don't go to a formal dinner party in dungarees – unless, as Aneurin Bevan did, you are using your clothes to make a political statement.

Some writers deliberately use non-standard grammar so as to give the impression that they are in the forefront of change. Smart-alec writing specializes in this. So we find writers in popular newspapers making deliberate grammatical 'mistakes' to show how unstuffy they are:

Curious, isn't it, the number of people falling over themselves to cast the first stone in the wake of Paddy Ashdown's confession of adultery?

Thus starts a signed column under the heading 'Current Events' in the *Sunday Express*, and though the grammar is non-standard I can see no harm in it. It's only the columnist trying to get off on the right foot with his readers, to show he's *talking* to them.

Lower down the column he says: 'Some folk are rather sniffy about the Poet Laureate.' That word *folk* is a nice rustic one. It's there for the same reason as the grammar. Plainly this bloke is one of us.

Once again it depends who you are writing for. And not just who for, but where. Free-and-breezy grammar which sounds all right in a viewy column would not do for the news columns of the same paper. The front page of that issue of the *Sunday Express* carried an indignant story about lax security at a royal residence, and we expect a much better standard of grammar here – it gives a more authoritative tone to the facts being offered. Actually there *was* a grammatical blunder:

Despite giving false personal details [wrote the reporter] to the royal household interviewer and estate manager, a full security check failed to alert police to my identity.

If you can't spot it, see page 189.

Rules should be learnt

It should be clear already that the grammar is part of the message. This was the point that Orwell missed. Needless to say, he was being perverse. He hardly broke any rules himself. If, like him, you want to pretend to be a simple rustic and are anxious not to be mistaken for an Old Etonian (which, of course, Orwell was), then by all means break the rules. But you won't be able to do it effectively unless you know what the rules are to start with.

And, one might add, unless you keep up to date with them. For obviously the conventions of grammar are not static. They are changing all the time – a process which has been going on for centuries. Nowadays if

---

What we regard as errors are often merely survivals from an earlier form of the language. – Anthony Burgess

---

you heard someone say 'If it be true' rather than 'If it is true' you would think either that they were talking dialect or that they were very old-fashioned. Yet there was a time when 'be' was right and 'is' was wrong.

Since so many readers feel strongly about these matters – as anyone who has edited the letters page of a broadsheet paper will know – the least you can do for them is to conform to *their* notions of what is right and proper. If in doubt we should lean on the side of the old-fashioned. And it doesn't take long to learn the parts of speech. Their functions are defined in the Glossary.

Split infinitives

'To go' is an infinitive; 'to boldly go' is a split one, because there is a word between the 'to' and the 'go'. The prejudice against split infinitives

---

What grammar is

For many years educational theorists discouraged the teaching of grammar in English schools. The idea was that since infants learned to talk without being taught any grammar, schoolchildren didn't need any either – indeed, said some teachers, it was more of a hindrance than a help since it demoralized less able children and made them reluctant to express themselves for fear they might lose marks for getting the grammar wrong.

These teachers were overreacting to an earlier misunderstanding about what grammar is. A grammarian is someone with a system for describing how language works. Grammarians are not interested in telling us how it *ought* to work, any more than botanists, whose business is the knowledge of plants, find it necessary to say which flowers they think are prettier than others. But teachers had thought of grammar as a set of unalterable rules which, like school rules, had to be obeyed, and had been using them as a stick to beat their pupils with.

This was foolish. But how much grammar should be taught? To change the analogy, we don't all need to become anatomists but we do need to know something about how the body works if we are to keep healthy, and to name its parts so as to explain to a doctor what we think is wrong with us.

---

may have come from teachers of grammar who based their systems on Latin; this was how grammar was taught in schools 50 years ago. Since Latin infinitives are expressed in one word and therefore can't be split, perhaps it was thought wrong to split them in English as well. Quite stupid, of course, but there you are.

At a time when it was thought rather daring to split infinitives, writers for left-wing protest groups and other minority interests deliberately split them as a trivial act of defiance against the Establishment, most of whose members were still carefully avoiding the habit. Thus the aim of the Government and its lackeys, we were told, was 'to totally smash the

> Our English grammar books are often shamefully out of date. –
> Anthony Burgess

genuine aspirations of working people' and so on. Indeed, the split infinitive was more or less compulsory among these writers.

Now, of course, nearly everyone does it and the gesture means nothing.

Whatever the rules, a widely split infinitive ('I decided to unilaterally, and before anyone began telling lies about me, issue a statement') is obviously hamfisted.

> For an explanation of grammatical terms, see the Glossary on page 209

'Who' and 'whom'

The distinction between these two small words can give rise to much strong feeling and is worth looking at.

Who is the form to use when it refers to the subject of the clause it introduces:

> Lord Fishcake, who recently evicted one of his tenants, is much disliked in the village.

Who is the subject of the clause 'who recently evicted one of his tenants'.

> Lord Fishcake, whom many villagers dislike intensely, recently evicted one of his tenants.

Whom is the object of the clause 'whom many villagers dislike'.

That is still the rule, but it is hardly observed in speech, and less and less in writing. When to stick to it and when to ignore it? That depends on how you think your readers would feel about it. Example:

> Dr James Dooley, who I consulted on this subject, finds a lot of gallstones which the owner was never aware of. – Dr John Collee in *The Observer*

A few sentences after this Dr Collee is writing:

> You can take drugs to dissolve gallstones but the stones may subsequently recur.

Someone who can write expressions like the rather pompous (and, incidentally, tautological) *subsequently recur* is the sort of person who would be expected to know when to write *who* and when to write *whom*. Most readers of *The Observer* probably knew the difference too. He should have put *whom*.

But Dr Collee likes to be one of the lads. He writes *it's* rather than *it is* and indulges in informal grammar ('Just because you're found to be carrying them doesn't mean they're causing your symptoms'). I suspect that the phrase *subsequently recur* came from the good Dr Dooley (whom he consulted, remember?) and that he forgot to reprocess it. My point is that one should be consistent in these matters.

Another example:

> Frank was my tutor at Oxford 45 years ago. He is very kind and a genuine Christian. His support for prisoners like Moors Murderers Ian Brady and Myra Hindley, who no one else would help, has been misunderstood.

This was James Pickles writing in *The Sun*. Of course *who* should have been *whom* here, but since most of his readers would never have bothered to say 'whom', he could be excused for breaking he rule himself. On the other hand, Mr Pickles was a retired judge and might be expected to talk proper. On the other hand again, Judge Pickles had enjoyed acting the Plain Blunt Man who wasn't frightened of the Lord Chancellor, so he wouldn't want to sound like a fussy old lawyer.

Personally, if I had been subbing the Pickles column at the time I would have put *whom*. It would have been a fault (if you can call it a fault) on the right side.

> It was a precision air strike designed to bring the war home to the man who Belgrade is holding personally responsible for the continued siege of federal army barracks. – From a *Guardian* report

Not much question about this one. Most *Guardian* readers would prefer a *whom*. A minority of them, however, whom some obscure reasoning has led to the belief that attention to grammar is 'elitist', might approve of the mistake.

Some people try hard to get their *who* and *whom* right and end up getting them wrong after all. The *who* in the following sentence is perfectly correct:

> The editor [of *Queen* magazine] was Beatrix Miller, a person of wonderfully balanced judgment, who Jocelyn recognised would never be frightened of him. – Quentin Crewe, autobiography

Many people would want a *whom* here, because they would say it was the object of 'Jocelyn recognized' – whereas in fact it is the subject of 'would never be frightened of him'. ('Jocelyn recognised' is just an aside.) So *who* is right. This mistake is often made, even by very good writers, as here by Kingsley Amis in *The Observer*, about the TV version of his novel *The Old Devils*:

> The toning-down canard started as a protective device run up by one of the cast who may not have read the book at all . . . Another, *whom* [my italics] one had presumed had read the book, enlarged on her grave doubts about the propriety of her accepting her part at all – only the toning down had laid those doubts to rest.

Or was it an over-officious sub-editor who altered *who* to *whom*? (If so, apologies to Sir Kingsley Amis.)

In the next example, however, *who* should clearly have been *whom*:

> A couple of telephone conversations with the mysterious Mr Weir, who Dr Bayliss had assumed to be in the 'spooks department', had been the firm's only contact . . .

The rule is summed up thus:

The mysterious Mr Weir, *whom* Dr Bayliss had assumed *to be* in the 'spooks department'	The mysterious Mr Weir, *who* Dr Bayliss had assumed *was* in the 'spooks department'

Whom in the left-hand column is the object of *assumed*. In the right-hand column *Dr Bayliss had assumed* is an aside and *who* is the subject of *was*.

Here is another well-meaning attempt to get it right:

> Daniel Barenboim is no stranger to controversy. All his life the brilliant pianist-conductor has competed in the public arena without much regard for whom he has offended. – Start of feature in the *Daily Mail*

For whom sounds terribly affected, does it not? *Without much regard for whom* is also somewhat square-wheeled. (The whole piece is overwritten, but I will not burden you with more of it.) Supposing the sentence had run:

> All his life the brilliant pianist-conductor has competed in the public arena without much caring whom he has offended.

At first sight this seems correct, *whom* being the object of the clause *whom he has offended*. But it still sounds stupidly pedantic and genteel, which indeed it is. What's wrong with 'without caring who he has offended'? Nothing.

But what about this?

> The Turkish incident should have alerted airline security chiefs to the potential menace of carrying unaccompanied baggage without checking to whom it belongs. – News item in the *Sunday Times*

You can't break the rules here. A slightly facetious friend can't say to a woman: 'Where is the lucky man to who you are engaged?' But you *can* say '. . . without checking who it belongs to', which is what the writer should have done here.

Propositions: a silly rule

It could just be that the *Sunday Times* man in the example above was trying to avoid ending his sentence with a preposition (*to*). There was a silly rule once, drummed into their pupils by second-rate schoolteachers, that this should never be done. It had in fact been done even by the best writers since at least the sixteenth century. In our own century (just – 1902 to be exact) we had John Masefield's

> And all I ask is a tall ship and a star to steer her by

which was for decades a favourite among teachers of English, and I doubt if any of them told their pupils that Masefield should have written

> And a star by which to steer her.

It was probably the name *preposition* which encouraged the idea that you shouldn't end with one. 'If it's a preposition', bad teachers would say, 'it must be *pre* something,' and indeed prepositions most often go in front of nouns or pronouns.

But we know it's a nonsense. 'They decided to heave *to*.' 'The general told his men to fight *on* .' 'Ah,' cry the pedants, 'but then it's an adverb!' It is doubtful where such arguments lead us to, or what principle we end up with.

'That' and 'which'

Some subs get themselves into a sweat worrying about when to use *that* and when to use *which*. I suggest you play it by ear.

This is the house that Jack built.	The house, which Jack built last year, is falling down.

Or you can leave the word off altogether:

The house Jack built has fallen down.

That is also optional as a conjunction in sentences like this:

Jack has honestly admitted that his house was jerry-built.	Jack admits his house was jerry-built.

Again, you play it by ear – and your ear immediately tells you that *that* is not needed in the right-hand column, but sounds better in the left.

But when in doubt, keep it in. It is often quite wrongly left out, as here (the subject is a City scandal in which the Department of Trade and Industry was criticized):

The Department now maintains the regulatory system set up by the 1986 Financial Services Act, with the Savings and Investment Board as the watchdog for funds like Barlow Clowes, is adequate to prevent another such scandal. – *Daily Telegraph*

Without a *that* after *maintains* we may well think that the Department *looks after* (maintains) the regulatory system, till we come across an *is* a whole three lines later – quite a shock. If the writer had put *says* instead of *maintains* he would not have needed a *that*.

Enough about that.

'Was' and 'were'

We can expect to see *whom* disappearing altogether from the language sooner or later, simply because it is hardly ever needed to convey the sense. Some of the examples I have given above may be poorly written but none of them is ambiguous. I like to use *whom* where it seems appropriate, but I am fairly sure that my great-grandchildren, if any, will never use it once in their lives.

It looks as though the same is happening to *were* in sentences like 'If I were you I would do such-and-such' or 'He behaves as though he were some sort of expert'. More and more of us are saying and writing *was* instead.

I think this is rather a pity, because this time there really is a difference of meaning. The rule, at least at the time of going to press, is:

> Use *were* for something which might happen now or *in the future* if it is to happen at all. ('If I were prime minister'; 'If I were a Russian'. Use *was* for things which may or may not have happened *in the past* ('If he was drunk, he didn't show it').

The rule is broken here by the Right Rev Richard Harries, writing in *The Observer*:

> The question to ask is, if there was no oil interest, would the war still be morally worth fighting? I believe it would.

At least I think it's being broken. It depends what he meant. As it stands the sentence means 'if oil hadn't been one of the reasons why the war was started', but it is more likely that he meant 'if there was no oil interest *now*', in which case he should have put *were*.

> Mr Patten redeemed himself yesterday with a polished performance in his first conference speech as party chairman. It was as if he was determined to disprove *The Guardian*'s suggestion that he wasn't a good platform speaker. – Ian Aitken in *The Guardian*

'Was determined' is right, because Mr Aitken was talking about the past.

> If the *Correspondent* was a disaster from the start and lacked the resources to relaunch, *The Independent* could launch in the spring with no competition. – Charles Wintour in *The Times*

Right again. Sir Charles is looking back to the start of the *Sunday Correspondent*. But this is wrong:

> He never asked me to temper an opinion if I were determined on it. – Quentin Crewe

Here Mr Crewe, a polished writer, has been over-anxious to be correct. A century ago he would have been, but, as I say, rules change. He is writing about something which might or might not have happened in the past, and should therefore have put *was*.

'If' and 'should'

I have already (see page 67) said what I think of people who say *should* where most if us would choose the *if* construction ('Should you wish to leave early' instead of 'If you would like to leave early'). But every so often it can be useful, as it is in this news item from *Today*:

Spurs managing director Terry Venables demanded the original £4.8m fee be augmented by another £1.8m should Gazza prove his fitness after a year.

The writer could have put 'if Gazza proves' but that would have sounded wrong because he was reporting something which happened in the past. He could have put 'if Gazza proved' but that sounds wrong too, because Mr Venables was talking about the possible future. The *should* construction avoids this dilemma. But it is best not used too often. It smells too much of the business letter.

Hanging participles

These are sometimes called 'unattached participles' because it is not always clear where, if anywhere, they belong. This sort of thing:

Walking down a crowded street the other day some rascal relieved me of my wallet.

Who was doing the walking, me or the rascal?

Despite giving false personal details to the royal household interviewer and estate manager, a full security check failed to alert police to my identity. – *Sunday Express*

Who gave the false details? It's only when you get to the last word but one ('my') that the context tells you that it must be the writer. The problem is not just that the grammar is 'wrong', but that it does nothing to help the reader.

Sometimes the meaning is obvious from the start so the hanging participle doesn't matter, except for its undoubted inelegance:

After questioning him closely, he at last broke down and told me what he had done.

'Questioning' is a hanging participle, but we know it belongs to the 'me' and not to the 'he'.

> Blinded and sweaty, sleepless and bitten, the afternoon becomes a matter of waiting for the sun to set and the mosquitoes to come out. – Cassandra Jardine, *Daily Telegraph*

We know what it means, but it still grates a bit, does it not? So, certainly, does this remark from an obituary in *The Times*, however clear its meaning:

> Fluent in at least four languages, his doctorate was gained in French at Strasbourg University in 1955 . . .

(For more Obitspeak, see page 86.)

Sometimes, though, such grammatical mistakes can lead to absurdities, as in this fragment from the *Daily Express*:

> . . . The roof in question is Naworth Castle, the Carlisle family seat and one of the most important medieval border strongholds. Largely rebuilt after a fire in 1844, the ravages of the 20th century have obliged Old Etonian Carlisle, 80, to carry out extensive repairs.

Frivolous readers will have tittered at this. Since ravages can't be rebuilt, it must have been poor old Carlisle who needed the repairs . . . The silly thing about it is that it could so easily have been avoided:

> It was largely rebuilt after a fire in 1844, but now the ravages of the 20th century have obliged Old Etonian Carlisle (etc).

And here is a puzzle from our old friend Nigel Dempster of the *Daily Mail*:

> Emma sent Fortnum and Mason parcels to James while he was in the Gulf and received loving letters in return. But after posing for photographs in a Rupert Murdoch rag for a five-figure sum and claiming James had become obsessed by the Princess, communication has ended.

The person who posed for photographs was probably the said Emma, but as far as the grammar goes it could equally well have been Fortnum, or possibly Mason. There also seems to be some muddle about the tenses (the *has* at the end is a bit of a surprise) but that is by the way. Why not start the second sentence 'But after [or since] she posed' etc.?

Better men than Nigel Dempster have also been guilty.

Sir: While following the logic of your leading article about events in Algeria, there is one lesson that you have failed to draw. – Letter from Sir David Steel to *The Independent*

The grammar is a stumbling-block: it tells us that *The Independent* is following its own logic, which makes no sense. 'I follow the logic . . . but . . .' would have met the case.

One more example, from the excellent Roger Cooper, writing in the *Sunday Telegraph* about a visit to his old school:

The occasion was the reunion of an age-group some 10 years younger than mine, which perhaps was just as well, as there was enough to surprise and embarrass me without failing to recognise once-familiar faces.

'Failing' is plainly a hanging participle, grammatically wrong, and not up to scrutiny. But it is perfectly clear. I think I would have put 'without the danger of failing' etc. That would have been better, as well as disarming the pedants.

'I' and 'me'

Children are often told that it is bad to say 'Me and Jim are going to play football' and that if they really want to get on in life and grow up to earn a good wage in the head office of a respectable firm they must learn to say 'Jim and I'. Unfortunately some of them overreact to this excellent advice and go on saying 'Jim and I' on every possible occasion, even when it is quite obviously wrong to do so. One of them is Dr John Collee, the already-quoted *Observer* doctor, from whom I take this sentence:

What's the final goal for you and I, for the NHS, or for the minister of health in Burkina-Faso?

Good question. But of course it should have been 'the final goal for you and *me*'. Politicians don't shout 'Vote for I', do they? What television interviewee can be heard saying 'Ask I another one'?

On behalf of my brother and I . . . – Kevin Maxwell, answering press questions after the death of his father Robert Maxwell

Kevin Maxwell ought to have known better. Saying or writing 'I' when it should be 'me' is an ignorant genteelism. It is becoming more and more common as I write, and in due course will doubtless be acceptable in the best circles. But not yet. So let's avoid it.

Charles Moore, writing in *The Spectator*, makes a similar slip in a witty article attacking western European diplomats:

> To such people, Mr Yeltsin is a figure from nightmare. They dream of rough beasts such as he slouching towards Brussels, burping and snarling and breaking the furniture and being irritatingly attractive to their women.

'Such as him' would be better. The 'him' goes with the beasts who are the object of the diplomats' dreaming. An argument *could* be made for 'he' (the beasts are doing the slouching and are therefore the subject of that part of the sentence) but it is not a strong one.

This again is a common mistake – and an old one.

> The boy stood on the burning deck
> Whence all but he had fled.

The famous lines by Felicia Hemans were written in the early nineteenth century.* But this is no excuse for our making the same sort of mistake in the twentieth or twenty-first.

Jane Austen, Mrs Hemans's yet more famous contemporary, often wrote 'the best of the two', which is now condemned as thoroughly bad practice. Anthony Trollope mixed up his *was* and his *were*. Oliver Goldsmith wrote 'different *than*'. More than 230 years later he is still held up as an exemplary stylist, but not for his 'different than', now generally frowned on, unless it can't be avoided. So it's no use defending a bit of poor grammar on the ground that better writers have done the same in the past. As I say, things can change – in either direction.

Numbers

Good writers know when to break a rule (and good subs will let them do it).

Most people would agree that it's wrong to say: 'Apples and pears *is* hard to get these days.' So is the following right or wrong?

> It is vital that the shape and structure of the peace is drawn up under the auspices of the UN and that it should have the full authority of the UN. – *The Observer*, during the Gulf War

* To see what is wrong, turn it round and substitute 'except' for 'but'. 'All had fled except he' can't be right.

It certainly breaks a rule – *is* after a single subject, *are* after two or more – 'shape and structure' obviously being a plural subject. But 'shape and structure', when you think about it, are a single *idea*: the same thing expressed in two words rather than one.* So the singular *is* turns out to be right after all. Only a nitpicker would want to change it.

Another puzzle:

> The possibility that an unregarded portrait by Leonardo may be about to emerge from a bank vault in Omaha is the stuff of which Hollywood movies, not real life, is made. – Godfrey Barker in the *Daily Telegraph*

Surely, since the subject of that part of the sentence is 'movies', which is a plural, it should be 'are made'? Quite right, quite right. It should read:

> . . . is the stuff of which Hollywood movies, not real life, are made.

Or should it? Your ears will tell you that it should *not*. We have a singular ('real life') just before the 'is', and it's this that the reader thinks of. Again it's a question of knowing when to break the rules.

Some odd plurals

A few Latin, Greek and other imported words have kept their old plurals. Examples:

One	*More than one*
Addendum	Addenda
Bureau	Bureaux
Consortium	Consortia
Criterion	Criteria
Curriculum	Curricula
Datum	Data
Graffito	Graffiti

---

*It is, in fact, a pleonasm (see Chapter 7). There is not much difference between shape and structure, at least in this context. Pleonasms can sound bombastic. Poets are allowed them, of course:

The very head and front of my offending Hath this extent, no more.
(Othello to the nobles of Venice)

'Head and front' is a ripe pleonasm. But Shakespeare was not writing leaders for *The Observer*. What the *The Observer's* man meant was, I fancy, 'the general shape of the peace' (leaving the parties concerned to sort out the details). More direct, therefore more effective – and beyond the reach of the plural/singular nitpickers. Or did he just mean 'the peace treaty should be drawn up . . .'? Hard to say.

Medium	Media
Memorandum	Memoranda
Phenomenon	Phenomena
Stratum	Strata
Thesis	Theses

Datum is hardly used. *Data* is simply the Latin for 'the things given', but is often used as a singular followed by 'is', much to the distaste of traditionalists. *Media* is a plural because it refers to various media of communication (newspapers, television, radio), each of which is a *medium*. However, *media* is used more and more as a singular now. Those who defend this habit confuse the issue by pointing out that *medium* (plural *mediums*) has its own special meaning of a person who communicates with (or is the go-between for) spirits from the other world. This should not prevent anyone from sticking to the old rule and keeping *media* as a plural when mentioning more than one medium of communication. Nor is it yet generally acceptable to refer to a single journal as a media.

These old plurals have been pretty well abandoned:

syllabi (syllabuses)
thesauri (thesauruses)
hippopotami (hippopotamuses)

And these are disappearing:

referenda (referendums)
stadia (stadiums)

'Hopefully'

I mention this word only because some people object to it in sentences like 'Hopefully he will be coming tomorrow'. They frighten us by calling it an Unattributed Adverb and complain that since adverbs are supposed to qualify verbs and adjectives, and there is no verb or adjective to go with it in the above instance, it must be an interloper and should therefore be thrown out.

Take no notice of such people. If we can accept 'Luckily he arrived yesterday' and 'Incidentally I shall be late', we can use *hopefully* in the same way. Also, incidentally, *thankfully*.

But we need to be careful of it when there is a danger of its gravitating towards a verb to which it doesn't belong, or where it might be ambiguous, as in this pay-off from a characteristic leader in *The Sun*:

. . . Homosexuality is either RIGHT or WRONG for clergymen. In an age of doubt and uncertain values, people hopefully turn to the Church for a lead. Not to wash its hands like Pontius Pilate.

Are the people turning hopefully or is *The Sun* hoping they are? Apart from such instances, there is nothing wrong with *hopefully*.

The *Sun* leader's last sentence (incidentally) is a nice example of the informal grammar sometimes favoured by leader-writers in the popular press. It's all right here but would hardly be acceptable in *The Economist* or the *Financial Times*.

'They'

In the interests of sexual equality, it is no longer wise to say 'he' in cases like these:

We ask the anonymous author, whoever he is, to declare himself to us.

No self-respecting doctor would claim that he has never made a mistake.

'He' was all right when doctors were always men. Must we now say

We ask the anonymous author, whoever he or she is, to declare him or herself to us'?

Of course not. We say:

We ask the anonymous author, whoever they are, to declare themselves to us.

Do not listen to anyone who complains that '*they* is plural so you can't have it after a singular'. They are just being old-fashioned. Too old-fashioned.

All change

I end this chapter with a list of words and expressions compiled in about 1927 by Professor J.Y.T. Grieg of Armstrong College, Newcastle Upon Tyne.

Boss	Tote	Goner
Not my funeral	Under the weather	Go the whole hog
Corner (verb)	Lengthy	Cold snap
High-falutin'	Lynch	Caption
Joy ride	Indian summer	Collide
Cut no ice	Filibuster	Fizzle out
Bunkum	Greased lightning	Itemize
Boodle	Belittle	Eventuate
Peter out	Side-track	Non-committal
Schoolmarm	Rowdy	Lobby (verb)

You may ask what these 30 expressions have in common. The answer is nothing – except that 15 years earlier, according to Professor Grieg, all had been regarded either as Americanisms or for one reason or another unacceptable by 'good' writers in Britain. It just goes to show how quickly not only the grammar, but also the vocabulary, of English can change.

12 BEWARE OF STATISTICS

> Drink deep, or taste not . . . – Alexander Pope

All good programmes for trainee journalists include something about the laws of libel and copyright. If I had my way they would also include a compulsory course on statistics.

We might then have been spared such things as the following item from the front page of a highly regarded British national daily:

MONGRELS FOUND TO BE THE MOST VICIOUS DOGS
By Celia Hall, Medical Editor

Laws to protect the public, particularly children, from savage dogs may have muzzled the wrong jaws.

A survey by West Midlands plastic surgeons of more than 100 bites and multiple bites makes the medium-sized mongrel the nastiest dog around.

This type was responsible for biting nine per cent of the children treated – but only one per cent of adults. The next least reliable dog was the Staffordshire bull terrier. Its bad temper accounted for eight per cent of the bitten children. But this may reflect geographical bias in the data . . .

By comparison, Rottweilers behaved like lambs, biting hardly anyone – 1 per cent of the children and 1 per cent of the adults.

Jack Russells bore the most frequent grudges against adults, accounting for 10 per cent of the sample . . . Most victims had been bitten at home or by dogs they knew.

Anyone taking this report seriously – and it certainly seems to have been written in earnest – might well conclude that it was safer to have a pet Rottweiler than a mongrel because the Rottweiler was less likely to attack the children.

In fact, of course, the plastic surgeons' little research exercise is value-less, because it doesn't tell us how many dogs of each kind there are. The RSPCA's estimate is that mongrels outnumber Rottweilers by 50 to 1, so it is hardly surprising to find that people have a bigger chance of being bitten by one. (But not, I imagine, if their neighbours keep Rottweilers.)

Newspapers which seek a reputation for reliability really shouldn't ped-dle such tosh. (This journalist was actually given a hint when she was told that the figures for the Staffordshire bull terrier might 'reflect geo-graphical bias', but she still drew the wrong conclusions.)

Successive reports have told us how little most people, adults as well as children, understand simple arithmetic, yet journalists go on merrily churning out figures even when they are not needed.

Around 50 per cent of fifth-form girls at this school do not make it into the sixth form to take A levels. – *Sunday Telegraph*

Why 'around 50 per cent'? Why not 'about half'?

Unemployment in the South-East has risen by 100 per cent. – **BBC** Television news announcer

In plain words, it had doubled. In my own apprentice days I was told to put as few figures into stories as possible – not merely because it was so easy to get them wrong, but because it was reckoned that most of the readers, not being at home with them either, would simply pass them

---

'Anything exciting is bound to be controversial for a percentage of the population.' (Managing director of Rover cars, quoted in the *AA Magazine*.) He meant 'for some people'. Saying 'a percentage' gave the misleading impression that he knew how many.

---

over. Nowadays hardly anyone takes this admirable advice. The feeling seems to be that a few percentages give the story a backbone of authority and authenticity.

This is almost certainly wrong. We know, for example, that the death of a friend from lung cancer is far more likely to stop someone smoking than any amount of statistical correlations. Batteries of figures in a story may actually diminish the attention it is likely to get. The readers' eyes glaze.

But if we must use them, let us by all means get them right. Here are a few of the more dangerous booby-traps.

Other things not being equal

There is always a natural temptation to give dramatic treatment to rows of figures which seem to 'prove' a trend, without thinking of all the possible reasons why the figures should have behaved in that way. Figures may show, for example, a startling increase in convictions for criminal offences. LONDON'S CRIME RATE SOARS, says the headline, followed by suitably frightening copy. But a moment's thought should remind us that a graph showing more criminal convictions doesn't necessarily imply more criminals. It may simply mean that the police are getting better at catching them, or neighbours readier to report them.

In 1991 the London correspondent of *Le Monde* was reporting (I translate):

> Though it could not be ranked among the most dangerous capitals in the world, London, too, is a crime-sick city, to judge by the latest annual statistics from Scotland Yard.

The report goes on to record a 19 per cent increase in street crimes and a surprising 54 per cent increase in domestic violence. It is honest enough to cite Scotland Yard's view that this 54 per cent is largely due to the victims, not their attackers, because the victims are readier to complain than they used to be, and the police more likely to believe them. Yet the correspondent still feels justified in describing London as a city *malade de la criminalité* and a sub-editor in putting up the strapline BIG GROWTH IN LONDON CRIME. It may be right and it may be wrong; the point is that the figures themselves neither support nor contradict it.

Another example:

> A league table of the most academically successful English independent schools last year suggested that single-sex day-schools – both girls' and boys' – had overwhelmingly better A-level results. Of the top 39 schools, only two had co-educational sixth forms. Girls' schools made up half the top 10, and more than half the top 39. – From an article on co-education in the *Sunday Express*

Here the reporter very sensibly smelt a rat. So she consulted an expert. His answer is at the end of this chapter.

It is easy to use bare figures to whip up excitement, as in this big splash from a popular Sunday tabloid:

708 DEAD
The faces and facts
behind a year of
British killing

Easy, but dishonest. The use of 'British' in the second deck suggests that Britain is a particularly bad place for people who don't want to get murdered, though in fact it is comparatively safe – about eight times as safe as the United States, for example. If the reporter knew this, he was deliberately deceiving the readers of the *News of the World* for the sake of giving them an enjoyable fright.

Election times are hazardous. It is too easy to come out with copy something like this:

> Mr Trueblue is highly popular in this constituency. 'I Love Trueblue' badges are to be seen everywhere – twice as many as those carrying the 'I Love Labour' message.

This tells us nothing about Trueblue's popularity. All it indicates is the availability of Trueblue badges. Unless a clear majority of voting citizens is seen wearing them they offer no guarantee of a parliamentary seat for Mr Trueblue.

Not much different from the above was the pro-Labour *Daily Mirror's* report of a pre-election poll about Britain's National Health Service:

> Voters from ALL parties – including the Tories – still don't believe the Health Service is safe in the Government's hands . . . A poll published yesterday reveals that most people think the NHS is getting worse under the Tories and will go further downhill if they are re-elected . . .
>
> Six out of ten people, and a fifth of Tories quizzed, do not believe ministers' assurances.

Six out of ten does not justify the word *most*. (And a *fifth* of those Tories who answered hardly supports the phrase *including the Tories*.) Saying *most* when what is meant is *a majority* is at best inaccurate, at worst – as I suspect it was here – dishonest. (Not that the political left has the monopoly in such matters.)

Sloppily used, statistics can be very useful for supporting readers' prejudices:

> Results of national tests of seven-year-olds confirm our worst fears. One in five cannot write and 27 per cent cannot count to 100 or do simple sums.

The *Daily Mail*, from whose leader columns this comes, goes on to call it a 'shameful revelation': shameful, that is, because the teachers haven't been listening to the Government and have gone on using progressive methods in their classrooms.

Again the *Daily Mail* might very well have been right, but there was nothing in the figures to show that it was. To do that the *Mail* would have had to find out how many seven-year-olds couldn't write or count in the days before teachers started using progressive methods. (In fact, there are figures from earlier times which 'confirmed the worst fears' of the *progressives*, but they would not have suited the *Daily Mail*.)

Suspect samples

Though I deplore the habit of putting in too many figures, it is also possible to put in too few. For instance, I think anyone writing up the results claimed for a survey should say how many people took part in it. And who were they anyway? Were they a representative sample of opinion? Here is part of an interesting item from *The Observer*:

> While most people are thankful to have put Christmas shopping behind them for another year, a significant minority of Britons cannot stop spending, whatever the season.
> Researchers at Lancaster University believe compulsive shopping is a psychological disorder that may affect up to 6 per cent of the population.
> With the easy availability of credit cards and shopping a favoured pastime, they fear some families cannot stop themselves from running up debts.
> Dr Richard Elliott, who leads the research team at Lancaster, said the team had placed an advertisement in a local newspaper to publicise the project: 'We were astonished to hear from 15 people, 12 of whom turned out to be genuine sufferers, through one small advertisement. We realised there must be a sizeable problem. We're talking here about an overwhelming urge which people can't control.'

The information is maddeningly incomplete and certainly doesn't make sense as it stands. Six per cent of the population works out at about 3 million people suffering from compulsive shopping. But how did Dr Elliott arrive at this alarming figure? He and his team discovered 12 people who had the disorder, and 12 is 6 per cent of 200. But the story as presented suggests that his sample was not of 200 people but of only 15, four-fifths of whom had the disorder.

Of course 15 is far too low a sample from which to draw any general conclusions about the country as a whole. But the real trouble with the story is that it is based on a biased sample. The people who bothered to answer the advertisement were more likely to suffer from squandermania than the people who didn't answer it.

A random sample, incidentally, is not as unmethodical as it sounds: it means a sample which has been chosen to ensure the widest mixture of people possible, given the numbers taking part in the survey.

Also incidentally, it was rash of *The Observer* reporter to write that a 'significant minority' of Britons can't stop spending. It sounds impressive, but it doesn't mean much. The word *significant*, on the other hand, has a clear meaning in statistics. A significant difference between two sets of figures – say, the number of stillbirths in two hospitals – is a difference which can't just be dismissed as due to possible mistakes in sampling. So the word should be used with care.

Opinion polls

Political opinion polls are notoriously unreliable, partly because we don't always vote the way we say we will, partly because the pollsters can't get the samples right: the people questioned are not representative of the electorate as a whole.

For a different reason, opinion polls in general should always be looked at with a cynical eye.

For example: the *Sunday Times* ran extracts from a book about the Prince and Princess of Wales which seemed to show how unhappy the Princess was in her marriage, and *The Observer* commissioned the distinguished pollsters Harris to find out what effect the book had had on the standing of the Monarchy. Well over a third of the answers said Prince Charles had 'come out of the recent publicity badly'. Since the book had been heavily biased against the Prince, this was hardly surprising. The reporter writing up the results concluded: 'Prince Charles has been badly damaged in public esteem', and the front-page puff said 'Boos for . . . Charles'.

In fact the Prince's popularity might not have suffered at all from the book. It all depended on what people thought the words 'come out of recent publicity badly' meant. If they meant 'Is this bad publicity for the Prince?' most people would answer yes; if they meant 'Does this convince *you* that the Prince is a bad husband?' many of the same people might well answer no. The reporter had no business to take the question in the second sense; but the real fault was with Harris for the ambiguous way it framed the question in the first place.

So beware of pollsters. Take all questionnaires with a generous pinch of salt, and ask yourself what the questions mean, or might be taken to mean, before analysing the answers to them. The pollsters won't do this for you.

Referenda on the 1992 Maastricht Treaty for European unity offered a famous object lesson. Some MPs urged a referendum asking the British people whether they were 'in favour of renegotiating the Maastricht Treaty'. What were the British people to make of such a question? And what would we make of our answers? Would a 'yes' mean we liked the Treaty but thought it could somehow be improved – or that we wanted it altered because we thought so little of it? Would a 'no' mean that we liked the Treaty as it stood, or that we didn't want anything to do with it?

Of course if you aim to make a good story out of the results of an opinion poll, or write up a statistical report in a way that confirms the prejudices of your readers, nothing could be easier. But perhaps you want to be a serious journalist.

Percentage of what?

Here is another example of statistics which *seem* to tell a story:

> The proportion of women police has doubled from five per cent to 10 per cent since 1975, but the proportion of women above the rank of constable has halved. – Reporter on BBC *Woman's Hour*

The idea was that policewomen weren't doing well in the Force, and this was how the media had interpreted the figures when they first came out. One newspaper, giving the details, reported:

> The overall number of women in policing increased from 5.4 per cent in 1975 to 10.5 per cent in 1988 but while there were 11.2 per cent of women officers above the rank of WPC in 1971, the figure had dropped to 5.8 per cent in 1988.

Its story was headed WOMEN FAIL TO REACH TOP IN POLICE. Another paper headed its report FEWER WOMEN POLICE PRO-MOTED, another ROUGH JUSTICE FOR POLICE GIRLS.

But without more details the figures could easily have meant something quite different. How recently had all those extra policewomen been recruited? If there had been a big influx of women in the past couple of years, say, it would hardly be surprising to find that many of them were still constables; in which case, of course, the *overall* proportion of police-women in the lower ranks would go up and the overall proportion in the higher ranks would go down. No story! Again I am not saying that the papers drew the wrong conclusions – the figures emerged at a time when a senior policewoman was claiming that her further promotion had been blocked because of her sex – only that they were not in a position to draw them from the statistical evidence given.

It is possible that some reporters misunderstood the basis of those percentages. Or rather, they may have forgotten what the '100' in 'per cent' represented. This is easily done. To say that 'there were only 5.8 per cent of women officers above the rank of WPC' might, if carelessly looked at,

---

Never say: 'Cases of malnutrition [or whatever] went up by 200 per cent last year.' Many readers will think it means cases have doubled, though in fact it means they have trebled (two more cases for every one the year before; a *doubling* would have been an increase of 100 per cent). Just forget the percentages and write naturally. Put 'trebled'.

---

be taken to mean that 'the percentage of all officers above the rank of WPC who were women was only 5.8'. And if you take out the word 'of' this is just what it *would* have meant.

The answer to all this is – one should always ask oneself: 'Percentage of what?'

Keep off the figures

A big feature in *The Times* on the day the above story broke seems on first sight to have clarified the situation, but in fact only confused it. The relevant passage read (my italics):

> . . . While women police officers have almost doubled *in number* from 5.4 per cent in 1975 to 10.5 per cent in 1988, the *number* above the rank of constable has halved from 11.2 per cent in 1971 to 5.8 per cent in 1988.

This must be nonsense. Numbers and percentages are not the same thing.

Let us suppose that a local force of 1000 police had 50 policewomen in it in 1975 and 100 policewomen 10 years later. As the report says, their number has doubled. We are told that about 10 per cent of them were above WPC in 1975, which makes five officers (10 per cent of 50), but that only 5 per cent of them were above WPC 10 years later, which again makes five officers (5 out of 100). So according to the percentages the number above WPC hasn't changed. But we are also told that the number above WPC has halved! If the percentages are right, the numbers are wrong; if the numbers are right, the percentages must be wrong.

To readers who have decided to skip the above explanation I would say only one thing. Keep off the figures.

Non-swimmers should stay out of the water.

Watch your language

Of course some stories need to make their point with figures – a report about a decline in the sales of daily newspapers, for example, would not be worth much without evidence to back it up. *The Guardian* carried just such a detailed report at the end of 1991. In the course of it the paper made the following more or less meaningless remark:

> The decline was steepest in both absolute and percentage terms among the tabloids.

I have said how important it is, if we are to offer some statistics, to get the language right. The same principle applies here as it does to the use of figures themselves: use statistical language only when you have to for the sake of clarity. *In percentage terms* is in any case an unlovely phrase. Presumably the author meant that the tabloids' circulations fell faster and farther than the other papers'.

If so, this would have been a rather more reader-friendly way of putting the point.

Not so stupid?

Intelligence tests are sometimes misunderstood. The IQ scale is organized in such a way that those of average intelligence fall around the 100 mark in a range between, say, 50 and 150, with most people at or near the 100 mark and the fewest people at either extreme. If the tests themselves fail to produce graphs showing this symmetrical distribution they can be altered till they do.

It is therefore unwise to complain of a person that they have an IQ of 'only 100', since this is a figure to which most people approximate. Nor should anyone be shocked – as some people have been when it has been mentioned to them – that half the population have IQs of less than 100.

The expert's answer for page 199

The reasons for these schools' comparatively poor showing in the academic league tables may have had nothing to do with their being co-educational. Perhaps there were fewer of them in the first place.

The reporter was fly enough to call an expert. Professor Ted Wragg told her: 'The tables don't compare like with like. A lot of the single-sex schools are very high-prestige, selective schools like Manchester Grammar School and Eton. They select the most able boys or girls.'

Appendix:
TOOLS OF THE TRADE

Spellchecks

Most word processing software includes the spellcheck facility, which is a great convenience and a clever piece of technology, but the help it can give is pretty limited. All it does is to highlight any words on the screen, including proper names, which are not in whatever dictionary the programmers have chosen. It will tell you if you have spelt a word wrong, but not whether it is the wrong word in that context.

It may also offer the correct spelling, or some ludicrous guesses as to what word you had in mind, which are worth a laugh if you have the time.

But of course a wrong word spelt right is still a wrong word. It is therefore no substitute for a good dictionary.

Dictionaries

There are usually at least four reputable one-volume dictionaries on the market at any given time, leaving aside their pocket versions. By the time you read this there may be more. All are roughly the same price, each has its virtues. Most give the commonest definitions first. The big *Oxford English Dictionary* and its small sister, the *Shorter Oxford*, are historical dictionaries, giving the earliest definitions first.

Some newspaper offices sensibly recommend a particular one which everyone should use, so there need be no arguments about variant spellings, hyphenations and so on. (A style book can't cover everything.) If there is no such recommendation, or if you are a freelance, my own advice is: choose the one which came out last.

Publishing houses are constantly vying with each other to produce the most up-to-date dictionary, and since they are all done on computers they are easy to revise. So the time between new editions becomes shorter. This has had the effect of getting new words, or new uses of old ones, accepted sooner than they would have been in the old days, and generally speeding up changes in the language. And the faster the language changes, the more anxious the publishers are to bring out fresh editions. It's a vicious circle.

So go for the latest one. If nothing else, this will give you the advantage over tiresome sub-editors who cut out words because they've 'never heard of them' or 'they're not in my dictionary'.*

Despite what I have just said, there is no such thing as a completely up-to-date dictionary. The fact that a word is not found in it does not mean that it does not exist; a word exists as soon as someone has used it.

A dictionary merely reflects that words were in use, and the way people used them, when it went to press. If we always followed the dictionary we would still be writing in the vocabulary of Dr Johnson. We need not become slaves to it, except, as I say, for the sake of a house style.

Thesauruses

For generations, writers at a loss for a word have made straight for *Roget's Thesaurus*, the original and still the most famous of them all. (Longmans is the best version.)

It is a wonderful thing. But it is a cumbersome way of finding straight synonyms. In fact it was never meant to be a synonym dictionary, but rather an aid to enlarging a writer's imaginative range and stock of ideas. Roget organized his words not in alphabetical order but according to the ideas they express, and despite its index anyone in a hurry for an answer can easily get lost. Ordinary synonym dictionaries are not nearly such fun, of course. The best, at the time of my writing this, is the *Oxford Thesaurus*, subtitled *An A-Z Dictionary of Synonyms*, which systematically ranks its words according to how close their meanings are to the word under which they are listed. As I hope I have made clear in Chapter 1, it is almost impossible to find a true synonym, and it recognizes this.

Two others worth mentioning, and still in print as I write, are the *Cassell Thesaurus* and the *Collins Dictionary and Thesaurus*. The Cassell is the only one I know which gives detailed advice about differences of nuance between near-synonyms, which is invaluable, but it covers far fewer words than most rivals. The Collins, a handy two-in-one, is also recommended.

* I do not, of course, imply that all sub-editors are tiresome. Some most certainly are; but so are some authors – particularly those stupid enough not to take the advice of a *good* sub when it's offered. (If a bad sub is a sore tribulation, a good one is beyond price.)

Grammar, usage

Fowler's Modern English Usage (Oxford), revised by Sir Ernest Gowers, is the best guide here. Though quirky and tetchy at times – its attitude towards the English language is a bit like the late Nikolaus Pevsner's towards English architecture – it is pleasingly unpedantic. Its only disadvantages are that it is best enjoyed in an armchair rather than at a desk – old Fowler takes his time; and that it is more than a quarter of a century since its last major revision. Most of it, however, is still sound.

GLOSSARY OF GRAMMATICAL
TERMS (with apologies to those who know it all already)

There is no proof that an acquaintance with grammatical terms leads to improved language use . . . But the knowledge that the pedal on the right is called the accelerator, the one in the middle is the brake and the one on the left is the clutch is essential to the learner driver. – Keith Waterhouse

Active See **Verbs**.

Adjective Describes or modifies a noun. A *good* girl. Nouns can be used as adjectives: A *goose* girl.

Adverb Describes or modifies a verb. A verb is something happening, and an adverb says how, when, etc. it happens: She sang *beautifully*. He hit the note *hard*. Or it can modify an adjective: a *very* good girl, an *annoyingly* vague man.

Clause A part of a sentence. Clauses have a verb in them but need not be the main part of the sentence. Thus:

Main clause: '*She sang . . .*'

Dependent clause: '. . . *while he accompanied her on the harpsichord.*' So called because it makes no sense on its own. This one is an

Adverbial clause because it describes the circumstances in which she *sang* (verb).

Conditional clause: clauses starting *if* or *should* (as in 'should it be necessary . . .') are conditional clauses.

Noun clause: 'She said *she was going to sing.*' The words in italics are the object of 'said'. 'They all wanted *to hear her.*' The words in italics are the object of 'wanted'.

Relative clause: 'The song, *which she had only just learned,* was the song [that] *they all loved best.*' 'The man *who accompanied her* was the one *we heard before.*' The words in italics are relative clauses.

Dependent clause See **Clause**.

Elision Omission of a bit of a word, usually indicated by an apostrophe (*Don't* for *do not*).

Finite sentence Has a main verb in it.

Genitive   See **Possessive**.

Grammar   System of describing how language works.

   Prescriptive grammar: rules about the mechanics of language, such as those once taught in all schools – based, inappropriately, on the grammar of another language, and a dead one at that, Latin.

Hanging participle   See **Participle**.

Infinitive   'I wanted *to go* . . .'

   Split infinitive: '. . . so I decided *to tactfully withdraw.*' (Nothing much wrong with split infinitives.)

Intransitive   See **Verbs**.

Metaphor   Describes one thing or idea in terms of another ('He's over the moon'), whereas a

   Simile makes a direct comparison ('He's like a dog with two tails').

Noun   Word describing a person, place, thing, or quality. Respective examples: '*Henry* of *Navarre* had a *face* of *character*.'

Object   'James loved *Mary*, but he loved *oysters* more.'

   Subject: 'But the *oysters* made him ill. *This* served him right.'

Participle   Part of a verb, thus: 'I am *taking* this seat', present participle. 'Sorry, it is already *taken*', past participle.

   Hanging or **dangling** or **unattached participles** have no subject to attach themselves to, which can sometimes lead to ambiguity.

Passive   See **Verbs**.

Phrase   A meaningful combination of two or more words, as distinct from a clause, which always has a verb in it.

Pleonasm   Using more words than necessary to express an idea. 'What a *tiny little* helping.' 'You're so *gluttonously greedy*.'

Plural   Of a word which is about more than one person, thing, etc.

Possessive   *My* book *of quotations* was once *John's*. Here *my* and *John's* are possessives; *of quotations* is a genitive.

Prepositions   Mean nothing by themselves and are used only to relate words or ideas to each other (*of, to, for, by, with, from*, etc.). So called because they are usually put before a noun or pronoun.

Pronoun   Word which refers to a noun (*he, she, it*). So called on the ground that it can't make sense unless there's a noun for it to refer to. '*He*'s a nasty man' means nothing unless *he* is identified. (*It* in sentences like '*It*'s good to see you' is a separate case and is called a subjective pronoun.) *Which, who, whom*, etc. are **relative pronouns**.

Relative clause   See **Clause**.

Relative pronoun   See **Pronoun**.

Simile   See **Metaphor**.

Split infinitive   See **Infinitive**.

Semantics   Study of the meanings of words.

Singular   Of a word which is about one person, thing, etc.

Subject   '*Oysters* made James ill, but *Mary* loved them.'

Object: 'It was James who made *Mary* sick.'

Subjunctive   'If I *were* you, if that *be* so, heaven *help* us all.' The italicized words are in the subjunctive mood, which is used for what might happen rather than what actually does.

Syntax   That part of grammar which is to do with the structure of sentences.

Tautology   Phrase or clause that says the same thing more than once in different words. ('The only living survivor.')

Tense   The form of a verb which decides whether it is concerned with the past, present or future, and their variations.

Transitive   See **Verbs**.

Verbs   Are words of doing and being. Verbs with objects ('She *loved him*, but he only *loved taking her to the theatre*') are transitive; those without ('But he *wept* when she *died*') are intransitive.

Active verbs: Verbs about people or things which are doing something or in some way making something happen ('Man *bites* dog') as opposed to having things done to them. Their opposites are

Passive verbs: ('Dog *is bitten* by man.') Too many passives make for poor prose, specially when in the form of the

Impersonal passive: 'It is thought that . . .' (by whom?).

INDEXES